The Really Useful Science Book

The Really Useful Science Book

A framework of knowledge for primary teachers

STEVE FARROW

 Falmer Press

(A member of the Taylor & Francis Group)
London • Washington, D.C.

UK The Falmer Press, 1 Gunpowder Square, London, EC4A 3DE
USA The Falmer Press, Taylor & Francis Inc., 1900 Frost Road, Suite 101, Bristol, PA 19007

First published in 1996
Reprinted 1997 (twice)

A catalogue record for this book is available from the British Library

Library of Congress Cataloging-in-Publication Data are available on request

ISBN 0 7507 0376 8 paper

Jacket design by Caroline Archer

Typeset in 10/12pt Garamond by
Graphicraft Typesetters Ltd., Hong Kong.

Printed in Hong Kong by Graphicraft Typesetters Ltd.

Contents

List of figures   xiii
Acknowledgments   xvii

SECTION ONE   *Introduction*   1

SECTION TWO   *Life processes and living things*   7

SOME KEY IDEAS IN LIFE SCIENCE   7

KEY IDEA 2.1   *The characteristics of living things*   9

CONCEPTS TO SUPPORT KEY STAGE 1   9
The characteristics of living things   9
CONCEPTS TO SUPPORT KEY STAGE 2   9
Organ systems   9

KEY IDEA 2.2   *Life processes*   11

CONCEPTS TO SUPPORT KEY STAGE 1   11
Feeding   11
Elimination of waste (excretion)   11
Respiration   11
Growth   12
Response to stimuli (sensitivity)   12
Movement   12
Reproduction   12
Differences between plants and animals   12
CONCEPTS TO SUPPORT KEY STAGE 2   13
Nutrition systems (feeding, digestion, egestion)   13
    Plant nutrition – photosynthesis   13
    Animal nutrition – digestion   14
The cardio-vascular system (circulation and respiration)   15
    The blood   15
    Circulation   16
    Respiration   17
The musculo-skeletal system (support and movement)   20
    Support in plants   20

CONTENTS

Support in animals – the skeleton   20

Movement in animals   21

The nervous system (sensitivity, coordination)   23

Human sense organs   23

The eye   23

The ear   24

Taste and smell   25

The skin (touch, temperature)   25

Plant responses to environmental stimuli   26

Coordination and control   26

The nervous system   26

The endocrine or hormone system   27

Reproductive systems   28

Asexual reproduction   28

Sexual reproduction   29

The biology of human reproduction   29

Puberty   30

The menstrual cycle   31

Sexual reproduction in flowering plants   31

Dispersal   33

KEY IDEA 2.3   *Optimum conditions for survival*   34

CONCEPTS TO SUPPORT KEY STAGE 1   34

Healthy plants   34

Healthy animals   35

CONCEPTS TO SUPPORT KEY STAGE 2   39

The defence systems of the body   39

External resistance to invasion   39

Responses following invasion   40

Conscious action which can promote health   40

Diet   41

Teeth   41

Personal hygiene   42

Life style   43

The effect of exercise   43

The need for rest   43

Harmful effects of drugs, alcohol and tobacco   44

KEY IDEA 2.4   *The variety of life*   46

CONCEPTS TO SUPPORT KEY STAGE 1   46

The classification of plants and animals   46

Kingdom: viruses   46

Kingdom: bacteria   47

Kingdom: protoctista   47

Kingdom: fungi   48

Kingdom: plants   48

Kingdom: animals   51

CONCEPTS TO SUPPORT KEY STAGE 2   53

The identification of plants and animals using keys   53

Similarities and differences: the basis of classification   53

The dichotomous or binary key   53

A dichotomous key to the five vertebrate classes   54

Lateral keys   55

KEY IDEA 2.5   *Adaptation to environment*   56

CONCEPTS TO SUPPORT KEY STAGES 1 AND 2   56

Charles Darwin's observations and deductions   56

FURTHER CONCEPTS TO SUPPORT KEY STAGE 2   58

The sources of variation in plants and animals   58

Genetic variation   59

Environmental variation   59

The mechanism of natural selection   60

Adaptation to environment   61

Examples from local habitats   61

Woodland environments   61

The inter-tidal zone: rocky shores   62

KEY IDEA 2.6   *The transfer of energy*   65

CONCEPTS TO SUPPORT KEY STAGES 1 AND 2   65

Photosynthesis   65

Energy transfer   65

Food chains and webs   66

The food cycle   67

FURTHER CONCEPTS TO SUPPORT KEY STAGE 2   67

Cycles of matter   67

The water cycle   67

The carbon cycle   68

The oxygen cycle   69

The nitrogen cycle   70

Energy transfer: micro to macro   70

CONTENTS

Life processes and living things:
National Curriculum coverage   71

SECTION THREE   ***Materials and their properties***   75

SOME KEY IDEAS IN MATERIALS SCIENCE   75

KEY IDEA 3.1   *The classification of materials*   77

Introduction   77

THE ORIGIN OF MATERIALS   77

CONCEPTS TO SUPPORT KEY STAGE 1   77

Natural and manufactured materials   78

CONCEPTS TO SUPPORT KEY STAGE 2   78

Natural materials from the physical environment   78

Natural materials from the biological environment   79

Manufactured materials   79

Types of manufactured materials   80

THE PHYSICAL PROPERTIES OF MATERIALS   83

CONCEPTS TO SUPPORT KEY STAGE 1   83

Questions about objects and materials   83

CONCEPTS TO SUPPORT KEY STAGE 2   84

Properties and characteristics of materials   84

   Density   84

   Hardness   85

   Strength   85

   Elasticity   86

   Stiffness (and flexibility)   87

   Toughness   88

   Compressibility   88

   Thermal and electrical conductivity   88

   Magnetic properties   90

   Composite materials   91

The characteristics of the main groups of materials   91

THE USES OF MATERIALS   92

CONCEPTS TO SUPPORT KEY STAGE 1   92

Fitness for purpose   92

CONCEPTS TO SUPPORT KEY STAGE 2   93

Considerations for the choice of materials   93

A materials case study: drinks containers   94

KEY IDEA 3.2   *The particulate nature of matter*   95

The kinetic theory   95

The states of matter: solid, liquid and gas   95

CONTENTS

Changes of state   95
The compression of gas   97
Elements, compounds and mixtures   97
The structure of atoms   97
The periodic table   98
Atomic bonding   99

KEY IDEA 3.3   *Changing materials*   102

CONCEPTS TO SUPPORT KEY STAGE 1   102
Change in shape   102
Heating and cooling everyday materials   103
CONCEPTS TO SUPPORT KEY STAGE 2   104
Separating mixtures   104
Changing materials   107
   Physical changes   107
   Mechanical changes   107
   Chemical reactions and heat energy   108
   Changes involving oxygen   108

KEY IDEA 3.4   *The rock cycle*   110

Igneous rocks   110
Sedimentary rocks   110
Metamorphic rocks   112
Soil formation and characteristics   113

KEY IDEA 3.5   *The water cycle*   115

Materials and their properties:
National Curriculum coverage   117

SECTION FOUR   **Physical processes**   119

SOME KEY IDEAS IN PHYSICAL SCIENCE   119

KEY IDEA 4.1   *Sources and forms of energy*   121

Introduction   121
Some definitions   121
THE PRIMARY SOURCES OF ENERGY   122
Bonding within and between atoms and molecules   122
FORMS OF ENERGY   123
Nuclear energy   123
   Radioactive decay   123

CONTENTS

Nuclear fission   124

Nuclear fusion   124

CONCEPTS TO SUPPORT KEY STAGE 2   125

Chemical energy   125

Long-term energy transfer   126

Electricity   127

What is electricity?   127

Electricity in simple circuits   128

Series circuits   130

Parallel circuits   131

Switches   132

Circuit diagrams   133

Work and power in electrical circuits   133

The generation of electricity   135

Static electricity   137

The electromagnetic spectrum   138

Strain energy   140

Potential and kinetic energy   141

Potential energy   141

Kinetic energy   141

Heat and temperature   142

The difference between heat and temperature   142

Heat transfer   143

LIGHT   144

CONCEPTS TO SUPPORT KEY STAGE 1   144

Sources of light   144

Light and seeing   145

Light and dark   146

CONCEPTS TO SUPPORT KEY STAGE 2   146

The behaviour of waves   146

Light waves   147

Straight line travel   148

The reflection and absorption of light   148

Shadows   149

Transmission   150

Refraction   150

SOUND   152

CONCEPTS TO SUPPORT KEY STAGES 1 AND 2   152

Sound waves   152

The speed of sound   153

FURTHER CONCEPTS TO SUPPORT KEY STAGE 2   154

The reflection of sound   154

CONTENTS

The absorption of sound   154

The transmission of sound   155

Pitch   155

Loudness   156

KEY IDEA 4.2   *Forces*   157

Introduction   157

CONCEPTS TO SUPPORT KEY STAGES 1 AND 2   157

Some more definitions   157

The effects of forces: the laws of motion   158

   The first law of motion   158

   Momentum   161

   The second law of motion   161

   Gravity   163

   The difference between mass and weight   164

   Falling objects   165

   The third law of motion   166

The effects of forces: change of shape   167

FURTHER CONCEPTS TO SUPPORT KEY STAGE 2   168

Pressure   168

Forces in action   169

   Friction   169

   Upthrust   171

   Displacement   172

   Floating and sinking   172

   Objects weighed in air and water   174

KEY IDEA 4.3   *The Earth and beyond*   176

Introduction   176

CONCEPTS TO SUPPORT KEY STAGES 1 AND 2   176

The solar system   176

Day and night   177

The seasons   178

The Earth and the Moon   179

   The orbit and rotation of the Moon   179

   The phases of the Moon   179

The solar system and beyond   180

   Galaxies   182

   Inter-galactic space   182

A cosmic address   183

CONTENTS

Physical processes:
National Curriculum coverage   185

Useful references   189

Appendix: Symbols used in drawing circuit diagrams   191

Index   193

List of figures

SECTION TWO **Life processes and living things**

2.1   The process of photosynthesis   13

2.2   The human digestive system   15

2.3   The circulation of the blood   17

2.4   The human thoracic cavity   18

2.5   The main parts of the human skeleton   21

2.6   The muscles and movement of the human arm   22

2.7   The joints in human limbs   23

2.8   The human eye   24

2.9   The human ear   25

2.10   A section of human skin   26

2.11   Conscious and reflex action pathways   28

2.12   Human sexual organs   31

2.13   The parts of a flower   32

2.14   Examples of seed dispersal mechanisms   33

2.15   The life cycle of a flowering plant   36

2.16   The main parts of a flowering plant   36

2.17   The main external parts of the human body   38

2.18   Sections of human teeth   42

2.19   Examples of the classification of a plant and an animal   47

2.20   A classification of the plant kingdom   49

2.21   A classification of the animal kingdom   50

2.22   An example of a lateral key   55

2.23   'Normal' and 'high-peaked' forms of Galapagos tortoise shells   57

2.24   The layers in a deciduous woodland   62

2.25   The zonation of some seaweeds and periwinkles on a rocky shore   64

2.26   A pyramid of biomass in a simple food chain   67

2.27   A food web: some feeding relationships in a pond ecosystem   68

2.28   The food cycle   68

2.29   The water cycle   69

2.30   The carbon cycle (after Shreeve, 1983)   69

2.31   The nitrogen cycle (after Shreeve, 1983)   70

SECTION THREE   **Materials and their properties**

3.1   A soil profile   78

3.2   A hexane molecule   81

3.3   Plastics from ethene   82

3.4   Examples of compressive, tensile and shear forces   86

3.5   Stress/strain curves for a variety of materials in tension   87

3.6   The states of matter and changes of state   96

3.7   The structure of a carbon atom   98

3.8   Periodic table entries for carbon and copper   98

3.9   Electron diagrams of some common elements   100

3.10   Covalent bonding: a chlorine molecule   100

3.11   The solubility curves of two different compounds   106

3.12   Features formed by igneous rocks   111

3.13   The deposition of sedimentary rocks   111

3.14   The rock cycle   113

SECTION FOUR   **Physical processes**

4.1   Series and parallel circuits   130

4.2   Changing effects in series circuits   131

4.3   The effect of resistance in a parallel circuit   132

4.4   A simple circuit and its corresponding circuit diagram   133

4.5   Stages in the generation of electricity   136

4.6   The electromagnetic spectrum   139

4.7   The six colours of the rainbow   139

4.8   A 'light and dark' box   146

4.9   Making wave forms with a skipping rope   147

4.10   The main features of wave forms   147

4.11   The straight line experiment   148

4.12   Angles of incidence and reflection   149

4.13   The refraction of light   151

4.14   The appearing coin 'trick'   151

4.15   The movement of molecules in a sound wave   153

4.16   Investigating reflected sound   154

4.17   The relationship between the mass and frequency (pitch) of tuning forks   156

4.18   Sound waves – pitch and loudness   156

4.19   Investigating the second law of motion   162

4.20   Measuring mass and weight   164

4.21   Equal and opposite reactions: forces in balanced pairs   167

4.22   An example of the effect of unbalanced forces   168

4.23   Investigating the force of friction   171

4.24   How the shaping of a hull effectively increases a vessel's volume   174

4.25   Forces acting on a mass being weighed in air and water   174

4.26   Simulating day and night   178

4.27   Summer and winter: the positions of the Earth and Sun   179

4.28   Simulating the phases of the Moon   180

4.29   The orbits and axial rotation of the Earth and the Moon   181

4.30   The relative sizes of the Earth, the Sun, and Betelgeuse   181

Acknowledgments

Many people and organizations have helped me during the production of this book, and I am pleased to acknowledge my debt of thanks to the following:

to Gareth Wyn Jones, the inspirational headteacher of Ysgol Gynradd Bontddu, who first made me welcome in his school and then encouraged me to teach science to primary children – diolch yn fawr iawn i chwi;

to the members of the Research Committee of the School of Education, University of Sunderland, who awarded me the one-semester secondment which allowed me to write the text;

to Professor Yvonne Stewart-Smith, the Director of the School of Education, who provided both encouragement and the resources needed to produce the typescript;

to the Sunderland primary teachers who were members of the 1993–94 '20 day' primary science course, who read and commented on early drafts of section 2;

to Professor Jack Yarwood, Director of the Materials Research Institute, Sheffield Hallam University, for much theoretical and practical encouragement;

to Jenny Begg, who read and made suggestions on each section, and to Anne Hussey, who read and commented on drafts of Sections 2 and 3;

to my former colleagues in the University of Sunderland – Colin Gill from the School of Engineering and Advanced Technology; Ian Yeomans from the School of the Environment; and from the School of Education: Neil Hutton, George Shield, Stephanie Atkinson, John McShea, Bob Stokoe, Chas Bowles, and Alex Dockerty, all of whom gave of their time and expertise, and to Carolyn Andrew – who read and commented on the entire typescript in draft form, and also suggested the book title;

and finally, to Malcolm Clarkson, Anna Clarkson, Jackie Day, Alison Woodhead and Teresa Jenkins of Falmer Press, for their encouragement and support during the production of the final version of the book.

Introduction

The nature and purpose of the book

WHAT THE
BOOK AIMS
TO DO

This book has been written with primary teachers and teachers-in-training in mind, and its main purpose is to **support and extend teachers' own science knowledge**.

Of course, the content has been chosen to reflect the structure and requirements of the National Curriculum (NC) in science, but there is more to the book than that. The hope is that, in using the book, teachers may gain insight into, and understanding of, the science which underlies the NC requirements, in the context of a wider knowledge base.

To that end, there has been a deliberate avoidance of the use of the science programmes of study for Key Stages 1 and 2 simply as a 'check list' for the contents of the book. Readers will find that some of the ideas and concepts presented are not included in, or are 'beyond', the current Key Stage 1 and 2 requirements. Even though such ideas and concepts may therefore be inappropriate *for primary school children*, an understanding of them may be of value and relevance to *teachers*.

An example may be useful here. The 'particulate nature of matter' and 'kinetic theory' are not components of the Key Stage 1 or 2 programmes of study, and it is not therefore a requirement for primary school teachers to be able to teach these concepts to children. Their inclusion may seem irrelevant in a book of this sort. However, some understanding of the particulate nature of matter may be useful for teachers, in order for them better to understand the behaviour of solids, liquids and gases (which *do* appear in the Key Stage 2 programme of study). The book therefore includes sections which deal with the particulate nature of matter and with kinetic theory, in the hope that they may provide useful insights for teachers who are preparing to investigate the properties of solids, liquids and gases in their own classrooms.

In dealing with the main areas of science – life science, materials science and physical processes – an attempt has been made to provide a whole picture of each area, rather than a mosaic of National Curriculum pieces. The hope therefore, is that coverage of the subject knowledge requirements of the science NC for Key Stages 1 and 2 is well within the scope of the book, and that there is much else besides which teachers may find engaging and interesting.

Part of the thinking behind the attempt to provide an 'overview' for each of the three main areas of science, is the belief that it is perhaps risky professionally only to 'know about' the particular part of the science NC with which you may be currently engaged in school. We may all have been 'one step ahead of the children' at some time in our own careers, but in my experience, it is an uncomfortable place to be! I hope that the content chosen, and the explanations given, will enable teachers, through the development of deeper understanding and greater confidence in their own science knowledge, to interpret more effectively the science National Curriculum for the children in their charge. There is now considerable evidence from 20 day science course evaluations, that increased subject knowledge can lead to increased confidence and to changes in the science learning opportunities presented to children – 'Now that I *know* more, I feel I'm a better teacher of science.'

WHAT THE BOOK *DOES NOT* DO

Since the book is specifically devoted to the subject knowledge of science, there are two areas of science education which have deliberately not been addressed.

■ Scl – experimental and investigative science

There is no overt consideration of science AT1, although many examples are given of investigations which relate to the science knowledge under consideration. Wherever appropriate, 'classroom' versions of these investigations are indicated, and teachers may wish to include them in their own schemes of work. For more direct consideration of the implementation of AT1, readers are referred to other publications (see list of references).

■ The planning, organization and management of classroom science

The book does not address the issues inherent in the day-to-day provision of science education in primary classrooms. Once again, there are a number of excellent publications available which deal specifically with these issues, and these too, are listed in the references section.

THE DEVELOPMENT OF THE BOOK

The starting point for the development of the book was a consideration of the programme of study in each of the three 'content' attainment targets of the science National Curriculum, i.e.:

■ Sc2 – Life Processes and Living Things
■ Sc3 – Materials and their Properties
■ Sc4 – Physical Processes

In order to gain a 'feel' for the scope of the content of ATs 2–4, each of the 'content' phrases or clauses in the old (1991) programmes of study was listed, and then a set of '**Key Ideas**' was drawn up for each of the areas of science represented by the attainment targets.

During the writing of the book, the 'Dearing' review proposals were published, with rewritten programmes of study containing shifts of emphasis in some content areas. These, in turn, were followed by the 'final' SCAA version of the new National Curriculum in science for Key Stages 1 and 2. In my opinion however, the Key Ideas identified as relevant to the science 'subject knowledge' attainment targets are not affected by the Dearing review and rewrite – life science is still life science, whichever 'pieces' are currently included in the NC mosaic – so the contents of the book have remained substantially unaltered by the rewrite.

The Key Ideas represent an attempt to encapsulate what is at the heart of the branch of science represented by the specific attainment target. Each has been expanded, section by section, to provide a description and explanation of the concepts involved. As has already been explained, some of these concepts are 'beyond' what is necessary for children at Key Stages 1 and 2, but their inclusion is seen as important in the development of teachers' fuller understanding of the science which underpins the Key Stage 1 and 2 requirements.

It is important to recognize that the book does not set out to provide material which can be used in the classroom in an unmodified form. It is not a book for children, but my hope is that it will be of value to teachers and students in supporting and extending their knowledge of science so that what they provide in the way of science learning experiences for children will be grounded in a broader and more secure knowledge base, and a deeper understanding of the subject knowledge context of the science National Curriculum.

THE STRUCTURE OF THE BOOK

The book contains three main sections, Life processes and living things, Materials and their properties, and Physical processes.

At the beginning of each section, the Key Ideas are listed, and are subsequently expanded in the following text. Concepts which relate to the Key Ideas are presented as 'Concepts to Support Key Stage 1' (or Key Stage 2, or both). The expectation is that the ideas presented will assist in teachers' understanding of the science involved, and hence will support their own teaching of the various components of the Key Stage 1 and 2 programmes of study. Where concepts are presented which are not Key Stage 1 and 2 requirements for children, but which may be helpful in terms of understanding science for teachers, this distinction is made clear in the text.

At the end of each main section there is a **National Curriculum coverage** listing for the attainment target concerned. This allows the reader to relate each component of the programmes of study for Key Stages 1 and 2 to the Key Ideas and concepts presented and described in the book, and may be useful as a 'quick reference' guide for those seeking help with particular and specific aspects of NC-related science knowledge.

THE LANGUAGE OF SCIENCE

Throughout the book, the aim has been to express scientific ideas in the most straightforward language possible, using examples from everyday experience. In each case, and at the appropriate place, the scientific terminology appropriate to the particular idea presented has been included in the explanation.

Where complex concepts are involved, scientific terminology becomes necessary for the accurate expression of ideas, as in such cases, oversimplification could lead to distortion, omission and/or a potentially misleading explanation, and every effort has been made to avoid this.

It is hoped therefore, that the self-avowed non-specialist will not be daunted, nor those with a science background feel patronized, by the use of the language chosen (simple or scientific) for the expression and explanation of ideas.

THE PROVISIONAL NATURE OF SCIENCE KNOWLEDGE

I believe that it is important to stress that science does *not* provide us, once and for all, with the *right* answers. What it can provide is a series of provisional explanations based on theory, observation and verification by experiment or investigation. In some cases these explanations offer a degree of predictability so high that they can be generalized into 'laws' – the laws of motion, for example. In everyday terms, the laws of motion first propounded by Sir Isaac Newton can still offer us a useful explanation of the forces acting on moving objects – it is these laws which are described and explained in the subsection of this book which deals with forces.

Further theorizing and experimentation however, may bring new discoveries which increase our understanding of the way the world works, and cause modifications to the explanations offered by science. Early in this century, the 'frontiers' of Newtonian physics were extended by the theory of relativity proposed by Albert Einstein, and Einsteinian physics may well be supplanted in future by the attempt to provide a 'unified theory' which can explain the behaviour of all matter.

Scientific knowledge then, is provisional, and gives rise to current explanations of the nature of things – explanations which may remain valid until further knowledge allows us to modify and improve them. In writing this book, every effort has been made to present the current and accepted thinking in science. Where alternative explanations or controversies exist (as with global warming, or 'cold' nuclear fusion, for example) these have been acknowledged and included.

| A NOTE ON UNITS |

Throughout the book, the attempt has been made to express units in the most easily understandable form. So for example, the units of density have been cited as **grams per cubic centimetre**, and have been expressed in terms of g/cm^3, rather than in terms of the more conventional $g\ cm^{-3}$. Similarly, **acceleration** is expressed in terms of **metres per second per second**, written as m/s^2, rather than as $m\ s^{-2}$.

Life processes and living things

2.1 *The characteristics of living things: All living things have a number of characteristics in common*

2.2 *Life processes: These characteristics are the observable outcomes of the processes which sustain and renew life*

2.3 *Optimum conditions for survival*

2.4 *The variety of life: There is a large variety of life forms on Earth*

2.5 *Adaptation to environment: Animals and plants tend to adapt to their environments (Natural Selection)*

2.6 *The transfer of energy: Life is sustained through the transfer of energy (from the Sun to the tissues of living organisms)*

The characteristics of living things

All living things have a number of characteristics in common

How do we know that things are alive? Young children have been known to describe a car as being alive because it can move, or a calculator, because numbers appear when you switch it on and press the buttons. A group of five-year-olds once explained that big boulders grew from little ones – a perfectly understandable five-year-old conclusion, as they had seen plants grow from seeds, and they knew that small young people grew into bigger older people!

It takes time and experience with a variety of living and non-living material to begin to develop the notion of 'alive', and the understanding that all living things have a number of characteristics in common. It may be helpful to remember that whilst some 'inanimate' objects may possess some of these characteristics, only living things possess them all.

The characteristics of living things

Living things, including humans: **feed, respire, excrete, grow, respond to stimuli, move, and reproduce.**

The characteristics of living things, (feeding, excretion, respiration, growth, response to stimuli, movement, and reproduction), outlined above, are all processes which occur as a result of the specialization of cells in the plants and animals concerned.

It is possible to visualize the processes on a 'micro to macro' scale:

- life processes at the most fundamental level involve the synthesis, breakdown and recombination of inorganic and organic **molecules**;
- these molecules are broken down, reassembled and incorporated into the individual units of life – the **cells**;
- cells of similar kind, having similar functions, are grouped together as **tissues**;
- tissues are grouped together in **organs**;
- and organs which contribute to major bodily functions are grouped in **organ systems**.

Organ systems

The organs and organ systems can be grouped according to their functions, and one convenient grouping for mammals is as follows:

System name	Functions	Mammalian organs
nutrition system	feeding, digestion, egestion	gut, liver, pancreas
cardio-vascular system	circulation, respiration, excretion	heart, lungs, kidneys
musculo-skeletal system	support, movement	skeleton, muscles, tendons, ligaments
nervous system	sensitivity, coordination	brain, sense organs
reproductive system	reproduction	sexual organs

In the next section (Key Idea 2.2), these systems will be decribed, with particular reference to humans, and where appropriate, to flowering plants.

Life processes

These characteristics are the observable outcomes of the processes which sustain and renew life

Life is sustained as a result of complicated chemical reactions which happen continuously in the cells and tissues of each animal or plant. The basic chemicals which secure this process (which is known as metabolism) are supplied to the cells through the feeding process.

Feeding

Green plants are unique in the living world in that they are able to make their own food. They do this by using the energy from sunlight to make organic molecules (carbohydrates) from simple molecules like carbon dioxide and water. This process is known as photosynthesis, and is the basic support system for life on Earth (see Key Idea 2.6: Energy Transfer).

Animals are not able to synthesize carbohydrates, so they need to feed either on plants (when they are known as herbivores), on other animals (carnivores), or both (omnivores).

However the food is derived, it is used to 'fuel' the life support systems of the individual plant or animal – the systems which ensure continued survival. In animals, the food is broken down by a process known as digestion, where the useful components of the food are broken down physically and chemically, absorbed into the blood, and finally taken in solution to the tissues where the processes of life take place.

Elimination of waste (excretion)

Living things are able to eliminate from their tissues the components of food which are of no value (e.g. the **egestion** of faeces in animals) and the byproducts of metabolism which are toxic (e.g. the **excretion** of carbon dioxide and urea).

Respiration

The food produced by plants, or eaten by animals, is broken down so that it can be used to provide energy to support the life processes of the organism. Energy is released by the breakdown of organic molecules (usually in the presence of oxygen), and the process is known as respiration.

Respiration consists of up to three processes:

a) **breathing** – the supply of oxygen to the surfaces for gaseous interchange;
b) **gaseous interchange** – the diffusion of oxygen into the organism and carbon dioxide out;

11

c) **cellular respiration** – chemical reactions in the cells which result in the release of energy.

Some organisms are able to respire in the absence of oxygen (anaerobic respiration), but the process is much less efficient than aerobic respiration.

Growth

Some of the food produced by plants, or eaten by animals, is used in the production of cells – the organism increases in size. Plants tend to grow throughout their lives, adding new tissue as time progresses. Animals tend to grow until they reach maturity, when tissue growth gives way to replacement.

A salutary thought is that old age ensues when replacement fails to keep pace with wear and tear, and death occurs when all metabolism ceases.

Response to stimuli (sensitivity)

Organisms are able to react and respond to stimuli. Animals are able to respond to some or all of: light, heat, sound, touch, and the chemical indicators of taste and smell. Plants respond to light and gravity (some respond to touch, e.g. Mimosa, Venus Fly Trap).

Movement

Animals are able to move by conscious decision and to travel using limbs or all of their bodies. Plants tend to grow towards favourable stimuli, e.g. light.

Reproduction

Organisms are able to produce offspring of their own kind, either through sexual (involving two parents), or asexual (cloning) reproduction.

Differences between plants and animals

Using the list of characteristics of living things, it is possible to draw up a table showing the main differences between plants and animals:

	Plants	Animals
Feeding	food synthesized from inorganic molecules	eat plants or other animals
Respiration	energy stored as starch	energy stored as glycogen
Elimination of waste	oxygen and CO_2, leaf fall	CO_2, urine, defaecation
Growth	branching, continues to death	compact, continues to maturity
Response to stimuli	slow (growth), no obvious nervous system	rapid, through nervous system and sense organs
Movement	anchored, rigid cell walls	mobile, skeleton and muscles
Reproduction	frequently asexual embryos as seeds	infrequently asexual embryos in eggs or live-born
Cellular structure	rigid cellulose cell-wall, chloroplasts present in green plants	thin cell membrane

**CONCEPTS TO
SUPPORT KEY
STAGE 2**

**Nutrition systems
(feeding, digestion,
egestion)**

A major difference between living and non-living things is that living organisms are able to replace, from outside themselves, energy lost in the maintenance of life. In order to do this they must supply themselves with energy-rich organic compounds which can be used to 'fuel' the processes of life, and they do this by feeding.

All life depends, directly or indirectly, on the most fundamental life process of all – the ability of green plants to make food from simple inorganic molecules – photosynthesis.

Plant nutrition – photosynthesis

Photosynthesis is a two-stage process. The first, or light, stage, involves the transfer of energy from sunlight to the molecules of chlorophyll (the green pigment) in the leaves of a plant.

The units of light energy, the photons, transferred through the chlorophyll, enter a chemical pathway and combine with hydrogen ions from water in the plant. At the end of the light stage, the hydrogen has combined with other energy carriers in the cells, and oxygen (from the water) is produced as a waste product and is released to the atmosphere through the tissues of the plant (see Fig. 2.1).

The second stage of photosynthesis does not need light, but can be affected by temperature. Essentially what happens is that the hydrogen from the light stage, via the energy carrying molecules, combines with carbon dioxide, absorbed from the atmosphere by the plant, to produce sugars, and eventually starch, which is the main energy-rich compound in green plants.

The chemical formula for the process is as follows:

$$6CO_2 + 6H_2O \xrightarrow{\text{sun's energy, through chlorophyll}} C_6H_{12}O_6 + 6O_2$$

carbon dioxide   water   glucose   oxygen

Fig. 2.1 The process of photosynthesis

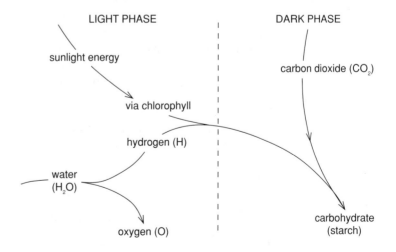

Animal nutrition – digestion

Animals are not able to synthesize energy-rich compounds, so they feed on plants, or on other animals (or both), in order to secure a supply for themselves. The body has developed a series of processes which cause the physical and chemical breakdown of the food, the absorption of the required components, and the elimination of waste material, as follows:

- physical processes – chewing, swallowing, churning in stomach;
- chemical processes – breakdown by enzymes;
- absorption of food into blood stream;
- reabsorption of water from waste – faeces;
- elimination of faeces from anus.

The physical process of chewing allows the food to be broken down into smaller pieces. The front, incisor teeth, act as shears to 'chop' the food, whilst the rear, molar teeth, help to grind the food to a pulp. The overall effect is to increase the surface area of the swallowed food, so that the digestive enzymes can act with greater efficiency.

The physical process continues after the food leaves the mouth, as swallowing regulates the amount and frequency of food reaching the stomach. The muscles of the gullet (oesophagus) wall contract once the food has passed and help to push it into the stomach (a process known as peristalsis), and the contractions of the muscular stomach wall 'churn' the food to allow better mixing with the digestive enzymes.

The basic function of the chemical process of digestion is to break down the food molecules into units which are soluble and small enough to be absorbed into the body through the gut wall. The digestion of the various components of the food is assisted by specific enzymes, which are biological catalysts. Enzymes speed up the rate of chemical reactions, and are 'added' to the ingested food at various places during its journey through the gut.

To start with, the salivary glands in the mouth secrete saliva, which is a mixture of mucus, to lubricate the food and make it easier to swallow, and amylase, an enzyme which helps the breakdown of starch in the food.

Once the food is in the stomach, glands in the stomach wall secrete gastric juice, a mixture of hydrochloric acid and pepsin, an enzyme which helps to break down proteins into peptides. When the food passes out of the stomach into the duodenum, bile (produced by the liver and stored in the gall bladder) is added. This has the function of emulsifying the fat from the food into small droplets. From the pancreas comes a mixture of enzymes which enter the duodenum and help with the breakdown of starch and glycogen to sugars, fats to glycerol and fatty acids, and proteins to peptides.

As the food passes from the duodenum to the ileum, millions of tiny finger-like processes in the gut wall, the villi, absorb into the blood stream the soluble molecules which are the products of digestion – sugars are digested as glucose, fats as glycerol and fatty acids, and peptides as amino acids (the building blocks of proteins).

What passes from the ileum to the colon is a mixture of undigested food and water. During its passage through the colon, water is absorbed into the bloodstream so that the remaining material becomes more solid, forming faeces

Fig. 2.2 *The human digestive system*

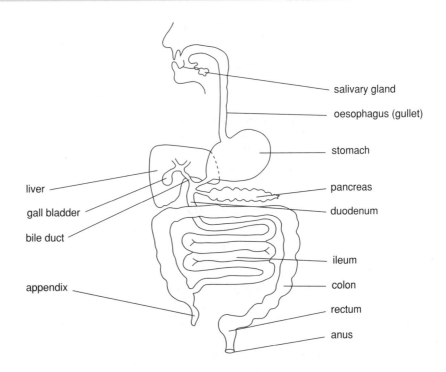

- salivary gland
- oesophagus (gullet)
- stomach
- pancreas
- duodenum
- ileum
- colon
- rectum
- anus

liver

gall bladder

bile duct

appendix

which pass out of the body through the anus (see Fig. 2.2 for a diagram of the human digestive system).

The cardio-vascular system (circulation and respiration)

The human cardio-vascular system has a number of components. These include the heart (a pump), the lungs (for oxygen supply), a network of branching blood vessels (arteries, veins and capillaries) which allows blood to reach every part of the body, and the blood itself (a vehicle for the transport of dissolved oxygen and food substances, and of the waste products of metabolism).

The blood

In examining the constituent parts of the blood it is possible to list the various functions of the system as a whole.

Plasma (a straw coloured liquid): transports dissolved food (glucose, fatty acids and amino acids) and mineral salts, waste products (carbon dioxide and urea) and hormones; contains antibodies and protein used in clotting (fibrinogen).

Red blood cells (erythrocytes): are shaped like flattened discs and have no nucleus, and are produced in red bone marrow. They transport oxygen in solution round the body. Haemoglobin is the oxygen carrying pigment.

White blood cells (leucocytes): are of two types:

a) phagocytes, which kill bacteria by engulfing them, and are produced in red bone marrow;

b) lymphocytes, which produce antibodies which dissolve into the plasma and kill invading bacteria, and are produced in the lymph nodes.

Platelets (thrombocytes): are fragments of blood cells, which help blood to clot and wounds to heal, and are produced in red bone marrow.

To summarize, the blood acts as:

- a **transport** system for oxygen, food and wastes;
- a **defence** system against invasion by bacteria and other antigens;
- a **sealing** system against wounds;
- a **regulation** system for body temperature and water and chemical balance.

Circulation (see Fig. 2.3)

The circulation of the blood round the body is basically a double system, with the heart acting as the double pump that drives it. The sequence is as follows:

Phase 1

- **de-oxygenated blood** from the tissues arrives at the right upper chamber (atrium) of the heart;
- the atrium contracts, sending the blood into the right lower chamber, or ventricle;
- the right ventricle contracts, sending the de-oxygenated blood to the lungs, via the pulmonary artery (the only artery to carry de-oxygenated, i.e. venous, blood);
- in the microscopic blood vessels which supply the lung surface, carbon dioxide diffuses out of solution from the blood plasma, and oxygen diffuses from the lungs, combining with the haemoglobin in the blood platelets to form oxyhaemoglobin – **the blood has been oxygenated**;

Phase 2

- the oxygenated blood returns from the lungs (via the pulmonary vein) to the left atrium;
- the left atrium contracts, sending the oxygenated blood to the left ventricle;
- the left ventricle contracts, **sending oxygenated blood round the body** via the aorta, and to the head via the carotid artery.

In practice, both atria contract at the same time, rapidly followed by the ventricles, so that the two circulations, one to the lungs, the other to the rest of the body, are running simultaneously. Non-return valves between the atria and the ventricles ensure that the blood always flows in the same direction. The left ventricular (systolic) contraction, which forces oxygenated blood round the body, can be felt from outside the body as the 'pulse', and is a direct measure of the speed of blood circulation. Heart rate is controlled naturally by specialized tissues within the atrium walls, or artificially by the implantation of a 'pacemaker' which delivers small, regular electrical impulses to the heart muscle, helping to stabilize the heart rate.

A variety of factors can influence heart rate:

- **increased exercise** leading to oxygen debt will cause the rate to rise to compensate;
- certain **hormones**, notably **adrenaline**, the 'fight or flight' hormone, can

Fig. 2.3 The circulation
of the blood

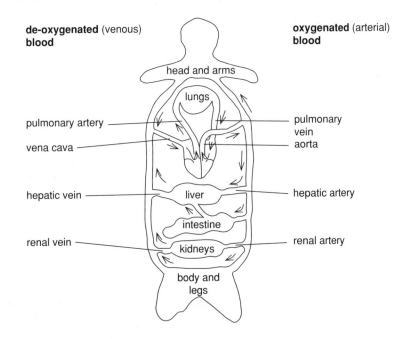

de-oxygenated (venous) **blood**

oxygenated (arterial) **blood**

head and arms

lungs

pulmonary artery

vena cava

pulmonary vein

aorta

hepatic vein

liver

hepatic artery

intestine

renal vein

kidneys

renal artery

body and legs

increase heart rate in order to allow the individual to react quickly and with great energy to particular situations;

■ **cooling of the outer body** can cause a compensatory increase in heart rate, e.g. in winter;

■ **alcohol** stimulates an increase in heart rate.

The oxygenated blood is carried away from the heart in arteries. These are capable of withstanding high pressure, and have strong elastic walls. As they divide into smaller and smaller vessels, they eventually become capillaries. These are very small tubes with walls only one cell thick, thus presenting the smallest barrier to the diffusion of oxygen and waste products into and out of the cells which they supply. Capillaries eventually combine to form veins, which are thin walled vessels carrying de-oxygenated blood towards the heart at low pressure. Veins contain a system of flaps or non-return valves which prevent blood from flowing back towards the tissues.

The organs which remove some of the waste products of metabolism are the kidneys. They are particularly concerned with the elimination of urea, which has a high nitrogen content, and is formed from the breakdown of proteins. As blood is pumped through the kidneys, excess water and urea diffuse as urine into the kidney tubules. These coalesce to form collecting ducts and eventually, via the ureters, urine is carried to the bladder, whence it is emptied to the outside by the relaxation of a muscular ring (sphincter) at the head of the urethra.

Respiration

Respiration is a sequence of processes which basically results in the oxidation of glucose molecules to form carbon dioxide and water, with an accompanying

Fig. 2.4 *The human thoracic cavity*

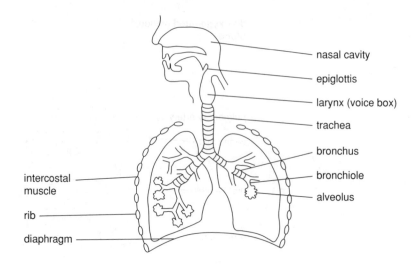

release of energy. The most efficient form of respiration takes place in the presence of oxygen and is known as **aerobic** respiration.

In order for aerobic respiration to take place, all organisms need a regular supply of oxygen, a medium for gaseous exchange, and a supply of glucose (either manufactured or consumed). Up to three processes are involved:

1. Breathing

Breathing (or ventilation) is the mechanism by which all land animals ensure that a regular supply of oxygen is delivered to the body. This is achieved by the inhalation of air into the lungs. In humans, the muscles between the ribs, the intercostal muscles, contract to lift the ribs upwards and outwards. At the same time the sheet of muscle at the base of the rib cage, the diaphragm, is pulled downwards by contraction. The net effect of these two movements is to increase the size of the chest (or thoracic) cavity, thus lowering the pressure and causing air to flood into the lungs. Conversely, when the diaphragm and intercostal muscles relax, the thoracic cavity contracts, pressure increases, and air is forced out of the lungs. Humans ventilate their lungs about 12 times per minute when at rest, exchanging about 0.5 litres of air as they do so. After exercise, this rate can increase to 60 breaths per minute, exchanging 2–3 litres at each inhalation.

In aquatic animals such as fish, the supply of oxygen is ensured by the passage of water, containing dissolved oxygen, across the gills.

Plants do not need a mechanism for breathing, as air can diffuse directly into plant tissues through pores (stomata) in leaves and other tissues.

2. Gaseous exchange

Air enters the lungs through the wind pipe or trachea (see Fig. 2.4). This is a tube of tissue, strengthened with cartilage rings to prevent it from collapsing. The trachea divides into two bronchi (one to each lung), and the bronchi divide into smaller bronchioles. At the end of each bronchiole are bunches of very small air sacs called alveoli, each one less than 1 mm in diameter. The alveoli have walls which are one cell thick, and they are covered with a network of extremely fine capillary blood vessels. The effect of this arrangement is to create a large surface area over which diffusion can take place – it has been estimated that the surface area of a pair of human lungs is equivalent to that of a tennis court!

The alveoli have a moist lining, and the closeness of the surrounding capillaries allows diffusion of gases in solution to take place at the surface of the lungs. Oxygen diffuses from the lungs into the red blood cells (platelets) in the capillaries, and carbon dioxide, a waste product of respiration, diffuses from the blood plasma into the lungs. The diffusion gradient is maintained by the continual replenishment of the oxygen supply (by breathing), and the removal to the tissues of the oxygen absorbed by the red blood cells (by circulation).

Inhaled air contains about 20% oxygen and 0.03% carbon dioxide; exhaled air contains about 16% oxygen and 4% carbon dioxide.

3. Cellular or tissue respiration

Cellular respiration is the set of chemical reactions which take place in the cells of the organism. It usually takes place in the presence of oxygen. The basic formula for aerobic respiration is:

$$C_6H_{12}O_6 \ + \ 6O_2 \ \text{------------} \ 6CO_2 \ + \ 6H_2O \ + \ \textbf{energy}$$

glucose   oxygen   carbon   water
                                          dioxide

This reaction is, apparently, a reversal of that of photosynthesis (see above), where carbon dioxide and water are combined using energy derived from sunlight, to produce glucose molecules, with oxygen as a 'waste' product.

The reaction is not however, a direct reversal. In the first phase of respiration, glucose is converted into pyruvic acid. This can then be respired aerobically, in the presence of oxygen, to liberate a relatively large amount of energy (as in the above equation), or be respired less efficiently in the absence of oxygen (anaerobically) to produce different waste products.

In the plant kingdom, the **anaerobic** respiration of yeast cells results in the production of ethanol (alcohol), a reaction at the heart of the brewing industry, and carbon dioxide, which forms the basis of the baking industry. In animals, anaerobic respiration of pyruvic acid produces lactic acid. This can occur in humans when oxygen demand exceeds supply, e.g. during strenuous physical exercise such as sprinting. The lactic acid produced by anaerobic respiration in humans is also the cause of 'stiff muscles' after unaccustomed exercise.

About 60% of the energy released by aerobic respiration is in the form of heat. This helps to maintain the body temperature of warm-blooded animals (mammals and birds). The remaining energy can be used for growth and repair, as some of the by-products of the oxidation process can be used in the production of other 'building blocks' such as amino acids and fatty acids, or for muscular movement, e.g. locomotion, or for the maintenance of heartbeat and breathing.

The musculo-skeletal system (support and movement)

As plants and animals have evolved larger forms, systems of support have become necessary.

Support in plants

Plants tend to grow upwards in the competition for light (the largest trees are over 100 metres tall), and they have evolved two main support systems:

1. **Water (hydrostatic) pressure.** Plant cells absorb water until they are inflated (turgid). The cell walls are strengthened with cellulose and this prevents the cells from bursting. The overall effect of this process is to 'stiffen' the plant tissue. A useful mental model of turgid plant cells is to imagine typical supermarket 1 litre cardboard containers full of fruit juice. A stack of such containers would not collapse as it would gain support from the liquid inside each 'cell'.
2. **Woody tissue.** Some plants (mainly in trees and shrubs) derive support from cells whose walls are thickened with **lignin**. The cells are thus mechanically strengthened, and make no energy demands on the plant.

Support in animals – the skeleton

Similarly, animals developed support systems as increasing size and range of activity brought larger forces to bear on the body forms which evolved.

Some animals without backbones (invertebrates) have evolved **exoskeletons**. These are rigid external coverings which offer protection to their owners, and also provide large internal surfaces for the attachment of muscles. The arthropods provide excellent examples of animals with exoskeletons – crabs, lobsters, and insects, for instance.

The five groups of vertebrate animals (fish, amphibians, reptiles, birds and mammals) have developed internal skeletons (**endoskeletons**) based on a remarkably similar pattern which demonstrates their common evolutionary ancestry. All have skulls and backbones containing brain and spinal cords, and land animals also have four limbs (again, structured on similar patterns) attached to the backbone via two limb girdles. One group, the sharks, dogfish and rays, have skeletons made of cartilage, but all the other vertebrates have bony skeletons. Fig. 2.5 shows the main parts of the human skeleton.

The tissues which comprise the skeleton in humans are bone, cartilage and ligaments.

Bone is a hard, strong and slightly flexible tissue made of calcium phosphate. This is secreted by bone cells arranged in cylindrical layers (for strength), which are connected to a network of fibres which give the bone its flexibility. Blood vessels and nerves run through canals in the structure of the bones. The bones of the skeleton provide a strong, rigid support for the body. The flexibility necessary in the skeleton in order for movement to take place is provided by joints which act as articulations between individual bones.

Cartilage is an elastic, rubbery protein which covers the ends of bones at joints. It can act as a smooth load bearing surface in a joint, e.g. the semi-lunar

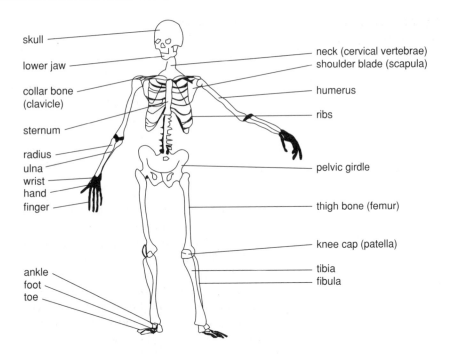

Fig. 2.5 *The main parts of the human skeleton*

skull
lower jaw
collar bone (clavicle)
sternum
radius
ulna
wrist
hand
finger
ankle
foot
toe

neck (cervical vertebrae)
shoulder blade (scapula)
humerus
ribs
pelvic girdle
thigh bone (femur)
knee cap (patella)
tibia
fibula

cartilage in the knee joint, and also as a shock absorber between bones, e.g. the 'discs' of cartilage between the vertebrae of the spine. The most obvious piece of cartilage which can be 'felt' is the end of your nose!

Ligaments are strong elastic groups of fibres which bind the bones tightly together at joints and help to prevent them from dislocating. The joints themselves are enclosed by a synovial membrane which secretes synovial fluid which lubricates the joint. Over-use of a joint can cause the over-production of synovial fluid, causing painful swelling at the joint – for example, in tennis elbow.

Movement in animals

Animals can move in a variety of ways: by swimming (fish, marine mammals, seals), crawling (lizards, toads), sliding (snakes), walking (humans), hopping (perching birds, kangaroos), running (gazelles, cheetahs), or flying (birds, bats).

In addition to the skeletal tissues above, two further tissues are involved in movement.

Muscles are tissues made up of fibres (mainly of protein), which are able to contract and so shorten their length. It is believed that this shortening is achieved by the muscle filaments sliding between one another rather than by the actual contraction of individual fibres.

Muscles which are involved in movement are examples of voluntary muscles, i.e. they are under conscious control. Whilst muscles can contract and shorten, they cannot lengthen again. They must be stretched back to full length by the

Fig. 2.6 *The muscles and movement of the human arm*

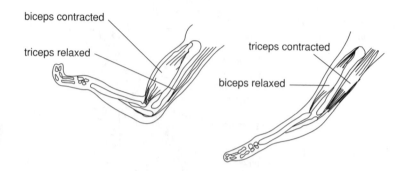

biceps contracted

triceps relaxed

triceps contracted

biceps relaxed

pull of an opposing or antagonistic muscle. So the muscles which control movement are found in opposing pairs.

A good example of this arrangement can be found in the human arm. The biceps muscle on the inside of the upper arm is a flexor muscle. When it contracts, it pulls on the forearm and moves it towards the shoulder, bending the arm. At the same time the opposing muscle, the triceps, on the outside of the upper arm, relaxes to allow the biceps to contract. When the triceps (an extensor muscle) contracts, it shortens and 'pulls' the arm straight, at the same time returning the biceps to its original, uncontracted length (see Fig. 2.6).

Similarly, the shin and calf muscles of the lower leg allow the foot to be 'waggled' up and down.

Some muscles cause internal movements in the body and are involuntary, i.e. they normally operate automatically and are not under conscious control. Two examples of involuntary muscles already described are the heart and the diaphragm (see previous section).

Tendons are strips of strong, inelastic tissue which attach muscles to bones. The inelasticity allows the 'pull' of the contracting muscle to act directly on the bone and so cause movement of some kind.

Muscles are able to cause movement because the bones articulate together at the joints. There are two basic types of joint:

- **fixed** and immobile joints where plates of bone are tightly interlocked like the pieces of a jigsaw; these joints are known as sutures, e.g. the bones of the cranium (skull);
- **movable** joints, of three types:
  ball-and-socket joints, which can move in more than one plane;
  hinge joints which can move in a single plane;
  sliding joints which have a limited rotary movement.

All of these joint types can be found in the limbs of humans, which have ball-and-socket joints at the shoulder and hip, hinge joints at the elbow and knee, and sliding joints at the wrist and ankle (see Fig. 2.7).

Movement can take place because of a sequence of events:

- **energy** is supplied by the **contraction** and shortening of muscles;
- the muscular contraction allows **bones** to **move** relative to each other;
- the **movement** of the bones **exerts** a **force** on the load-bearing surface in contact with the environment. For example, the tail of a fish 'presses' against

Fig. 2.7 *The joints in human limbs*

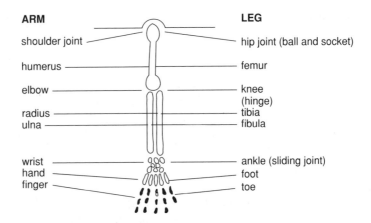

the water, the hoof of a horse grips the ground, the wing of a bird 'pushes' the air.

The nervous system (sensitivity, coordination)

In order to survive, plants and animals need to be able to respond to the variety of conditions presented by the environment in which they live. These conditions may be long term and therefore demand a long term response, e.g. bears respond to the onset of winter by hibernating, or may be sudden and potentially life-threatening, e.g. bears will fight or move away when attacked by another, larger animal.

Animals are able to respond to the stimuli presented by the environment because they have a number of specialized organs for sensing the environment in which they live and by which they are affected, and a system of specialized tissues – the nervous system – capable of receiving, relaying, analysing and responding to 'messages' about that environment.

Human sense organs

The specialist organs, or sensors, which allow mammals (including humans) to monitor the state of their environment are:

- the **eyes**, which respond to **light**, and allow humans to see colour, shape and movement;
- the **ears**, which respond to **sound and gravity**, and allow people to hear, and to be aware of 'where they are in space' – hence the ability to remain balanced;
- the **tongue**, which responds to **chemicals** in solution, and which can distinguish bitter, sweet, salty and sour tastes;
- the **nose**, which responds to airborne **chemicals** as smells;
- **skin sensors** respond to touch **(pressure), heat** and **cold**.

The eye

It is perhaps important to remember that the eye is an organ specialized for the collection and focusing of light. The 'seeing' is done when the signals

Fig. 2.8 *The human eye*

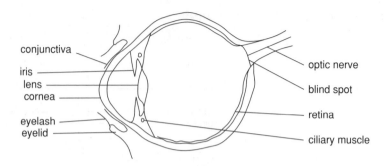

conjunctiva
iris
lens
cornea
eyelash
eyelid

optic nerve
blind spot
retina
ciliary muscle

received by light sensitive cells in the eye are relayed as impulses by the optic nerve for interpretation by the brain.

The human eye (see Fig. 2.8) is a fluid-filled sac housed in a bony socket. The front surface of the eye, the **cornea**, is protected by **eyelids**, which can 'blink' or stay closed to keep out dust, smoke, or other irritating substances, and by fluid (tears) which lubricate the eyeball and also help to wash out any solid or liquid irritants. The cornea also acts as an external lens and helps to focus light into the eye. Behind the cornea lies the **iris**, which gives the eye its 'colour', and which can enlarge or make smaller the hole (**pupil**) which admits light to the eye. It is easy to watch the pupil size change as light intensity varies, for example, by alternately shading the eyes, then looking towards a light – torchlight is sufficient – **never** use direct sunlight.

Behind the iris is the **lens**, the shape of which can be changed by the contraction or relaxation of a ring of muscle (**ciliary muscle**) which surrounds it. When the ciliary muscle is relaxed, the ligaments which suspend the lens are stretched and it becomes thin, and able to focus distant objects. When the ciliary muscle contracts, the strain on the **suspensory ligaments** is lessened, the lens becomes fatter, and can focus near objects. Finally, the lens inverts the image of the 'seen' object onto the **retina** – a thin layer of light-sensitive cells on the back of the eye. Impulses from these cells, some of which detect 'black-and-white' and others of which detect 'colour', travel along the **optic nerve** to the brain.

The ear

The ear has two basic functions: hearing, and sensing changes of position (hence, balance).

The outer ear (**pinna**) collects sound waves as vibrations in the air (see Key Idea 4.1: Sound) and channels them down the ear canal to the **ear drum**. Behind the ear drum are three small bones, the ear **ossicles**, which vibrate as the ear drum resonates with the incoming sound waves. This vibration is passed on to a fluid-filled spiral tube (the **cochlea**) where sensitive hair cells pick up the vibrations and send impulses along the **auditory nerve** to the brain. The upper part of the inner ear forms three **semi-circular canals** which are arranged in three planes. They too, are fluid-filled, and because the fluid tends to 'stay put' (as a result of inertia) when the canals move with the body, sensitive **ampullae** in the canals can detect movement in any direction,

Fig. 2.9 The human ear

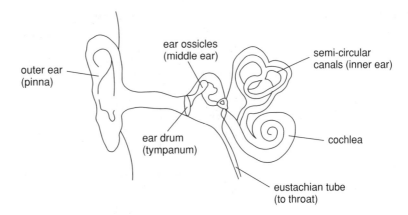

and impulses sent to the brain allow it to 'decide' what actions will be necessary to maintain balance (see Fig. 2.9).

Taste and smell

Taste and smell are closely linked, relying as they do on groups of sensory cells in the mouth and nose cavities. The taste buds on the tongue are able to sense bitter, sweet, sour and salty flavours. Since the mouth and nose cavities are linked, the sense of smell also adds to our appreciation of a full range of flavours. This is noticeable when the nasal passages are blocked, for example by a head cold. Not only is the sense of smell impeded, the sense of taste is also diminished, and food seems 'flavourless'.

The skin (touch, temperature)

Sensory nerve endings in the middle layer of the skin (dermis) enable us to feel pressure, and temperature. So, in addition to 'feeling' the touch of an object on the skin, we are able to tell whether it is hot or cold. If pressure on the skin is large, pain sensors in the upper layer of the skin (the epidermis) send impulses to the brain, and avoiding action can be taken (see Fig. 2.10).

In addition to this sensory capacity, the skin also has the following functions:

Protection
- the skin is waterproof, so it prevents water entry to, or loss from, the body;
- it prevents the entry of harmful bacteria and viruses;
- it produces the pigment melanin, which protects the body from the harmful ultraviolet component of sunlight;

Excretion
- some urea and salts are lost in sweating;

Temperature regulation
- hair in mammals traps layers of warm air;
- sweating assists heat loss by the evaporation of perspiration from the skin surface;

Fig. 2.10 *A section of human skin*

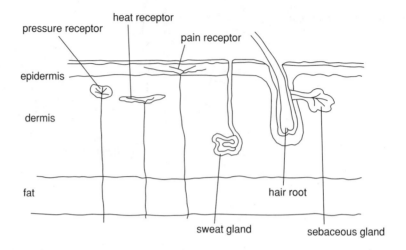

■ surface capillaries can open in warm weather (vaso-dilation) to flush the skin surface with blood, assisting cooling, or close in cold weather (vaso-constriction), restricting blood flow and conserving heat;

■ the fat layer under the skin provides heat insulation.

Plant responses to environmental stimuli

Plants respond in three main ways to the environments in which they grow:

a) they **grow towards light**: the shoots of green plants grow towards the sunlight they need for photosynthesis (positive phototropism);

b) the **roots** of plants **grow** downwards **towards gravity** (positive geotropism). This helps to stabilize the plants, and to reach sources of ground water; the **shoots** of plants **grow** upwards **away from gravity** (negative geotropism), thus helping with the search for light;

c) they **respond to changes in day length** (photoperiodism). A blue pigment (phytochrome) in plant leaves reacts as day length increases, producing a hormone (florigen) which triggers flower formation.

Coordination and control

It is important for an animal to give a coordinated response to information received about the state and nature of the surrounding environment. Random response is inefficient and may be ineffective, if not fatal.

There are two basic body systems for coordination and control: the **nervous system**, and the **endocrine** or **hormone system**.

The nervous system

At its most basic, the nervous system represents a communication system which connects environmental sensors (the sense organs) to effectors (muscles and glands) by means of a switchboard or relay system (the spinal cord) and a computer (the brain). The system allows for very rapid coordination and control of actions and responses.

The brain and spinal cord form the **central nervous system** (CNS), and the network of nerve cells linking the CNS with receptors (in the sense organs) and effectors (the muscles, glands etc.) all over the body, is known as the **peripheral nervous system** (PNS).

Nerve cells, or neurones, occur in bundles known as nerve fibres. These are long and narrow cells which are specialized to allow for the one-way passage of impulses similar to those of an electrical current. The impulses are caused by changes in the concentration of sodium (chemical symbol: Na) and potassium (K) ions in the neurones, and can travel at up to 120 metres per second. Unlike the wires in an electrical circuit, neurones in the nervous system do not make direct contact with other neurones, but are separated by small gaps (or synapses). When a nerve impulse reaches a synapse, it causes the secretion of a transmitter substance which allows the passage of the impulse across the synapse, so triggering an impulse in the next neurone along the line.

An example of the basic stimulus-response sequence for conscious action is as follows:

- information from the environment is received by sensory cells in the body, e.g. hair cells in the cochlea of the inner ear (see above) are stimulated by vibration;
- an impulse, triggered by the sensory cells, passes along the sensory neurones to the spinal cord;
- relay neurones in the spinal cord carry the impulse to pyramidal neurones in the brain;
- the pyramidal neurones, with many connections to others, allow the brain to decode and 'perceive' the stimulus (e.g. a doorbell ringing), and 'decide on' a course of action;
- the pyramidal neurones pass on the impulse to motor neurones which activate muscles;
- movement begins to 'answer the door'.

If the stimulus is of an urgent, painful or life-threatening nature – an object moving rapidly towards the eye for example – the relay neurones in the spinal cord would route the impulse direct to motor neurones, speeding up the response time, and an automatic, or reflex, action would result – the eyelids would quickly close – the 'blink' reflex (see Fig. 2.11).

The endocrine or hormone system

In contrast to the nervous system, where rapidly transmitted impulses tend to result in rapid and relatively short-term responses, hormones are 'chemical messengers' which are secreted in glands and released into the bloodstream. Hormonal 'messages' therefore travel more slowly (at the speed of the blood circulation), their actions therefore tend to take effect more slowly, and tend to be longer lasting.

A summary of human hormones, production sites and effects is as follows:

Hormone	Gland	Effect
growth hormone	pituitary gland (base of brain)	increases growth in young maintains size in adult
thyroid stimulating hormone	pituitary	acts on thyroid, thereby controlling metabolic rate
prolactin	pituitary	mammary gland development, milk production
thyroxine	thyroid gland (throat)	controls cellular energy release (metabolism)
insulin	pancreas	absorption of glucose from blood into storage deficiency causes sugar diabetes
adrenaline	adrenal glands (near kidneys)	raises blood sugar levels, preparing the body for action (the 'fight or flight' hormone)
oestrogen	ovaries	controls female sexual development and menstrual cycle
testosterone	testes	controls male sexual development and sperm production

Fig. 2.11 Conscious and reflex action pathways

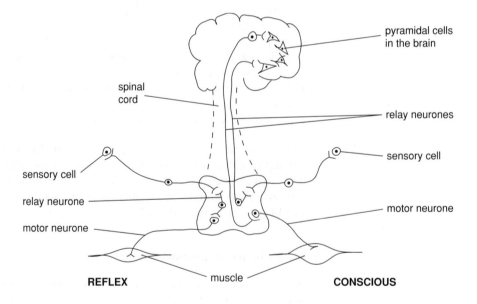

Reproductive systems

Asexual reproduction

Asexual reproduction occurs when an organism reproduces a genetically identical copy (clone) of itself. It is a process which is common in simple animals and many plants, and which can take the following forms:

Fission – the splitting of the original organism into two equal parts, each of which grow to form new individuals. Fission is a common method used by bacteria, resulting in exponential growth potential as one individual becomes 2, 2 become 4 and so on;

Budding – the parent produces an outgrowth which detaches and develops into a new individual, e.g. yeast cells;

Spore formation – the parent produces single celled bodies which detach and disperse themselves and can grow into new individuals under suitable conditions. An excellent method of surviving adverse environmental conditions, or for increasing the distribution of the species. Examples include bacteria and simple plants;

Vegetative reproduction (propagation) – part of a plant can develop into a new individual, eventually becoming detached and independent. Examples are the overground runners of strawberry plants, the underground rhizomes of marram or bracken, the tubers of potatoes, and the bulbs of daffodils and onions.

The advantages of asexual reproduction are that it can take place with a single individual, and can produce identical copies of a particularly favoured strain. In addition, asexual reproduction can allow for rapid population expansion, both in terms of numbers and distribution. Areas of grassland of up to 400 m^2 are known to be covered by clones of a single individual.

The disadvantages of asexual reproduction are:

a) that it limits the genetic variability, and hence the evolutionary potential, of a population, as it does not involve the mixing of genetic material from different individuals;
b) that a population composed of genetically identical individuals would be more vulnerable to disease than one with the genetic variability generated by sexual reproduction.

Sexual reproduction

Sexual reproduction takes place in all higher animals and plants, although it is possible for plants to revert to vegetative reproduction if environmental conditions are not suitable. Many plant populations survive by a mixture of asexual and sexual reproduction.

The key biological feature of sexual reproduction is that specialized cells (gametes) from a male and a female individual fuse to form a zygote cell, which then develops to form a new individual.

The biology of human reproduction

In humans, the female gametes (egg cells or ova) are produced, usually singly and at approximately 28 day intervals (under hormonal control) in the ovaries. Each ovum, containing half the number of chromosomes of all other cells in the body, is released (at ovulation), and begins a journey down the Fallopian tube (oviduct).

When sexual intercourse (copulation) takes place, sperms, produced in large numbers by the male testes, are released from the erect male penis by reflex muscular spasm during orgasm, into the female vagina. Sperms begin to swim towards the oviducts, where fertilization may take place if copulation has occurred within three days or so of ovulation.

Fertilization involves the surrounding of the ovum by sperms, and the eventual entry into the ovum of the head of a single sperm. The head of the sperm also contains half the chromosomal material of all other body cells, and the fusing of the sperm head with the nucleus of the ovum restores the full chromosomal complement to the fertilized egg (zygote).

As the zygote continues its journey down the oviduct towards the uterus, cell division begins, and after about one week the developing embryo arrives in the uterus as a hollow ball of cells (blastocyst) and implantation occurs into the wall of the uterus.

Finger like villi grow into the uterus wall to form the placenta, and it is here that the exchange of food and waste products takes place by diffusion between the blood vessels of the mother and the embryo. There is no direct connection of the two blood supplies.

The embryo becomes surrounded by a fluid-filled protective membrane (the amnion) which supports it and cushions it from shock. It continues to develop, and after two months is a recognizably human foetus. Nine months after fertilization, at the end of the period of internal development (or gestation), the baby is born.

The muscular wall of the uterus begins to contract regularly and forces the baby down the widened uterus-cervix-vagina – the 'birth canal'. The contractions become more frequent and powerful, eventually bursting the amnion and releasing its fluid to the outside. The most difficult part of the birth (from the point of view of the mother) is the passage of the baby's head through the birth canal. This is effected by the continuing (involuntary) muscular contractions of the wall of the uterus, assisted by the 'pushing' of the mother. Once the head of the baby has emerged from the birth canal (most babies are born head-first), the remainder of the birth is usually easier.

After the birth, the cord connecting the baby to the placenta (the umbilical cord) is ligatured and cut, and some minutes later, after further contractions, the placenta is expelled from the mother's uterus.

Puberty

Humans are not able to reproduce until they are sexually mature. Development towards that maturity is triggered by male and female sex hormones and is signalled by the onset of puberty.

In girls aged 10–12 years this causes:

- the development of secondary sexual characteristics (breasts, pubic and armpit hair);
- the onset of ovulation and menstruation;
- widening of hips.

In boys aged 12–14 years it causes:

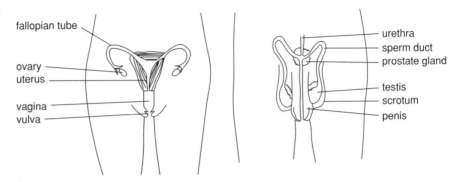

Fig. 2.12 *Human sexual organs*

- the development of secondary sexual characteristics (voice breaks, pubic and armpit hair);
- the onset of sperm production.

The menstrual cycle

The female menstrual cycle is, in the absence of fertilization, a 28-day cycle of egg production and release (ovulation), and the breakdown and expulsion from the body of the remains of the wall of the uterus (menstruation).

During the first two weeks of the menstrual cycle, the female sex hormone oestrogen, produced by the ovaries, causes the thickening of the uterine wall, and the stimulation of the pituitary gland to produce luteinizing hormone, which causes ovulation. If fertilization and implantation occurs, another hormone, progesterone, is produced which stops any further production of ova during pregnancy. If fertilization does not occur, or if implantation fails, the ovum dies and the uterus wall begins to break down.

The expulsion of the remains of the uterine wall and the accompanying 4–7 days of bleeding, is known as the 'period' of menstruation. After menstruation, oestrogen promotes the repair of the uterine wall, and a further hormone – follicle stimulating hormone (FSH) – causes the development of the ovum to be released at the next ovulation.

Sexual reproduction in flowering plants

As plants grow towards maturity they produce flower buds, which eventually develop into flowers (see Fig. 2.13). These are, in effect, a series of modified leaves, each set of which is specialized to perform a specific function. In general terms, a flower would consist of:

an **outer ring of sepals** (the calyx) which protects the contents of the flower bud during development;
an inner **ring of petals** (the corolla) which may be coloured and scented, and which attracts and provides nectar for visiting insects;
a **ring of stamens** (the male parts of the flower), each comprising a stalk (filament), and a pollen sac (anther);
a **central carpel** (the female part of the flower), comprising an ovary at its

31

Fig. 2.13 *The parts of a flower*

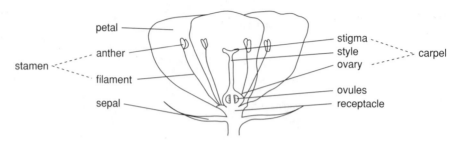

base, and a style or stalk which supports a stigma (a surface specialized for the receipt and germination of pollen).

This arrangement allows for self-pollination, i.e. the transfer of pollen from the anthers to the stigma, either in the same flower or to another flower on the same plant. Modifications include the ripening of anthers and ovaries at different times so that self-pollination is avoided, the presence of only male (or only female) parts on individual flowers, or the presence of only male (or female) flowers on individual plants, thus requiring cross-pollination for successful sexual reproduction. Some plants have 'fail safe' mechanisms which guarantee self-fertilization if cross-pollination does not occur, e.g. as flowers wither in late season, the anthers bend to touch the stigma, so ensuring pollination.

The sequence of events in the life cycle of a flowering plant (see Fig. 2.15) may proceed as follows:

Germination

■ the seed swells as it absorbs water. The root, then the shoot emerges;

Growth to flowering

■ the plant grows by branching. Flower buds emerge and flowers open;

Pollination

■ pollen grains mature in the anthers, which split on ripening, releasing pollen to the outside;
■ the pollen grains are transported, either by insects which have visited the flower to collect nectar, or by the wind, to the stigma of a flower of the same species (each plant produces species-specific pollen);
■ a number of pollen grains germinate on the stigma, and within minutes pollen tubes begin to grow towards the ovary. The pollen tubes eventually reach the ovary and penetrate the embryo sac. The nuclei from the pollen grains fuse with egg cells (ova), and fertilization has taken place;

Development of seeds and fruit

■ each fertilized ovum develops into a seed containing a shoot (plumule), root (radicle), and one (monocotyledons) or two (dicotyledons) seed leaves;
■ the ovary containing fertilized seeds develops into a fruit. The seeds may be

Fig. 2.14 *Examples of seed dispersal mechanisms*

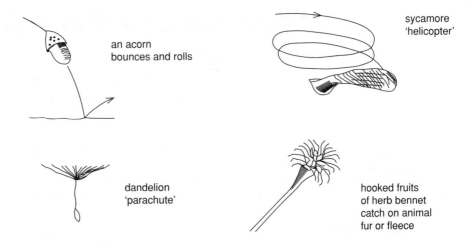

an acorn
bounces and rolls

sycamore
'helicopter'

dandelion
'parachute'

hooked fruits
of herb bennet
catch on animal
fur or fleece

borne internally, as in apples and tomatoes, or externally, as in blackberries and strawberries, where the 'fruit' is the swollen base (or receptacle) of the flower bud.

Dispersal

■ the seed pod dries out and splits. Seeds are shaken out and fall to the ground, where they in turn may germinate under suitable conditions.

Dispersal

The advantage of sexual reproduction, and particularly fertilization by cross-pollination, is the potential increase in variability (and therefore survival chances) which it provides.

In order to maximize the impact of this variability, and to minimize direct competition for scarce resources, plants have developed a number of ways in which their seeds can be dispersed, and hence the range and distribution of the species increased (see Fig. 2.14).

Examples of different dispersal mechanisms include:

■ 'bouncers and rollers' – acorns, horse chestnuts;
■ 'parachutes' – dandelions, thistles;
■ 'helicopters' – sycamore, ash;
■ 'pepper pots' – poppies;
■ 'edibles' – blackberries, strawberries, apples;
■ 'hookers and stickers' – burdock, goose grass (cleavers), herb bennet (wood avens);
■ 'splitters' – wallflowers, lupins, laburnum.

In addition to dispersal as a method for increasing range and distribution, seeds also allow plants to survive hostile environmental conditions, as they may lie dormant for long periods of time, for example during drought or extreme cold, before germinating when conditions have improved and survival chances are better.

Optimum conditions for survival

For animals and plants in hostile environments, survival may simply be a matter of 'hanging on', or of being able to tolerate conditions which other organisms cannot (e.g. desert, salt marsh). For most organisms however, it is possible to identify optimum conditions in which they will flourish.

Healthy plants

For successful establishment and growth to reproduction, plants need:

A 'safe site' for germination – a place where a seed can settle, preferably in well drained, well aerated soil, with space to grow, and with little likelihood of being blown or washed away. Much of the autumn 'seed rain' dies without ever reaching a safe site. Either there is no space available, or the seeds are washed or blown away, or collected and eaten by predators.

Water availability – plants need water in order to synthesize food, as a medium for metabolic reactions and internal transport, and for support (this can be seen when a plant begins to wilt if it is not watered regularly). Most of this water comes from the soil, and reaches the plant tissues through the root system. A small amount is absorbed directly from the leaves.

Oxygen (for photosynthesis) and carbon dioxide (for respiration) – both of these gases enter the plant by diffusion through small pores (or stomata), usually on the underside of the leaves.

Nutrients (minerals from the soil) – iron and magnesium salts are used in the production of chlorophyll, nitrates and sulphates are used in protein and DNA production, phosphates are used in 'energy carrier' molecules (ATP), and calcium is laid down in the middle layer between plant cell walls.

Sunlight (after germination) – is essential for photosynthesis, and is the source of energy which sustains life on Earth.

Space to grow – all plants in a natural environment are competing for available moisture, nutrients etc. Those which have the largest spaces into which to grow, will usually be the most successful. This principle can be very easily demonstrated by sowing different numbers of seeds into the same size pots of soil, and then observing the difference in size of the germinated plants.

Warmth – the chemical reactions which occur in the cells of plants, will 'work' better at higher natural temperatures. That is why growth is so luxuriant in equatorial forests, and why gardeners 'force' the growth of plants in glass-houses. Plant growth generally stops when the temperature falls below 6°C, or rises above 40°C.

A system of pollination – in order for a plant to set seed, pollen from the male parts of a flower needs to reach the female parts of a flower so that the gamete cells can fuse. Some plants rely on insects for pollination. Insects visit the flowers to collect nectar, and in doing so brush against the pollen bearing structures of the plant. When visiting another plant in search of nectar, some of the pollen is brushed off onto the female parts of the new flower, and pollination has taken place. Other plants rely on the wind 'shaking' the pollen out of male flowers and carrying it to female flowers of the same species.

Healthy animals In order to survive, grow, and stay healthy, animals need:

Food – animals cannot make their own food, so they have to eat plants or other animals. For healthy living a balanced diet is necessary, and should contain carbohydrates and fats (for energy), proteins (for body building), and vitamins and minerals (for maintenance). The table below shows some food types, examples and functions.

Type of food	Examples	Functions
Carbohydrate	glucose; starch	energy supply; plant cell walls; 'building blocks' of other molecules
Fats	animal fat; oils in plants	energy supply (double the 'energy per gram' of carbohydrates); insulation
Proteins	muscle; tendons; enzymes and hormones used in metabolism; haemoglobin	movement; insulin used to control blood sugar levels oxygen carrier
Vitamins	**A** (retinol) from vegetables and liver oils	helps night vision
	B$_1$ (thiamine) from wholemeal bread	builds strong muscles
	B$_2$ (riboflavin) from liver and yeast	helps respiration
	B$_{12}$ (cobolamine) from liver	helps make red blood cells
	C (ascorbic acid) from citrus fruit and fresh vegetables	strengthens skin; helps heal wounds
	D (calciferol) from butter and egg yolk	assists calcium and phosphate deposition in bones
Minerals	**Ca** (calcium) and **P** (phosphorus) from cheese and milk	bones and teeth are 66% calcium phosphate
	Fe (iron) from liver and egg yolk	part of haemoglobin (oxygen carrier)
	Na (sodium) salt	helps nerves and muscles to work properly
	I (iodine) from sea foods and table salt	makes the hormone thyroxine which helps to control metabolism

35

Fig. 2.15 *The life cycle of a flowering plant*

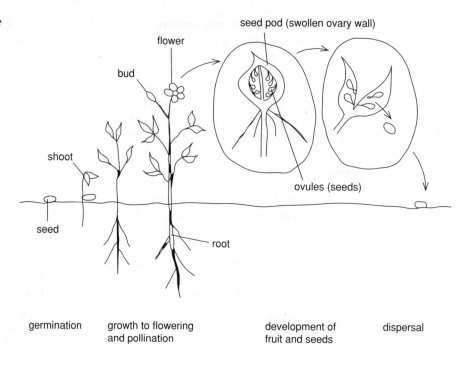

germination   growth to flowering   development of   dispersal
                 and pollination   fruit and seeds

Fig. 2.16 *The main parts of a flowering plant*

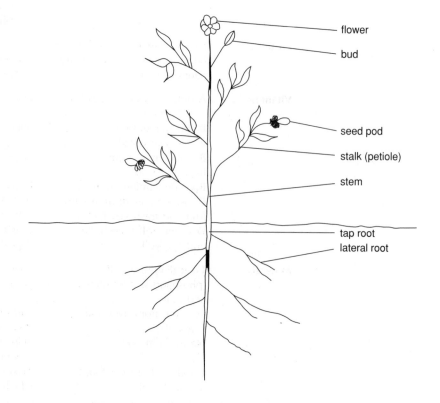

The main parts of a balanced diet will consist of carbohydrates, fats and proteins. Vitamins and minerals are needed in very small quantities, but their absence will often have a serious effect on health and well-being. The importance of a balanced diet is now better understood, as are the dangers of overeating. Eating 'more than is necessary' to sustain health can lead to obesity (being overweight), and is an increasing problem in children and young adults. Eating too much of one kind of food (particularly fatty and sugary food) can increase the likelihood of a person suffering from heart disease, high blood pressure, or strokes (cerebral (brain) haemorrhage).

Water – it has been estimated that human beings consist of 70% water. We need water for the processes of metabolism which go on inside the cells in our bodies, for the internal transport of metabolic products, and for the movement (diffusion) into our bodies of the oxygen for respiration, and out of our bodies of waste carbon dioxide. In addition to the water which is part of our food (cabbage, and banana are about 90% water, meat about 60%), we need to drink the equivalent of 1.5 litres of water a day in order to survive.

Oxygen – the air, which is a mixture of gases, contains about 20% oxygen. Almost all animals (and certainly all vertebrate animals) use oxygen in respiration. Oxygen is carried into the bodies of land animals in the air which is breathed into the lungs. On the damp surfaces of the lungs are very fine blood vessels (capillaries), where the oxygen from the air dissolves into the blood. At the same time, carbon dioxide, which is a waste product of respiration, comes out of solution in the blood and is exhaled from the lungs. The dissolved oxygen in the blood is then transported all round the body where it can be used for cellular respiration – the 'oxidation' of energy rich molecules such as glycogen or fats to produce energy, carbon dioxide and water.

Warmth – two of the groups of vertebrate animals (birds and mammals)are 'warm-blooded', i.e. they maintain a constant body temperature. This characteristic has allowed the two groups to colonize almost every area of the Earth, as the processes of life are not controlled by outside temperatures, although they may be influenced by them. Outside the tropics, most animals have evolved some system to retain body heat and so ensure a stability of temperature which will allow them to survive. The body covering is significant here: feathers for birds and hair or fur for land mammals. Other adaptations include the slowing down of the body systems during cold weather (hibernation in mammals), and migration to warmer places during the worst of the winter weather.

Safe site – animals also need safe sites, to lessen the chances of attack by predators, and for undisturbed breeding. Again, the birds and mammals are groups which pay particular attention to the rearing of young, and one reason for this is that they produce far fewer offspring than do the 'cold-blooded' vertebrate groups – fish lay eggs in thousands, and amphibians and reptiles in hundreds. In order to rear young beyond the stage of dependency, a sheltered and safe site is needed over a period of weeks or months. In many (most) animal species, the female is responsible for rearing the young, and this is one reason why female animals are often well camouflaged, so that they are less likely to be noticed by predators during the breeding phases of their lives.

A further salutary thought is that the activities of people have often been responsible for denying animals the 'safe sites' they need to breed successfully, whether through ploughing, building on, or changing in some other way, the animals' original habitat.

The idea of safe sites can also be extended to people, who are just as much in need of security as any other group. For people, and particularly young people, this implies a safe home environment and enough knowledge to deal with the parts of their environment over which they have no control. This knowledge may include procedures for road safety, how to deal with approaches from strangers, and so on.

Exercise and rest – animals in the wild are continuously exercising – frequently they are hunting or being hunted! In order to allow the body to grow and be healthy, it is important for people to take regular exercise too. This ensures that the heart and lungs are strengthened, and that all the 'moving parts' are in working order. Exercise also frequently results in a feeling of well-being, although excessive or obsessive commitment to an exercise regime can be harmful both physically and mentally.

An important part of healthy living is the requirement of the body for rest. It is not possible to 'keep going' for ever, and the human system needs to rest and recover on a daily basis. Most people need about eight hours sleep per night, and young people probably need more. Lack of sleep causes inattentiveness and irritability (which primary teacher has not noticed that during a morning session?), and whilst it is not appropriate to 'moralize' about how children should live their home lives, it may be worth pointing out the noticeable effects that lack of sleep can cause.

Fig. 2.17 The main external parts of the human body

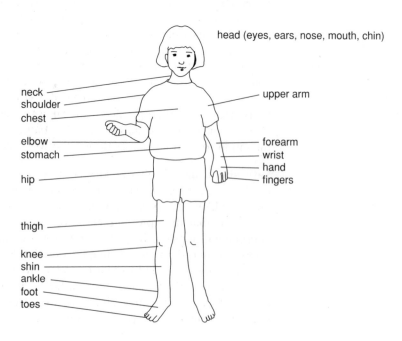

head (eyes, ears, nose, mouth, chin)

neck
shoulder
chest
elbow
stomach
hip
thigh
knee
shin
ankle
foot
toes

upper arm
forearm
wrist
hand
fingers

The defence systems of the body

A number of factors are involved in the establishment and maintenance of human health and well-being. Some of these factors relate to the defence systems of the body and others are under conscious control.

The human body is continuously at risk of invasion by potentially harmful agents. Some of these are inanimate, and take the form of atmospheric or water pollutants. Historical examples would include coal dust from mining, soot from coal fires (a substantial cause of the 1952 London 'smog' which caused over 2,000 deaths from bronchial disease), and asbestos fibres which were a primary cause of lung disease. Although these potential dangers have largely been removed (by the Clean Air Act and by Health and Safety legislation), modern examples would include the exhaust gases from motor vehicles (which may be the cause of a two-fold increase in the incidence of childhood asthma over the past 20 years), and increased levels of heavy metals such as lead, absorbed into human systems. Contentiously, we are told that there is no apparent connection between locally higher incidences of childhood leuk-aemia, and closeness to sites which emit ionizing radiation (nuclear power stations, for example).

The second group of agents are those living organisms which can 'invade' the body, and these are mainly viruses, bacteria, and parasites. Life style and personal habits play a part in the prevention of infection by such organisms, and these are considered below (see **conscious action which can promote health**). In addition to conscious action to maintain health, the body has its own defence systems which can prevent or deal with invasion and infection, and these are now described.

External resistance to invasion

The 'first line of defence' for the body is the skin (see Key Idea 2.2). The skin forms a physical barrier which prevent the direct entry of pollutants or infectious organisms. Secondly, there are a number of other devices used by the body to contain invasion. These include:

- 'filter' systems such as nasal hairs, which prevent or slow down the inhalation of airborne particles;
- mucous membranes, again for example, those in the nasal cavity, which secrete sticky mucous to trap airborne particles or bacteria;
- (although it may possibly be an unpleasant topic for discussion, both of these examples can be used to show the importance of blowing the nose to remove such matter, rather than sniffing and swallowing into the stomach);
- specialized areas of cells (ciliated epithelium) with a surface of very small hairs (cilia) which can 'waft' unwanted particles in a certain direction. An example of such tissue is the ciliated epithelium at the top of the trachea or windpipe. Dirt particles and bacteria which are trapped by mucus are swept by the cilia towards the throat, where they are either swallowed or coughed up, in either case removing the risk to the lungs;
- the conjunctiva, the surface membranes of the eye, sense dirt and dust particles or other foreign bodies and trigger the production of tears to 'flood out' the irritants.

Responses following invasion

The **innate** or **natural immune response** – immediately following infection, groups of cells in the body act to limit the damage which can be done by the invading organism. The action can take the form of engulfment (e.g. by phagocytes), or destruction or inactivation by chemicals produced by a variety of different cell types.

Adaptive immune response – this process is triggered when an invading organism 'escapes' the innate immune response. It involves the processing and recognition of the invading organism (the antigen) and the production of soluble factors (antibodies) which will lead eventually to its elimination.

The adaptive immune response has been successfully exploited in the production and action of vaccines. If dead or inactive infectious organisms (in the form of a vaccine) are injected into a human, the adaptive immune response will cause antibody producing 'memory cells' to be formed. These cells will 'recognize' and resist the effect of any live forms of the injected organism which may invade the body at a later date.

The immune response is not always successful in combating disease. One of the most urgent modern examples is the apparent inability of the human system to deal with the human immunodeficiency virus (HIV) which causes AIDS (acquired immune deficiency syndrome). Basically the action of HIV is to destroy the cells in the body which are able to resist infection, leading to a decreasing ability to mount immune responses. Eventually, the immune system of the body is unable to deal with infections and the individual may suffer from a combination of illnesses. It is at this stage that the sufferer is said to have AIDS, a condition for which there is no known cure.

The virus is known to be transmitted through unprotected sexual contact (particularly between homosexual and bisexual men), the administration of infected blood or blood products, exposure to blood-containing needles and syringes, or through the placental wall of a mother to an unborn child.

Conscious action which can promote health

In addition to the defence work which our bodies do on our behalf, there are a number of areas relating to health over which we have a degree of control. We can decide on various aspects of our life styles and can develop personal habits which can affect our health, and whilst it is arguable as to the extent to which a teacher should promote aspects of life style which relate to health, it is important for people to know the possible implications of any health-related decisions they may make. Areas of consideration include:

diet	types and balance of food eaten regularity of feeding
prevention of infection	washing of self and clothing oral hygiene toilet routines use of handkerchief if suffering from cold food hygiene
life style	attention to personal fitness; exercise regime rest and sleep patterns awareness of the dangers of substance abuse

Diet

Diet is one of the most important factors affecting health, and a balanced diet should contain:

carbohydrates   for oxidation and energy release; for storage as starch (plants) or glycogen (animals); cellulose strengthens plant cell walls, and provides fibre roughage for animals.

fats   for oxidation and energy release (twice the energy per gram of carbohydrates); energy storage; insulation.

proteins   for growth and repair (muscles, tendons, ligaments, skin, hair are made from proteins); enzymes control metabolic rate.

minerals   for building bones and teeth; for nerve function; for haemoglobin (oxygen carrier) in red blood cells.

vitamins   to help control metabolic reactions.

water   for transport inside the body; as a medium for metabolic processes.

fibre   indigestible plant tissues for 'roughage' help the passage of food through the gut.

'Healthy' diets are those which derive the above 'ingredients' from a range of foods, contain plenty of fresh or unprocessed foods, including fruit and vegetables, which cut down on saturated (animal) fat products, and which contain dietary fibre.

A useful idea is that, literally and metaphorically, **'we are what we eat'**. Awareness of the importance of a balanced diet has increased recently, but many nutritionists (and teachers) are concerned about the effect on the long-term health of children of convenience foods, monotonous diets and irregular mealtimes, all of which are potentially unhealthy. It has been suggested, for example, that a daily intake equivalent to five pieces of fruit or vegetables, can significantly decrease the chance of heart disease, cataracts (which occur when the lenses of the eye become opaque), and some cancers. (See also Key Idea 2.2: Nutrition Systems).

Teeth

A related component of healthy living is the need for people to look after their teeth. The pattern of teeth (dentition) in humans reflects an omnivorous diet, and comprises 8 incisors (for cutting), 4 canines (for tearing – relics of the carnivores' fangs), 8 premolars (for grinding and crushing) and 12 molars (adults only, also for grinding and crushing). The basic structures of human teeth are shown in Fig. 2.18. The outer coating of enamel is almost entirely made of calcium phosphate, and is harder than the dentine it covers, which in turn is harder than the bone of the jaw. The pulp cavity at the centre of the tooth contains the blood supply and the nerve endings.

Tooth decay (dental caries) can begin when acids are formed in the mouth

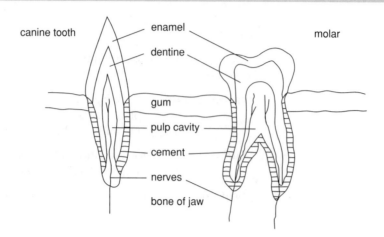

Fig. 2.18 *Sections of human teeth*

during the breakdown of sugars by bacteria. These bacteria form a layer on the teeth (known as plaque), and the acids they produce literally dissolve the tooth enamel and dentine. Toothache results when the nerves in the pulp cavity are affected.

It is important to maintain healthy teeth for as long as possible, both to ensure that food can be properly chewed, and to prevent or limit the discomfort and pain of toothache. Methods of preventing or slowing down tooth decay include:

- the regular brushing of teeth to remove plaque (toothpaste is slightly alkaline and this also helps to neutralize mouth acid);
- cutting down on sugary foods and drinks (less acid is likely to form);
- regular dental check-ups (and filling of cavities if necessary);
- the use of a fluoride toothpaste or tablets (strengthens enamel);
- fluoridation of water supply.

Personal hygiene

At the heart of personal hygiene is the attempt to prevent infection (and perhaps a wish not to offend the noses of companions!).

Leaving aside the persuasive advertising copy of the cosmetics industry, some important practices and functions of personal hygiene can be listed as follows:

- the washing of self and clothing will minimize the possibility of bacteria multiplying in sweat on the body or clothes;
- regular brushing of teeth will neutralize mouth acid and remove or slow down the build-up of bacteria in the mouth;
- the washing of hands after visiting the lavatory lowers the risk of infection, as does the regular disinfection of toilet areas;
- food hygiene may be practised by the prevention or slowing down of decay by refrigeration, the minimizing of risk of infection by use of clean utensils and the careful protection of food, appropriate cooking at the correct temperature (boiling kills most bacteria), the washing of hands before eating, and the proper disposal of unwanted food;

- the use of a handkerchief when suffering from a cold will remove infected mucous from the nasal cavity, and will lessen the 'droplet cloud' effect of an unprotected sneeze.

Life style

The effect of exercise

In order to maintain physical fitness, the body needs regular exercise. In recent years, concern has been expressed about the lack of fitness of the population caused partly by lack of exercise, and health promotion programmes exhort people to increase their rates of exercise in order to stay healthy. Conversely, the 'jogging' and 'aerobics' booms of the '80s and '90s indicate that large numbers of people are serious about the state of their fitness.

Whatever form the exercise takes, it should have the common effect of raising the heart rate through physical activity. This increases the circulation of blood round the body and allows the increased development of the blood capillary network, making for a more efficient transport system for the action of cellular respiration. Exercise allows all the 'moving parts' to develop, particularly the muscles, and the increased blood supply promotes the maintenance of healthy tissues. In addition, exercise frequently brings with it a sense or feeling of well-being, perhaps associated with the exercise-induced release into the blood stream of substances known as endorphins. It has even been suggested that these self-generated substances are mildly addictive, hence the obsession of some people with fitness and exercise!

Just as it is unwise to do too little exercise, it is also unwise to over-exercise. It is not a good idea to overload the muscles, joints and bones of children who are still growing, as this can cause deformity, breakdown or burn-out. This can be seen by the numbers of prodigious young athletes who, as adults, fail to fulfil the promise shown in their younger years.

The need for rest

No organism can simply 'keep going' for ever. After any long period of sustained physical and/or mental activity, the body 'tires' – it becomes less efficient, and a recovery period becomes necessary. In physical terms this need may be signalled by muscle fatigue (caused by the build-up of waste products such as lactic acid), the 'making of mistakes' when undertaking some mental activity such as counting or typing, or lack of coordination in some physical activity like driving a car or hitting a ball.

To restore the body to its full capacity again, a period of rest is needed. During the day this can take the form of stopping the present activity and beginning a different one (what teacher has not introduced a completely different activity to rejuvenate a jaded class?), or rest and relaxation in a position of comfort with little or no activity going on.

The daily pattern of activity and rest is an important consideration for people, particularly those with repetitive jobs, such as assembly workers, or those with jobs which demand long periods of high concentration such as bus or train drivers. Variation in physical and mental activity is important in the establishment of a healthy life style.

The body's main mechanism for rest is sleep, and most adults need about

8 hours sleep (preferably unbroken) each night, in order to recover from the exertions of the previous day. Children, whose metabolic rates tend to be higher because of general growth and activity levels, need correspondingly more sleep in order to recover fully. The frequent lack of sleep caused by modern life styles (late night TV watching, for example) has obvious effects on children in classrooms – inattentiveness, listlessness, irrational and sometimes anti-social behaviour. It may be appropriate for teachers to point out the effects of sleep deprivation, even if they are in no position to change things.

The harmful effects of drugs, alcohol and tobacco

A number of substances can affect the central nervous system and cause phyiological changes in people.

Drugs, some of which can be used for medical purposes, and some chemical solvents, affect the nervous system (possibly by altering the way in which nerve impulses are transmitted), causing changes in perception. If used regularly, the body becomes tolerant to low doses of a drug, and increasingly high doses are needed to produce the same effects. Eventually, with continued use, an individual becomes drug-dependent (or addicted) and has a physiological need for the drug. Once a person is habituated to the use of a drug, its withdrawal would be accompanied by the symptoms of serious illness. A common behaviour pattern is that such a person may have no effective life outside the need to satisfy the drug dependency, often resorting to crime to finance the necessary supply.

Examples of drugs derived from medicines are those which depress the awareness of pain (analgesics), e.g. morphine and heroin, and those which slow down the nervous system (sedatives), e.g. barbiturates.

Those which distort perceptions (hallucinogens) include plant derivatives (cannabis or marijuana) and manufactured substances (LSD and solvents).

Alcohol is a sedative drug. In small quantities it is said to be beneficial, as it can relieve tension, and bring about a feeling of well-being. Physiologically it is vasodilatory, i.e. it causes blood vessels to expand (hence a 'flushed' appearance after alcohol intake). This property is said to be beneficial in the prevention of heart disease. Also, it is a diuretic, i.e. it promotes the passing of urine, which can cause dehydration of the body (said to be one of the causes of the 'hangover' headache).

An excess of alcohol turns the feeling of well-being into an abandonment of caution, causes serious impairment of judgment, coordination, speech and vision, and eventually leads to unconsciousness, and in severe cases, coma and death.

Long-term addiction to alcohol causes an impairment of liver functions due to liver cell death, and the destruction of brain cells. The social effects can be similar to those of the pursuit of any drug dependency – lack of personal and social effectiveness, violent and irrational behaviour, and the allocation of all possible resources (to the point of indebtedness) to the purchase of alcoholic drinks.

Tobacco, like alcohol and the other drugs described, has two types of effects. Firstly, it is a stimulant, and is an example of that group of drugs which speed up nervous activity and increase alertness (cocaine and pep pills also fall into this category). The nicotine in tobacco makes it an addictive substance.

Secondly, inhaled tobacco smoke has a number of effects on the physiology of the body:

- tar irritates the ciliated epithelium of the trachea, causing an increase in mucus secretion, and a paralysis of the cilia which would otherwise remove unwanted particles. This results in mucus congestion of the bronchial tubes and a resultant 'smokers cough', and a likely increase in infection (bronchitis);
- tar also causes the break-up of the alveoli – the small air sacs at the end of the bronchioles (see Key Idea 2.2: The Cardio-vascular System). This has the effect of decreasing the surface area for gaseous exchange. Clinically this condition is known as emphysema, and causes chronic shortage of breath;
- tar is carcinogenous (causes cancer). It can cause the cells in the lungs to divide rapidly, eventually uncontrollably, forming a malignant tumour;
- carbon monoxide in inhaled tobacco smoke combines with haemoglobin in the blood, making the oxygenation of the blood less efficient and reducing the capacity for physical exercise;
- carbon monoxide also increases the sclerosis (deposition of fat) of the arteries, increasing the likelihood of a heart attack.

The variety of life

There is a large variety of life forms on Earth

There are, supposedly, more than two million different kinds of plants and animals on Earth. In order to study, or even to identify them, they have been classified into groups. The basis of classification is similarity and difference – how are the members of a group similar, and how do they differ from all other groups? These questions can be asked repeatedly until it is possible to identify individual types of plants or animals (these ideas are explored further in Concepts to Support Key Stage 2, below).

It is now commonly accepted that present day plants and animals have arisen by adaptation of previous forms, (see section on natural selection below) and most classifications of plants and animals are evolutionary, with groupings based on common ancestry. People involved in the science of classification (taxonomy) take into account the outward appearance, the internal organization, biochemical, and chromosomal evidence, when assigning organisms to their appropriate groups.

The classification of plants and animals therefore involves the division of large groups of organisms into progressively smaller groups with similar features. The hierarchy is as follows:

Kingdom; Phylum (from the Greek word for tribe); **Class; Order; Family; Genus; Species**.

To borrow an idea from mathematics, each succeeding refinement within the classification represents a 'sub-set' of the previous grouping. Two examples are shown in Fig. 2.19.

Conventionally, the generic name begins with a capital, and the specific name, with a small letter. Hence: *Erica cinerea* (Bell Heather); *Panthera leo* (Lion).

It is common to view all life forms as grouped into either the **plant** or **animal kingdoms**. Some modern classifications include four other kingdoms, and these are **viruses, bacteria, protoctista** and **fungi**. From the point of view of children's understanding of classification, the awareness of animals and plants is probably sufficient for Key Stages 1 and 2, but brief details are given here of the other four groups, as each has some significance for, or potential effect on, people.

Kingdom: viruses

Viruses are very small (about one-hundredth of the size of a bacterium), and so are beyond the resolution of a light microscope. They are sub-cellular

Fig. 2.19 *Examples of the classification of a plant and an animal*

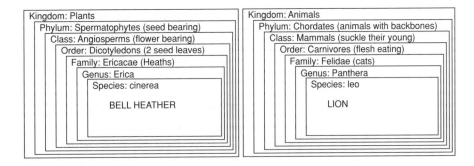

structures, which exist as chemicals outside of living cells, but which are able to reproduce once they have invaded their hosts. Viruses 'inject' their nucleic material (DNA) into host cells and 'take over' the host enzymes for their own metabolism. The virus DNA continues to replicate until eventually the host cell ruptures, releasing the newly produced virus copies to invade further host cells. They have obvious significance for human health, as their replication destroys the tissues which they have invaded. Examples of diseases caused by viruses:

Plants – tobacco mosaic disease
Humans – measles, mumps, herpes (cold sores), influenza, smallpox, HIV

Kingdom: bacteria

Bacteria represent the smallest life forms which are organized on a cellular basis (although they have no distinct cell nucleus). They are about one-hundredth of the size of a human cheek or liver cell. They can be spherical, rod-like or spiral in shape, and can occur in chains or clumps.

Most bacteria obtain their energy from the breakdown of living or non-living organic matter. They play an important role in the decomposition of plant and animal remains, and the eventual recycling of nutrients.

Some bacteria are valuable – they are involved in the production of yoghurt and cheese, and others are sources of antibiotics, e.g. Streptomycin.

Those which are parasitic on living organisms are potentially harmful, and examples of bacterial diseases are diphtheria, leprosy, tuberculosis and typhoid. These diseases are often transmitted through poor water supply, when personal hygiene is of a low standard, or when bacteria are airborne in small water droplets (resulting from coughing or sneezing). Again, the implications for healthy living are obvious.

Kingdom: protoctista

Single celled organisms. The plants are sometimes classified within the Algae, as they contain chlorophyll, but all are single celled, or colonial, and some are motile, i.e. they are self-propelled. As a group they have huge significance, as they make up much of the plankton in the oceans. It is thought that the plant component of plankton (phytoplankton) is responsible, through photosynthesis, for most of the Earth's oxygen supply (certainly for a significantly larger proportion than that produced by equatorial forest). Similarly, the phytoplankton provides the 'plant layer' which is at the base of all the marine food webs (see Key Idea 2.6, below). Some of the blue-green algae produce toxic waste products which can threaten water supplies if the summer time algal 'bloom' is extensive enough.

The animals (Protozoa) are almost all motile. Each individual cell contains organelles, specialized to perform certain functions – digestion, protein synthesis, transport etc. Two groups of marine protozoa secrete hard shells which on their death form the marine sediments which can eventually become chalk or limestone. Some protozoa are harmful parasites, causing Malaria (*Plasmodium*), Dysentery (*Entamoeba*), or Sleeping sickness (*Trypanosoma*).

Kingdom: fungi

The Fungi used to be classified as a group within the plant kingdom, but as they contain no chlorophyll they are now commonly excluded, so that the plant kingdom contains only **green** plants.

Since Fungi contain no chlorophyll they gain their food from dead organic remains (saprophytic nutrition), or from living hosts (parasitic nutrition). They consist of multi-cellular filamentous threads called hyphae which grow over the substrate, secreting enzymes which digest the plant or animal remains before being reabsorbed. As with bacteria, fungi thus play an important role in the decomposition of dead remains and the recycling of nutrients in the soil. Fungi are useful too, in the production of alcohol (a product of the anaerobic respiration of yeast cells), and antibiotics (Penicillium produces penicillin).

Their harmful effects include moulds spoiling food, plant diseases e.g. potato blight, dry rot in timber, and parasitic attack of animals, including humans, e.g. athlete's foot and ringworm.

The main division of classification however, is into plants and animals, and Figs. 2.20 and 2.21 summarize the main groups in each kingdom.

Here is a brief description of the major groups within the plant and animal kingdoms.

Kingdom: plants

Phylum: Algae

The multi-cellular versions include **filamentous forms** (*Spirogyra*, *Cladophora*), and more complex forms are brown, red, green and blue-green **seaweeds**.

Phylum: Lichens

Lichens are a **symbiosis** (living together for mutual benefit) of specific **fungi**, which provide protection, and unicellular **algae** which photosynthesize food. They are simple plants which are often the first colonizers of bare rock – the first soil formers. They grow very slowly and are sensitive indicators of atmospheric pollution.

Fig. 2.20 *A classification of the plant kingdom*

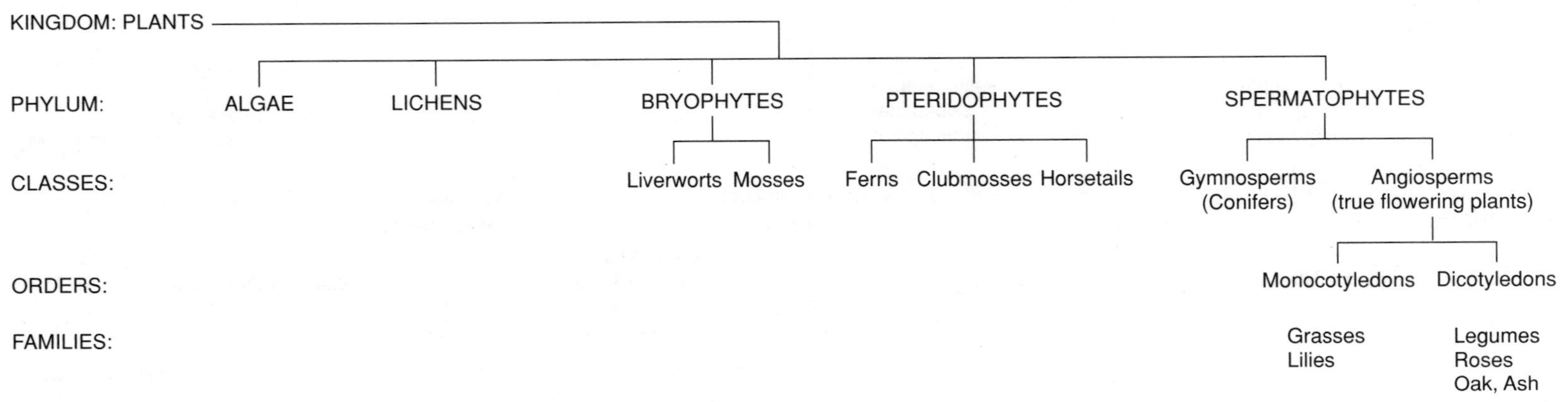

KINGDOM: PLANTS

PHYLUM:

CLASSES:

ORDERS:

FAMILIES:

ALGAE

LICHENS

BRYOPHYTES
- Liverworts
- Mosses

PTERIDOPHYTES
- Ferns
- Clubmosses
- Horsetails

SPERMATOPHYTES
- Gymnosperms (Conifers)
- Angiosperms (true flowering plants)
  - Monocotyledons
    - Grasses
    - Lilies
  - Dicotyledons
    - Legumes
    - Roses
    - Oak, Ash

Fig. 2.21 *A classification of the animal kingdom*

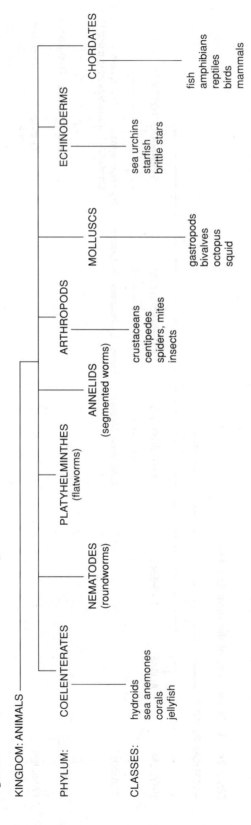

Phylum: **Bryophytes**

Classes: **liverworts and mosses**. Each of these groups favours damp situations and most can tolerate shady conditions.

Phylum: **Pteridophytes**

Classes: **ferns, club-mosses and horsetails**. The forerunners of the flowering plants. Many fossil forms were very large, and in some cases grew in the forests from which coal deposits have developed.

Phylum: **Spermatophytes**

The **seed bearing plants**.

Classes:

gymnosperms:	**conifers:**	**pines, spruces, firs, larches, yews**
angiosperms:	**monocotyledons:**	**iris, lily, bluebell, grasses**
	dicotyledons:	**rose, dandelion, birch, oak**

This classification is 'scientific' and is based on similarities between groups of like kind, arranged in ascending order of complexity. It also reflects an evolutionary series, evidence for which exists in the fossil record. However, it will be difficult for children to see the common sense behind a system which places grass plants from a meadow or playing field in the same group as oak trees, blackberry bushes or daffodils. They are however, all examples of flowering plants!

Kingdom: animals

Phylum: **Coelenterates**

Classes: **hydroids, sea anemones and corals, jellyfish**. Two basic layers of cells with a single body cavity. Stinging cells help with food capture.

Phylum: **Nematodes**

Unsegmented, cylindrical worms. Many are parasitic and cause diseases in plants, animals and humans.

Phylum: **Platyhelminths**

Flatworms. Many are parasitic and alternate between two hosts, causing disease in humans and animals.

Phylum: **Annelids**

Segmented worms – earthworm, lugworm, leech. Separation of the gut and body wall allows movement and digestion to take place independently. Earthworms are useful in improving soil aeration, drainage and nutrient availability.

Phylum: **Arthropods**

The largest and most successful animal phylum

Classes:
crustaceans – woodlice, barnacles, crabs, shrimps
centipedes (carnivores) and **millipedes** (herbivores)
spiders and ticks – 2 body regions, 4 pairs of legs. Some are parasitic and carry disease.
insects – 3 body regions, 3 pairs of legs. The power of flight has allowed worldwide colonization (adaptive radiation). Insects can be helpful – honey bees, pollination of crop plants, control of harmful organisms (ladybirds eat aphids), or harmful – destruction of crops (locusts), carrying disease (malarial mosquito), domestic pests, (clothes moth, house fly, death watch beetle)

Phylum: **Molluscs**

Animals with shells (may be absent or internal)

Classes:
gastropods – snails, winkles
bivalves – cockles, mussels, oysters
octopus and squids.

Phylum: **Echinoderms**

starfish and sea urchins. 5-way symmetry

Phylum: **Chordates**

Sub-phylum – **Vertebrates** – animals with backbones

Classes:
Fish
Cartilaginous – **sharks, rays and dogfish**
Bony – **cod, herring, mackerel**.

Fish live all their lives in water and breathe through gills (lungfish represent the evolutionary 'move onto land'). Cold-blooded, external fertilization, body covering of bony scales, limbs are fins.

Amphibians – frogs, toads, newts.

Larval forms (tadpoles) breathe through gills, adults have 'legs'. Cold-blooded, fertilization is external and aquatic, body covering of smooth skin.

Reptiles – lizards, snakes, crocodiles, turtles.

Mainly terrestrial, adults have legs (vestigial in snakes). Cold-blooded, internal fertilization, eggs laid in soft shell, body covering of leathery scales.

Birds – sparrow, raven, ostrich.

Power of flight has allowed worldwide adaptive radiation. Forelimbs are wings. Warm-blooded, internal fertilization, egg laid in chalky shell, body covering of feathers.

Mammals – shrew, cat, elephant, bat, dolphin, humans. Warm-blooded, internal fertilization, young born live and fed milk from female mammary gland, body covering of hair (except marine mammals).

Again, this classification represents a supposed evolutionary sequence of development. The ordering of the groups makes the assumption that the history of the animals has involved firstly, an increase in the variety of life forms, and secondly, a 'migration' from the water to the land. Hence, successive groups in the classification represent more complex life forms. (Note that there is no such group as 'minibeasts'. In terms of scientific classification that particular grouping is unhelpful.)

The story is not so simple however. It is believed, for example, that the marine mammals – whales, dolphins and porpoises – have 'gone back' into the sea in evolutionary terms, and that their ancestors were probably land-dwelling animals.

It is generally accepted that the increasing variety of life forms, and their migration from the sea onto land, can be explained in terms of the theory of evolution, and this is dealt with in a later section (Key Idea 2.5).

Similarities and differences: the basis of classification

CONCEPTS TO SUPPORT KEY STAGE 2	

The identification of plants and animals using keys

How is it possible to identify an unknown plant or animal? As has been seen in the previous section, all plants and animals can be assigned to groups in a scientific classification. There are a number of these, each containing variations, but all agree on the main groupings of plants and animals, and the groupings in a classification allow for the construction of 'keys', the use of which will enable the naming of an unidentified organism.

Classifications and keys are based on grouping together organisms which are similar to each other, but different from all other groups. The grouping begins at a general level and proceeds through increasingly detailed levels of organization until it is possible to identify the individual species of organism. As a reminder, the various levels of classification (reflected in the construction of identification keys) are:

Kingdom; Phylum (from the Greek word for tribe); Class; Order; Family; Genus; Species.

Identification keys have been produced in a variety of detail. Many field guides contain keys to the species described in them, for example the wild flowers, or birds, of Britain and Europe. Other keys have been specifically produced for smaller groupings of organisms, for example woodland mosses, seashore lichens, water animals, or deciduous trees. Some are pictorial, or combine illustration with text-based questions, but all are based on similarity with, and difference from, smaller and smaller groupings of organisms.

The dichotomous or binary key

This is the most common type of identification key, so named because it is based on a 'splitting into two'. The basic feature of such a key is a progressive series of questions, each of which has only two possible answers, which relate to characteristics of the unidentified plant or animal. If these characteristics are directly observable features of the 'look' of the organism, the key is said to be a 'morphological' key. Plant keys which depend on descriptions of the flowers are of limited use out of the flowering season, and in these cases it is possible to use keys based on 'vegetative' characters alone. In working through the layers of questions, more and more specific details can be considered until eventually, the individual species can be identified.

Some keys expect the user to be familiar with morphological and structural details, and these are perhaps of limited use in classroom or field situations, but it is possible to find (or even produce) keys based on questions about general features, including information about life-cycles. Many teachers produce their own identification keys for use in well-known local habitats, or to support a study of major groups of plants or animals.

Here is a simple example of a dichotomous key for the five groups (classes) of vertebrate animals. It is based on some of the diagnostic characteristics of each of the classes, and is structured in such a way as to identify one class per question.

A dichotomous key to the five vertebrate classes

Q1. Does the animal spend all or most of its life in water? Does it 'breathe' for all or most of its life through gills? (other questions could include: body covering of bony scales?; cold-blooded?; external fertilization?)
Yes? – the animal is a fish. No? – go to Q2

Q2. Does the animal live part of its life in water and part on land? Does the animal produce larval forms (tadpoles) which breathe through gills? (other questions could include: body covering of soft skin?; cold-blooded?; external fertilization?)
Yes? – the animal is an amphibian. No? – go to Q3

Q3. Does the animal live all or most of its life on land, have a scaly body covering and lay soft-shelled eggs? (cold-blooded?; internal fertilization?)
Yes? – the animal is a reptile. No? – go to Q4

Q4. Does the animal have a body covering of feathers; does it lay hard-shelled eggs? (warm-blooded?; internal fertilization?)
Yes? – the animal is a bird. No? – go to Q5

Q5. Does the animal suckle its young? (warm-blooded?; internal fertilization?)
Yes? – the animal is a mammal.

The questions in the above key have been chosen to avoid pitfalls. Here are some which could cause problems for general identification:

'Does it live in water? Yes? – the animal is a fish.' – Not necessarily true, as the marine mammals (whales, dolphins and porpoises) also live in water, and some fish spend most of their lives in mud.

Fig. 2.22 An example
of a lateral key

	Body Covering				Limbs			Mouth parts		
	Hair	Feathers	Scales	Other	Legs	Wings	Fins	Teeth Obvious	Teeth small or absent	Beak
Goldfish			√				√		√	
Pigeon		√			√	√				√
Human	√				√			√		
Frog				√	√				√	
Mouse	√				√			√		
Sparrow		√			√	√				√
Lizard			√		√					
Herring										
Crocodile										
Newt										

'Can it fly? – Yes? – the animal is a bird.' – Again, not necessarily true, as animals other than birds can fly (bats), and not all birds can fly.

So, some care is needed when selecting questions for the production of keys.

Lateral keys

Lateral keys are based on the principle of comparison. The features of the unidentified plant or animal are compared against a list of general characteristics. The exhibition of a particular set of these characteristics allows the organism to be placed in a group which shares the set.

Using the example of the five classes of vertebrate animals again, the list of characteristics could include: type of body covering, type of limbs, and type of mouth parts. To use the lateral key, each of the animals to be classified would be compared against the list of characteristics, and those belonging to the same group would be seen to have the same 'set' of features.

The diagram (Fig. 2.22) shows an example of a lateral key designed to classify vertebrate animals into groups.

Adaptation to environment

Animals and plants tend to adapt to their environments (Natural Selection)

The explanation of the theory of evolution is generally credited to Charles Darwin, although another 19th-century naturalist, Alfred Wallace, had separately come to similar conclusions. In the end, they 'launched' the theory with joint papers to the Royal Society in 1858, and Darwin published his book 'The Origin of Species by means of Natural Selection' in 1859.

Between 1831–36, Darwin had been the naturalist on board the admiralty ship HMS Beagle, which had made a round-the-world voyage of scientific discovery. During his travels Darwin had gained an appreciation of the huge variety of plants and animals on Earth, but he was particularly struck by one location. Having rounded Cape Horn, the Beagle visited the Galapagos Islands, 600 miles west of the coast of Ecuador, in South America. Darwin noticed that the animals of the Galapagos Islands bore a resemblance to those of the South American mainland. Two things struck him however: firstly, the island populations were not identical to the mainland animals of a similar kind, and secondly, each island appeared to have its own separate population of animals. Examples which Darwin recorded and collected included the so-called Darwin finches, and the giant tortoises.

Darwin had noticed that whilst all the islands were of volcanic origin, were roughly the same height and experienced the same climate, each had its own population of finches, which appeared to be adapted to feed on the available vegetation of the island concerned. Similarly, the populations of tortoises had adapted to feed on the particular vegetation of each island. A striking example of this was the shape of the shells of the giant tortoises. Those which lived on grass covered islands had normal shaped shells, whilst those that lived on bouldery, scrub covered islands had shells with high peaks which enabled the animals to raise their heads to browse on overhanging vegetation (see Fig. 2.23).

All of these insights were eventually to lead Darwin to the realization that species of animals and plants were not created and immutable, but that by slow and small steps, new species gradually evolved from previously existing forms. A distillation of Darwin's work can be presented in terms of four observations, from which three deductions are possible, as follows:

Charles Darwin's observations and deductions

Observation 1: organisms show the potential for 'geometric' increase.

In modern terms, 'geometric' means 'exponential', i.e. 2, 4, 8, 16, 32, 64 . . . and so on. This is true both for plant and animal populations. A single grass head

Fig. 2.23 '*Normal*' *and* '*high-peaked*' *forms of Galapagos tortoise shells*

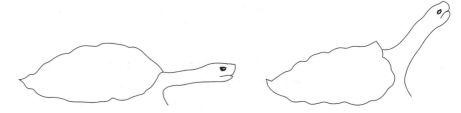

could contain 1,500 seeds, and some fish produce millions of eggs each time they spawn.

Observation 2: but populations remain relatively stable.

Although populations do rise and fall in numbers, the fluctuations bear no resemblance to the potential for 'geometric' increase cited by Darwin.

Deduction 1: there is a 'struggle for existence'.

Since in all plants and most animals there is a very high wastage of embryonic or juvenile forms, there must be a continuing struggle for survival. Birds like the house sparrow or greenfinch commonly lay 4–6 eggs, and may produce three broods in a season – a potential production of 12–18 offspring per pair per year. Clearly however, the population of either of these species does not increase 6–9-fold annually.

Observation 3: individuals vary, and some variations confer advantage.

Darwin had noticed, as had many naturalists before him, that all individuals vary, that is, they are all different from all other individuals of the same species (except as we now know, in the case of identical twins). Some of the variations between individuals were advantageous to survival in specific environments. So the high-peaked tortoises on shrubby islands which were able to 'crane their necks' to browse on overhead vegetation were more likely to survive than normal shelled individuals living on the same island. The 'high peak' gave them an advantage in the battle for survival.

Deduction 2: organisms which survive are those best adapted to the environment – the 'survival of the fittest'.

In the Darwinian sense, 'fitness' means 'best adapted to the particular environment', and is not necessarily a function of size, strength, etc. To continue the tortoise example, both normal and high-peak shelled forms would survive on a grassy island – neither would be disadvantaged by grazing the ground plants. On a shrubby island however, the high-peak shells would have a distinct advantage over the normal forms, and would be the 'fittest' for that particular environment. There is a 'cart before horse' danger here. The high-peaked tortoises do not **become** high peaked because of 'craning their necks' to browse on overhead vegetation; those tortoises which are **born** high peaked are more likely to survive because they are **able** to 'crane their necks' to graze the shrubs above them.

Observation 4: characters which confer advantage tend to accumulate (and tend to be inherited).

As long as the environment remains stable and unchanged, the characteristics which confer advantage will tend to accumulate. This is because there is more chance of 'fitter' forms surviving to breed, and therefore of the advantage being inherited by subsequent generations. Sadly, Darwin did not know of the work of Gregor Mendel, who first laid out the principles of 'inheritance' (modern day genetics). Had he done so, it would have 'completed the story' for him.

Deduction 3: natural selection gives rise to new species.

This, in a sense, is the final explanation of Darwin's observations of the animals of the Galapagos Islands. It is possible that all of them descended from ancestors from the mainland populations. Over very long periods of time however, each island population responding to the natural selection of each separate island environment, would slowly adapt to become the 'fittest' form for that particular island, and would of necessity look different from similar species of island neighbours. Natural selection, driven by the different environments on each of the islands, had given rise to different species on each island.

It is worth remembering that the ideas implicit in natural selection represent a theory – not established fact. Although much of the evidence points to the theory being a reasonable one, it cannot be verified on a short time scale. It has taken much of geological time to produce the variation in life forms which we see today!

A further point is that it is possible to offend religious sensibilities by proclaiming the theory of evolution as fact – with these, as with many ideas in science, we tread the boundary between knowledge and belief – it is unwise to declare as fact something which cannot be verified.

| FURTHER CONCEPTS TO SUPPORT KEY STAGE 2 |

The sources of variation in plants and animals

At the heart of the theory of evolution is the idea that natural selection acts on the great variability within individual species of plants and animals in an area to bring about the survival of the fittest – those best adapted to the particular environment of the area concerned.

Remembering Darwin's 3rd observation:

individuals vary, and some variations confer advantage,

it is appropriate now to ask what causes the variation between individuals of the same species. A useful idea can be expressed in the form of a simple formula:

Phenotype = Genotype × Environment

The phenotype of any organism is the totality of its expression as a living thing – the way it looks and functions. All individual phenotypes (with the exception of those of identical twins) are unique. An individual's phenotype will result from the interaction of its genotype – the total genetic capacity inherited from its parents – with the environment in which it finds itself. All individual plants and animals look as they do because of the way in which their environment has acted on their own genetic coding.

This concept is particularly helpful when considering the 'nature versus nurture' debate. Much heat has been generated in the past over the extent to which characteristics such as intelligence or musicality are governed by heredity or environment. Will intelligent parents produce intelligent offspring? Can a child become musical if surrounded by the wherewithal of music? $P = G \times E$ shows us that these are not the correct questions to ask. A child's intelligence will be a function of the way in which its capacity for intellectual activity (genotype) is acted on by the environment in which it finds itself (or which is provided for it). A child surrounded by music will achieve little unless it has inherited some capacity for musical activity.

Environment can have a significant effect on phenotypes. Hydrangea flower colour can be controlled by soil additives, resulting in flowers ranging from blue to purple depending on the calcium content of the soil.

Genetic variation

So, the variation shown by all individuals (phenotypes) can be related to the genetic coding inherited from their parents. The code is made up of sequences of bases, strung together in long molecules of the chemical **deoxyribonucleic acid** (DNA), which is the main constituent of the cell nucleus. The bases are arranged in pairs which are linked in a 'double helix'. The particular sequence of the bases in the DNA strand allows for the assembly of particular amino acids, and these are the building blocks of the proteins used in each cell in the organism.

The base sequences are grouped together in **genes**, and are linked together on the DNA molecules to form **chromosomes** (a useful model is of carriages – the genes – making up a train – the chromosome). At fertilization, the two parental gametes, each containing half the required number of chromosomes, fuse to form the embryo, restoring the full chromosomal complement to the new individual. Each individual is thus a unique 'mixture' of its parents' genetic coding. The variation achieved by this continual mixing of genetic material as a result of sexual reproduction is the 'raw material' which is tested by natural selection for the ability of the species to adapt to changing environmental circumstances.

Environmental variation

Individual plants and animals also vary within species depending on the nature of their environments. A well-fed animal will tend to be bigger and stronger than a malnourished one, with a correspondingly greater chance of survival to reproduction. The important feature of environmental variations – characteristics 'acquired' during the lifetime of the individual – is that they cannot be inherited. A tree that grows tall simply because it germinates in a favoured position, will not produce tall offspring as a result. A person who has put on weight because of a programme of body-building will not produce large and well-muscled offspring as a result.

The mechanism of natural selection

Given then, the variability within species of plants and animals, how does natural selection operate? The answer comes from Darwin's 2nd deduction:

organisms which survive are those best adapted to the environment – the survival of the fittest.

It is clear from any study of plants and animals and their habitats, that particular (and generally predictable) groups of plants and animals are associated with particular habitats. It is important to remember that plants and animals are able to survive in specific locations because they are able to **tolerate** the conditions found there, not because they '**like**' them. Salt-marsh plants survive in salt marshes because they can tolerate high levels of sodium in their systems, not because they 'like' salt. Conversely, meadow grasses do not grow on salt marshes because they cannot tolerate sodium in their systems. Similarly, rhododendron bushes will not survive on calcium-rich (chalky) soils (they are said to be calcifuges – 'fleeing from calcium'), but they can tolerate acid soil conditions, and will thrive in the absence of calcium.

In Darwinian terms, the survivors in any habitat will be those plants and animals best adapted to that environment – the 'fittest' – and it is the environmental conditions, which 'select' the survivors. Whilst the environmental conditions remain relatively stable the characteristic plant and animal species in the area will tend to be unchanged. However, any changes in conditions will immediately favour those plants and animals best suited to coping with the changes, and natural selection will operate to 'filter out' those organisms unable to survive.

The environmental conditions are governed by physical factors such as rock type, soil type and depth, slope gradient, aspect (the direction a slope faces), climate and seasonality (temperature, water availability, length of growing season, day length), and biotic factors such as availability of food, shading, presence of predators etc.

Using the 'micro to macro' theme again, it is possible to imagine **individual plants and animals** in a particular habitat forming **breeding pairs**. The total grouping of individuals (or breeding pairs) of a species in the habitat concerned would constitute a **population** of that species. Populations of individual species in a habitat interact with populations of other species to form a **community** or **assemblage**, and the community of species in a habitat interact with the environmental conditions to form a self-sustaining **ecosystem**. Examples of ecosystems are woodlands, grasslands, rocky shores, ponds, and so on. The sum total of all the Earth's ecosystems is called the **biosphere**.

Some care is needed when interpreting such ideas, as the terms used are not very precise. A population could mean a species grouping at a number of different levels; for example, the population of caterpillars on an oak tree, of mistle thrushes in a wood, of red kites in Wales, of elephants in Africa, or the world population of blue whales.

Similarly, the general idea of 'community' is usually a positive one based on mutual tolerance, respect and well-being. This is emphatically not the case in 'communities' of plants and animals (hence the alternative, but not so descriptive term, assemblage). If Darwinian theory is correct, all plants and animals are competing fiercely with each other all the time for the essentials of survival – food, water, shelter, space, light, etc.

All ecosystems are dynamic and evolving. Even though it may appear that a particular habitat is stable and unchanging, slow change is always taking place. As young trees in a woodland grow to maturity over many years, the woodland floor becomes more shaded, particularly during summer months, and the ground flora of the wood gradually changes from 'open clearing' to shade tolerant plants. Similarly, the colonization of bare ground by plants and animals can show a succession in time, as in the 'reclamation' of abandoned farmland by woodland, or in space, as in the succession of vegetation commonly visible when moving inland from a belt of seashore sand dunes. Most natural environmental change takes place slowly, allowing organisms time to respond and adapt over many generations. A disturbing modern trend is the rapid environmental change brought about by human activity, e.g. mining or quarrying, and the subsequent despoilation as plants and animals are unable to respond at a suitable evolutionary speed.

Adaptation to environment

As a result of natural selection, the plants and animals in a particular habitat are those best adapted to survive the environmental conditions found there. The adaptation may be seen in terms of:

- **changes in appearance**, e.g. 'dwarf' forms of plants growing on exposed upland surfaces;
- **modifications to life-cycle**, e.g. seeds which fall in autumn 'overwintering' in the soil before germination the following spring with increased chances of survival;
- **specialized physiology**, e.g. tolerance to toxic levels of heavy metals in the soil, and so on.

Some of these adaptations are best examined by looking at the plants and animals found in a variety of differing habitats.

Examples from local habitats

Woodland environments

Very few of the woodlands in Britain are completely natural. Since neolithic times, and particularly since the middle ages, the native woodlands of the UK, which are broadleaved deciduous woodlands, have been managed to a certain extent – even if this has meant the slow depletion of trees by felling through the centuries.

A typical surviving woodland would show four 'layers' of vegetation, conforming to the 'skyscraper' model, the **ground layer** of low lying mosses, liverworts and fungi, the **field** or **herb layer** of ferns and flowering plants (grasses and wild flowers), the **shrub layer** of woody shrubs (holly, hawthorn, elder) and the **canopy layer** of large trees (oak, ash, elm, beech, birch) (see Fig. 2.24).

Examples of adaptation to the woodland environment include:

- some of the plants of the woodland floor have little or no strengthening tissue – they are 'floppy' – a response to the sheltered conditions in woodland (example: wild garlic);

Fig. 2.24 *The layers in a deciduous woodland*

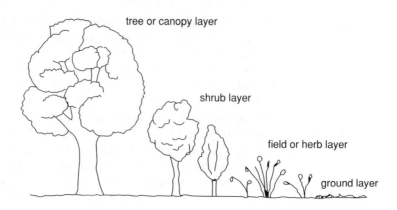

tree or canopy layer

shrub layer

field or herb layer

ground layer

- many woodland plants have large flat leaves, presenting the maximum surface area to the light – woodlands are dark places, particularly in summer, when limited sunlight penetrates the canopy (examples: dog's mercury, wild garlic);
- many of the plants of the field layer flower early in the year – flowering and seed set is complete before the canopy trees are in full leaf and the woodland floor darkens for the summer (examples: wood sorrel, wood anemone);
- later flowering plants are shade tolerant (example: bluebell);
- animals are specialized for feeding in woodlands – on tree trunks (examples: woodpeckers, tree creepers, nuthatches, squirrels), or in the canopy (examples: pied flycatchers, wood warblers);
- woodland birds have short rounded wings for rapid manoeuvring between trees (examples: sparrowhawk for hunting, warblers and flycatchers for hunting insects and escaping predators).

Many of these adaptations to the woodland environment can be easily seen, particularly if it is possible to visit a local wood at different times of the year, so building up a seasonal picture of the changing nature of the woodland. In some deciduous woodlands the shrub layer appears to be missing. This may be because animals have been allowed to graze the wood during winter seasons in the historic past, or that the shrub layer plants have been cut for firewood or for cottage industries such as hurdle or furniture making.

Coniferous woodlands in the UK are formed almost entirely from introduced species (with the notable exception of the scots pines of the Rothiemurchus forest). They tend to have a much simpler structure. Whilst the thinned open plantations may have ground and field layers present, the canopy of mature coniferous plantations is so dense that the shrub and field layers are usually absent, and the ground layer is formed from shade tolerant mosses and liverworts.

The inter-tidal zone: rocky shores

The inter-tidal zone is one of the most hostile environments on earth. It is exposed to drying winds, rainwater, large temperature fluctuations and inundation by sea water. In simple terms, because of the pattern of tides on the coast, a large part of the zone is covered at least twice a day by sea water (along most of the British coast the time interval between successive high tides is about 12 hours 50 minutes). In addition to the daily pattern, there is also a 28-day pattern to the range of the tides, linked to the phases of the moon. Following the appearance of the full and new moon, when the gravitational pull of the moon and the sun are at their greatest, the spring tides will produce the greatest range of movement, with the highest and lowest water levels in the cycle. One week after each spring tide, when the moon is at 'first and last quarter' phase and the combined 'pull' of the sun and moon is at its least, the smallest range of movement, the neap tides, result. The sequence during a complete lunar cycle would be:

Day 1 – new moon – spring tides – maximum range of high and low water;
Day 8 – first quarter – neap tides – minimum range;
Day 15 – full moon – spring tides – maximum range;
Day 22 – last quarter – neap tides – minimum range.

It is interesting to check this range from tide tables or from almanacs (available in the reference section of most public libraries) and to see how the pattern repeats itself throughout the year. The very highest (and lowest) tides of the year coincide with the equinoxes in March and September.

The plants and animals of the inter-tidal (or littoral) zone are basically marine organisms which have adapted to the changing conditions imposed by the pattern of the tides. Some examples of adaptation to life on a rocky shore include:

- plants (seaweeds) are tough and flexible – to resist the destructive action of waves;
- they have strong fixing points (holdfasts, not roots) attaching them to rock surfaces or boulders – to prevent them from being torn loose and carried out of their 'zone';
- they secrete a slimy mucilage which prevents them from drying out when exposed to the air, and which lubricates the movement of the fronds to minimize physical damage;
- some seaweeds have air bladders which help to buoy up the fronds in the waves;
- some animals are able to 'shut down' on exposure to the air – periwinkles close the 'trap door' (the operculum) to their shells, limpets attach themselves firmly to the rock, anemones withdraw their tentacles and become 'blobs of jelly'.
- other animals, mainly worms, burrow into sand to avoid drying out.

Because of the tidal patterns described above, the time spent exposed to the air varies according to position on the shore. The plants and animals of the upper shore are covered least often, and for the shortest time – perhaps for a few hours on two or three days in every fourteen. Those of the middle shore will be covered for half their lives, (12 hours in 24). Finally, those of the lower shore will spend almost all their lives covered with sea water, drying out only for a few hours during the 'low spring tide' phase of the tidal cycles – a 'mirror image' of the upper shore conditions.

Consequently, seashore organisms are to be found in broad 'zones', according to the extent to which they are able to tolerate drying out (desiccation) during

Fig. 2.25 *The zonation of some seaweeds and periwinkles on a rocky shore*

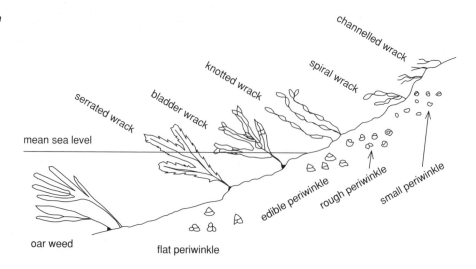

periods of low water. Two good examples of this zonation are provided by the seaweeds known as 'wracks', and by the periwinkles. Fig. 2.25 shows the positions of these organisms relative to tidal levels on a rocky shore. As well as linear zonation across the inter-tidal zone, it is also possible to see vertical zonation on rock 'islands' on the shore.

An important consideration when studying seashore life is that any plants or animals collected should be returned not simply to the shore, but to the approximate position of collection in the appropriate zone. Many organisms would not survive for long if replaced in a position different from the zone to which they are adapted.

The transfer of energy

Life is sustained through the transfer of energy (from the Sun to the tissues of living organisms)

As shown above (Key Idea 2.2), all living things need energy in order to sustain the processes of life. The initial source of this energy is light from the Sun. The basic process of energy transfer starts in green plants, which differ from all other life forms in that they are able to make their own food. They do this by combining simple molecules – water (H_2O) and carbon dioxide (CO_2) – into energy-rich sugars (carbohydrates) using the light energy from the Sun.

The process is known as photosynthesis (from Greek words meaning 'light' and 'putting together'), and the energy from the sunlight is transferred to the plant through the molecules of a green pigment called chlorophyll. This tends to be concentrated in the leaves of the plant.

Photosynthesis

The process of photosynthesis has already been described in Key Idea 2.2, (Plant nutrition – photosynthesis), but a summary would be as follows:

$$6CO_2 + 6H_2O \xrightarrow{\text{sun's energy, through chlorophyll}} C_6H_{12}O_6 + 6O_2$$

carbon dioxide   water   glucose   oxygen

Carbon dioxide (from the atmosphere) and hydrogen (from water in the plant) are converted into glucose, and oxygen (also from the water) is released to the air through the pores (or stomata) in the leaves of the plant.

The **energy** from the sunlight has been **transferred** into the chemical bonds of the glucose molecules, which can be:

■ converted to sucrose, for transport elsewhere in the plant;
■ converted to starch, for storage;
■ converted to cellulose, for cell walls (growth and support);
■ used in respiration;
■ used in amino acid or fat synthesis.

The factors which can affect the rate at which photosynthesis takes place include: the amount of light, water, carbon dioxide and minerals available, and the temperature of the environment.

Energy transfer

The green plants then, are the **producers** – they are able to synthesize their own food. They represent the first trophic (nourishment) level in any ecosystem, and they support, directly or indirectly, all animal life on Earth.

Much of the light energy 'trapped' by plants is used to sustain the plants themselves, for respiration, growth, reproduction, and so on. It has been estimated that up to 90% of the energy 'fixed' by the plant may be used by the operation of these life processes or be converted through decay, by bacteria or fungi for example.

This means that only about 10% of the energy fixed by plants is available for transfer to animals, which cannot produce their own food, and which therefore rely on plants to provide it for them. These animals, the **primary consumers**, are known as **herbivores**, and they have developed digestive systems which will deal with plant tissues in such a way as to make the products of photosynthesis available to them in a useful form. The herbivores represent the second trophic level in an ecosystem, and because of the small transfer of energy from producer to primary consumer, the herbivores in an ecosystem will be less numerous than the plants, and will produce less total living matter, or biomass.

Similarly, the animals which themselves live on the herbivores – the **carnivores** – represent the less numerous third trophic level, and those animals which live on carnivores, the top carnivores, will represent the smallest numbers, and lowest biomass in the ecosystem.

In its simplest form, this concept can be seen in terms of an 'ecological pyramid', and at each step up the pyramid there will be a large drop in both numbers of organisms and biomass (see Fig. 2.26).

Since only about 10% of the total energy within a particular trophic level is available for transfer to the organisms of the next level, it is easy to see how small a proportion of 'original' energy from green plants is available to top carnivores. If the original energy available at the first level (plants) was 100 units, then there would be 10 units available to the herbivores, 1 unit to the carnivores, and 0.1 units available to the top carnivores.

Food chains and webs

This transfer of energy through the trophic levels of an ecosystem is often described in terms of food chains:

Environment	Producer	Consumers		
		primary (herbivore)	secondary (carnivore)	tertiary (carnivore)
urban garden	cabbage	caterpillar	blackbird	sparrowhawk
pond	pondweed	tadpole	stickleback	perch
ocean	algae	herring	shark	
woodland	oak leaves	caterpillar	flycatcher	owl
grassland	grass	rabbit	weasel	

In natural environments however, such food chains rarely exist. It is unusual for a plant to be the only food species of a particular herbivore, or for that herbivore to be the only food for one particular predator. Most edible plants act as food for a number of herbivores (or omnivores), and similarly, most

Fig. 2.26 A pyramid of biomass in a simple food chain

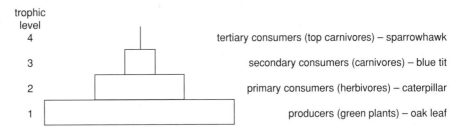

predators feed on a variety of prey species. If for any reason, the preferred food of any consumer begins to decline or disappear, possibly due to environmental change or population reduction, there are a number of options open:

- the consumer can seek other food (different species);
- the consumer can move to an area where the preferred food is in greater supply;
- the consumer may die.

Given these kinds of interactions, a more useful idea is that of a food web (see Fig. 2.27), with a variety of possible interrelationships between the trophic levels.

The food cycle An often neglected component of food webs is the role played by the 'decomposers' in an ecosystem. These include the small animals which live in the soil, such as woodlice and earthworms, which feed on dead and decaying organic matter, and the fungi and bacteria which decay plant and animal remains by 'digesting' them with enzymes.

The activities of the decomposers cause the breakdown of once living material into mineral salts and inorganic molecules (such as CO_2), thereby making them available once again to producers (plants). This results, in effect, in the recycling of nutrients and other mineral salts back into the food webs (see Fig. 2.28).

FURTHER CONCEPTS TO SUPPORT KEY STAGE 2

The biosphere, the totality of life on Earth, exists in a narrow band at or near the Earth's surface. It is now thought that the earliest life forms appeared on Earth about three billion years ago, and the sustaining, evolution and expansion of life forms since then has required a series of mechanisms for recycling the 'raw materials' of life.

Cycles of matter Some of the key raw materials of life are water, carbon, oxygen and nitrogen. The ways in which these elements and compounds are cycled through the biosphere are now described.

The water cycle (see also Key Idea 3.5)

Water is removed from the biosphere by:

- drainage – the 'run-off' of surface and ground water into rivers and lakes, and their drainage into the oceans;
- evaporation from water surfaces – lakes, rivers, the ocean – , from rocks and soil, and from plant surfaces – leaves, stems etc.;

Fig. 2.27 *A food web: some feeding relationships in a pond ecosystem*

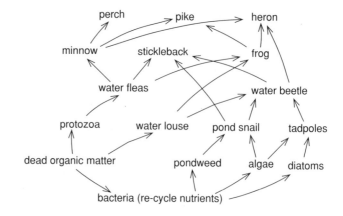

Fig. 2.28 *The food cycle*

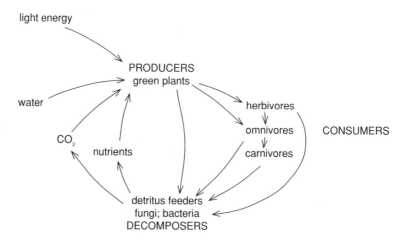

- transpiration – the diffusion of water as vapour from the aerial parts of a plant;
- perspiration – the excretion of water, as sweat, by animals;

water is returned to the biosphere from the atmosphere when water vapour condenses to form droplets which fall as rain or snow. Most rainfall occurs over the oceans, but that which does occur over the land masses, replenishes the ground water on which most plants depend for their supplies of water for photosynthesis (see Fig. 2.29).

The carbon cycle

Carbon, an essential ingredient of carbohydrates, is available in the atmosphere as a component of carbon dioxide gas. This is used by plants in the process of photosynthesis, and is then transferred through the trophic levels of the ecosystem, being combined with other elements and compounds in the tissues of living organisms. Most of the carbon is returned directly to the atmosphere as a waste product of the organisms' respiration processes, but some is 'fixed' in the form of undecayed plant and animal remains, or in the shells of animals as carbonate (see Fig. 2.30). It is thought that the formation

Fig. 2.29 The water cycle

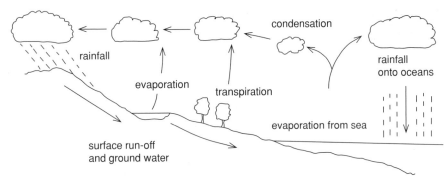

Fig. 2.30 The carbon cycle (after Shreeve, 1983)

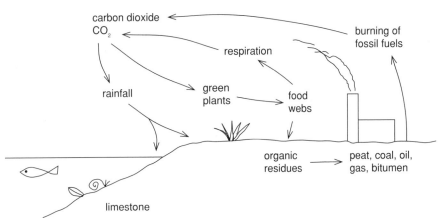

of limestone in the geological past removed large amounts of carbon from the atmosphere, as did the formation of coal and oil – the 'fossil' fuels. The rapid rate at which fossil fuels are now being used is the cause of an increase in atmospheric carbon dioxide (the present level may have doubled by the mid-21st century). There are at least two opposing theories as to the possible effects of this increase.

Theory 1 expects that the increase in carbon dioxide in the atmosphere will prevent heat loss by radiation from the Earth, so causing 'global warming', with the possible implication of the melting of the polar ice caps, the subsequent rise in sea level (up to 70 metres is predicted), and the 'drowning' of many of the world's largest cities.

Theory 2 states that the increase in the burning of fossil fuels will cause an increase in the layer of dust particles in the upper atmosphere. This in turn will cause a reflection of the sun's rays back into space, with a consequent cooling of the Earth's surface and atmosphere (a lowering of average temperatures by 3°C is predicted, sufficient to cause the onset of an ice age).

Time will tell!

The oxygen cycle

Most of the oxygen present in the atmosphere is produced by green plants as a by-product of photosynthesis. It is used by plants and animals for respiration,

Fig. 2.31 *The nitrogen cycle (after Shreeve, 1983)*

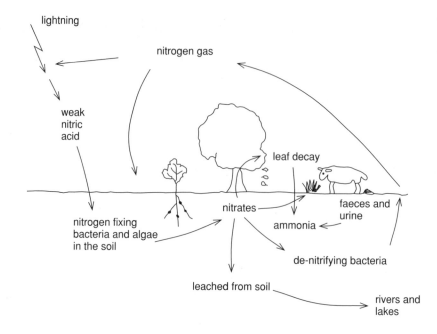

and becomes combined with carbon to form carbon dioxide, and with hydrogen to form water, as waste products of this process. It is thus a component of both the water and the carbon cycles.

The nitrogen cycle

Nitrogen, a gas which comprises 80% of the atmosphere, is 'fixed' by bacteria and algae in the soil as nitrate, in which form it can be absorbed in solution by plants. It is then incorporated into amino acids and proteins in the tissues of plants and then animals, and returned to the soil in faeces and urine, or in decaying plant and animal remains. Decomposers in the food cycle convert nitrogenous wastes to ammonia, which is in turn converted to nitrates again. These either re-enter the food cycle at this point, being absorbed by plants, or are denitrified and returned to the atmosphere as nitrogen gas (see Fig. 2.31).

Energy transfer: micro to macro

During photosynthesis, **photons** of light energy, enable **hydrogen ions** from the **water molecules** in green plants to combine with **carbon dioxide** absorbed from the atmosphere, forming **carbohydrate molecules**. These carbohydrates help to form complex molecules within the **cells** of the plant and help to supply energy for the metabolism of the **individual organism**. The individual plant forms part of the **producers trophic level**, and energy is transferred through the trophic levels of the **ecological pyramid** of the particular habitat.

Life processes and living things: National Curriculum coverage

Below is listed each of the component parts of the relevant programme of study of science in the National Curriculum (SCAA, 1995). In the bracket below each component the relevant Key Idea is shown, together with the section heading(s) in this book where further specific details may be found.

KEY STAGE 1

Pupils should be taught:

1. Life processes
  a the differences between things that are living and things that have never been alive;
    (KEY IDEA 2.1: The characteristics of living things)
  b that animals, including humans, move, feed, grow, use their senses and reproduce.
    (KEY IDEA 2.2: Feeding, Growth, Response to stimuli, Reproduction)

2. Humans as organisms
  a to name the main external parts, *e.g. hand, elbow, knee*, of the human body;
    (KEY IDEA 2.3: Healthy animals)
  b that humans need food and water to stay alive;
    (KEY IDEA 2.3: Healthy animals)
  c that taking exercise and eating the right types and amount of food help humans to keep healthy;
    (KEY IDEA 2.3: Healthy animals)
  d about the role of drugs as medicines;
  e that humans can produce babies and these babies grow into children and then into adults;
    (KEY IDEA 2.2: Reproduction)
  f that humans have senses which enable them to be aware of the world around them.
    (KEY IDEA 2.2: The nervous system)

3. Plants as organisms
  a that plants need light and water to grow;
    (KEY IDEA 2.3: Healthy plants)
  b to recognize and name the leaf, flower, stem and root of flowering plants;
    (KEY IDEA 2.3: Healthy plants)
  c that flowering plants grow and produce seeds which, in turn, produce new plants.
    (KEY IDEA 2.3: Healthy plants)

4. Variation and classification
  a to recognize similarities and differences between themselves and other pupils;
  b that living things can be grouped according to observable similarities and differences.
    (KEY IDEA 2.4: The classification of plants and animals)

5. Living things in their environment

a that there are different kinds of plants and animals in the local environment;
   (KEY IDEA 2.5: The mechanism of natural selection)
b that there are differences between local environments and that these affect which animals and plants are found there.
   (KEY IDEA 2.5: Examples from local habitats)

KEY STAGE 2

Pupils should be taught:

1. Life processes

a that there are life processes, including nutrition, movement, growth and reproduction, common to animals, including humans;
b that there are life processes, including growth, nutrition and reproduction, common to plants.
   (KEY IDEA 2.2: Life processes)

2. Humans as organisms

Nutrition

a the functions of teeth and the importance of dental care;
b that food is needed for activity and for growth, and that an adequate and varied diet is needed to keep healthy;
   (KEY IDEA 2.3: Conscious actions which can promote health)

Circulation

c a simple model of the structure of the heart and how it acts as a pump;
d how blood circulates in the body through arteries and veins;
   (KEY IDEA 2.2: Circulation)
e the effect of exercise on pulse rate;
   (KEY IDEA 2.3: The effect of exercise; The need for rest)

Movement

f that humans have skeletons and muscles to support their bodies and to help them move;
   (KEY IDEA 2.2: Support in animals – the skeleton; Movement in animals)

Growth and reproduction

g the main stages of the human life cycle;
   (KEY IDEA 2.2: Reproduction)

Health

h that tobacco, alcohol and other drugs can have harmful effects.
   (KEY IDEA 2.3: The harmful effects of drugs, alcohol and tobacco)

3. Green plants as organisms

Growth and nutrition

a that plant growth is affected by the availability of light and water, and by temperature;
   (KEY IDEA 2.3: Healthy plants)

b that plants need light to produce food for growth, and the importance of the leaf in this process;
(KEY IDEA 2.2: Plant nutrition – photosynthesis)

c that the root anchors the plant, and that water and nutrients are taken in through the root and transported through the stem to other parts of the plant;
(KEY IDEA 2.3: Healthy plants)

Reproduction

d about the life cycle of flowering plants, including pollination, seed production, seed dispersal and germination.
(KEY IDEA 2.2: Sexual reproduction in flowering plants)

4. Variation and classification

a how locally occurring animals and plants can be identified and assigned to groups, using keys.
(KEY IDEA 2.4: The identification of plants and animals using keys)

5. Living things in their environment

Adaptation

a that different plants and animals are found in different habitats;
(KEY IDEA 2.5: The sources of variation in plants and animals)

b how animals and plants in two different habitats are suited to their environment;
(KEY IDEA 2.5: Examples from local habitats)

Feeding relationships

c that food chains show feeding relationships in an ecosystem;
(KEY IDEA 2.6: Energy transfer; Food chains and webs)

d that nearly all food chains start with a green plant;
(KEY IDEA 2.6: Photosynthesis; Energy transfer; Food chains and webs)

Micro-organisms

e that micro-organisms exist, and that many may be beneficial, *e.g. in the breakdown of waste*, while others may be harmful, *e.g. in causing disease.*
(KEY IDEA 2.4: Kingdom: Bacteria; KEY IDEA 2.6: The food cycle)

| SECTION THREE | *Materials and their properties* |

SOME KEY IDEAS
IN MATERIALS
SCIENCE

3.1 *The classification of materials: Materials or substances can be classified according to their origin, properties or uses**

3.2 *The particulate nature of matter*

3.3 *Changing materials: Materials can be changed, and these changes can be permanent or reversible*

3.4 *The rock cycle*

3.5 *The water cycle*

* Please note that Key Idea 3.1 has been subdivided into three sections for easy reference: The origin of materials, The physical properties of materials, The uses of materials.

The classification of materials

Materials or substances can be classified according to their origin, type, properties or uses

Introduction

Since the beginning of human history, people have been using a variety of materials to help them in their daily lives. As technology progressed, the materials became more sophisticated, from the stone tools of the neolithic people to the metal weapons of bronze and iron age people. In general, materials were used to make objects with specific purposes – sharp bone needles for sewing, wooden rollers and wheels for transport, golden ornaments for decoration – all designed to improve the quality of life in the period concerned.

Today, we are surrounded by a bewildering variety of materials, capable of being put to many uses. Some are related to the necessities of life – the need for food, clothing and shelter. Others are more related to wants than needs – 'domestic consumer goods' like washing machines, video recorders, cars and so on. There are many ways in which to classify or group these materials, and the first part of this section will deal with some of them.

No matter how they are classified, it is important to remember that all of the materials that are available to people are derived from the resources of the Earth. In some cases the materials are 'natural' and can be used with little or no modification, whilst in other cases the natural (or raw) material needs to be processed in some way before being used to make something else. An issue of increasing concern is the awareness that the Earth's resources are not limitless, and that it will not be possible to go on depleting those resources at the present rates of consumption. Attention is now turning to the importance of 'renewable' resources when seeking new supplies of materials for people to use.

The origin of materials

CONCEPTS TO SUPPORT KEY STAGE 1

A simple first classification is to divide materials into natural and manufactured (or processed, or synthetic) types. The main groups of materials can be listed as:

Natural and manufactured materials

natural:	**rocks, soil, air, water, wood;**
manufactured:	**metals, glass, ceramics, plastics (including rubber), paper, fabrics.**

Fig. 3.1 A soil profile

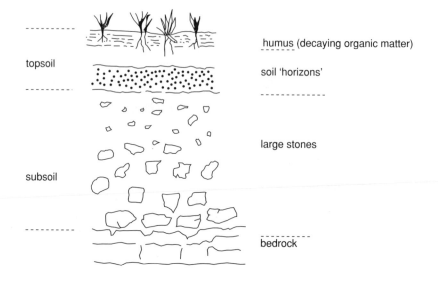

humus (decaying organic matter)

topsoil

soil 'horizons'

large stones

subsoil

bedrock

**CONCEPTS TO
SUPPORT KEY
STAGE 2**

**Natural materials
from the physical
environment**

In terms of human survival, one of the most important natural materials is the soil.

Soil is composed of weathered remains of bedrock, which contains the mineral nutrients needed for plant growth, mixed with humus – the decaying remains of dead organisms. In addition, soil contains water from rainfall and air from the atmosphere (see Fig. 3.1). It is the combination of these components which makes it a suitable growing medium for the plants which form the base of the ecological pyramid (see Key Idea 2.6).

Most other natural materials derived from the physical environment of the Earth are the products of geological processes which have been operating in and on the crust of the Earth for millions of years (see Key Idea 3.4: The rock cycle). These 'geological' raw materials are the products of extractive industry – mining, quarrying, dredging, drilling etc. They are rarely usable in their completely natural state, and some minor processing, usually physical, takes place before they can be used for their intended purposes. Quarried stone is broken into movable pieces, dredged sand is washed, and gravel is sorted for size, for example.

'Geological' raw materials include:

- granite, dolerite, and other 'hard' **rocks** which are quarried for roadstone;
- limestone, which is quarried for cement production and metal smelting;
- sand and gravel, which are dredged or dug for use in the building and glass-making industries;
- clays which are dug for the production of earthenware and ceramics;
- coal, which is deep mined or open-cast for fuel;
- oil, which is drilled from deep wells for fuel.

(It could be argued that the last two examples were of 'biological' materials as they are 'fossil' fuels.)

Two other important natural materials from the physical world are air and water.

Air is the mixture of gases which make up the Earth's atmosphere, and the relative abundance of the components, together with their uses, can be seen in the table below.

Gas	% Present in air	Uses
nitrogen	78.0	nitrates in soil (plant nutrients) used in ammonia production
oxygen	21.0	respiration oxidation, smelting medical applications
argon	0.9	domestic light bulbs
carbon dioxide	0.03	photosynthesis 'dry ice'
neon	trace	lighting
helium	trace	airships (non-flammable)
krypton	trace	high temp. light bulbs
xenon	trace	high temp. light bulbs

Water is a colourless, odourless liquid which originally derived from the Earth's atmosphere. It is 'recycled' from the atmosphere to the crust of the Earth and the oceans (see Key Idea 3.5: The water cycle). It is important because it supports life on the planet, as almost all the significant reactions at cellular level depend on aqueous solutions. It is also a key component in many industrial processes – as an ingredient in the brewing industry, as a coolant in the steel making process, or as a power source in the generation of hydro-electricity, for example.

Natural materials from the biological environment

From the biological environment comes:

- **wood** (timber);
- vegetable fibres (wood pulp, cotton, flax, hemp, sisal, coir);
- vegetable waxes, oils and sap (carnauba wax, linseed and sunflower oil, latex);
- animal fibres (wool, alpaca);
- animal products (leather from skins and hides, tallow for candles, lard).

Again, whilst each of these materials is natural, some processing is required before they can be used to their best advantage – timber is sawn to size, fibres are spun into yarn, latex is cured to make rubber, leather is tanned, and so on.

Manufactured materials

Manufactured materials are made from raw materials which have been processed in a variety of ways. Basic manufacturing frequently uses relatively simple processes, often involving irreversible chemical reactions (see below, Key Idea 3.3), in order to provide further raw materials for more complicated secondary processes.

The manufacturing of materials derived from 'physical' raw materials would include the following processes:

- the refining of **metals** from ores;
- the firing of **ceramics** (bricks, tiles, and porcelain) from clays;
- the making of **glass** from sand and other minerals;
- the fractional distillation of paraffin and petrol from crude oil;
- the production of coke (for smelting) from coal.

The basic manufacturing processes involving 'biological' raw materials would include:

- the sawing of timber;
- the production of **paper**, card and board from wood pulp;
- the production of **fabrics** from plant and animal fibres;
- the production of **rubber** from latex.

Secondary industries would include the production of:

- **plastics** (including synthetic fibres such as nylon and terylene) from crude oil derivatives;
- detergents, paint, and perfume from coal.

Types of manufactured materials

The basic processes used in the production of the main groups of manufactured materials are now described.

Metals rarely occur in their pure form. Those that do tend to be unreactive, and valuable, e.g. gold. Most other metals occur as ores, which are compounds of the metal and unwanted impurities, and in order to produce the metal, a process of smelting is necessary. Metals commonly used in manufacturing industry include **iron, copper, lead, tin, zinc, and aluminium**.

The most common method of producing metals is by removing the oxygen from the ore by a process known as reduction. In the production of iron, this involves the following sequence:

- **Iron ore** (haematite – iron oxide) is loaded into a blast furnace along with **coke** and **limestone**;
- **Hot air** is blasted into the base of the furnace and **carbon** from the coke reacts with **oxygen** from the air to form **carbon monoxide**;
- The **carbon monoxide** reacts with **oxygen** from the **haematite (iron oxide)** to form **carbon dioxide** and **iron**;
- The **limestone** combines with **impurities** in the ore (mainly silicates) to form **slag**;
- The **molten iron** is tapped from the base of the furnace and solidifies into billets known as **'pigs'** – hence **'pig iron'**.

At this point the iron is impure. To form steel, which is an alloy of iron and carbon, it is necessary to reheat the iron to drive off the impurities, and then to add up to 1.5% of carbon. Other metals can give the steel particular properties – the addition of chromium will produce stainless steel, for example.

Fig. 3.2 *A hexane molecule*

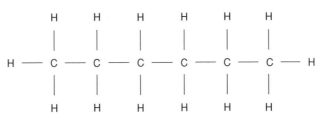

(H = a hydrogen atom, C = a carbon atom)

Other alloys (mixtures of metals) include:

- **brass** (copper and zinc), which is used for electrical contacts and corrosion resistant fixings (screws, bolts etc.);
- **bronze** (copper and tin), used for decorative or artistic purposes;
- **solder** (lead and tin), which is used for electrical connections;
- **duralumin** (aluminium, magnesium, copper and manganese), which is used in aircraft production.

Ceramics include those products which are made by baking or firing mixtures of clay, sand and other minerals – **bricks, tiles, earthenware, pottery, china**. There is a sense in which the kiln firing process is creating 'artificial metamorphic rocks' by using heat to fuse together the individual ingredients of the product into a matrix. The main constituent of all these products is silicon – clay is aluminium silicate; sand is silica dioxide.

This category would also include those products made by 'curing' mixtures of sand, gravel, water, and a setting agent (usually cement) to form **concrete**, and **mortar**, a sand, water and cement mixture.

Glass is also produced by the melting together of minerals. The basic ingredients are sand (silica dioxide), calcium carbonate and sodium carbonate. The resulting mixture of calcium and sodium silicates cools to form glass. Again, additives can change the character of the product. The addition of boron will produce heat resistant 'Pyrex' type glass, and added lead will produce hard 'crystal' glass.

Plastics are products of the oil industry. When crude oil (petroleum) is refined by fractional distillation, petroleum vapour is fed into a fractionating column, and different products condense out at different temperatures. Bitumen collects at the base of the column, followed (at increasing height) by heavy fuel oil, lubricating oil, diesel oil, paraffin, petrol and petroleum gas. The chemical differences between the fractions result from the number of carbon atoms present in the molecules. The general arrangement of hydrogen and carbon atoms in a hydrocarbon molecule is shown in Fig. 3.2.

Heavy fuel oils have 20–30 carbon atoms per molecule, whilst petrol has 5–10 carbon atoms.

In a separate process, those molecules with 8–12 carbon atoms per molecule (i.e. between paraffin and petrol) are chemically 'cracked', or split, into smaller units, one of which is ethene. **Ethene** is the basis of much of the plastics

Fig. 3.3 *Plastics from ethene*

MONOMER   POLYMER

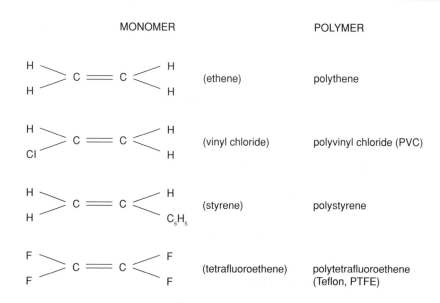

industry. Under conditions of high temperature and pressure, and in the presence of a catalyst, molecules of ethene, (**monomers**), can link together in long chains (**polymers**) – hence **polythene**. If the ethene monomer is modified by the replacement of one of the hydrogen atoms by another atom or molecule, further monomers result which lead to the production of other plastics on polymerization (see Fig. 3.3).

Rubber is an example of a natural polymerized material, produced by the curing of latex, the sap of the rubber tree. The natural rubber is heated with a small amount of sulphur (about 3%) in a process known as vulcanization, which hardens and strengthens the rubber. (The white sap which exudes from the broken stem of a dandelion plant is a type of latex. Its rubbery and sticky nature can be felt if it is rubbed between the fingers.) Synthetic rubbers include neoprene, widely used for wetsuit material, and butyl, which is used for pond linings.

Paper is basically a product derived from wood. Wooden billets, usually of softwood (the coniferous Sitka spruce is most frequently used), are shredded to a pulp, both by mechanical and chemical means. Chemical binders and bleaches are added, and the water is removed from the pulp, either by sieving it in thin layers or by feeding it from vats in a continuous strip. The resulting sheets or strips of paper are dried and pressed, and finished according to the required properties (see next section).

A sheet of paper is therefore a mat of wood fibres (which can easily be seen with a hand lens held to the torn edge of a sheet of paper). Some paper is made up of more than one layer, with the fibres 'laid' in a particular direction. Kitchen roll and table napkins are good examples of 'two-ply' laid papers. The individual layers can usually be separated, and the sheets can be torn into narrow strips very easily in one direction (usually 'along the roll'), but not at all easily 'across the roll'.

Paper is a material that is relatively easy to recycle, and 'paper bank' containers are increasingly common in public places. It is also possible to produce paper from rags, in particular those made from 'natural' fabrics.

Fabrics are usually made from woven fibres, which may be natural or synthetic. Natural fibres derived from plants such as cotton, flax and hemp, or from the fleeces of animals such as sheep, alpaca or angora rabbits, can be spun together to form a thread or yarn. These yarns can then be woven into cloth, braid, rope etc.

In a similar fashion, yarns can be spun from synthetic fibres made from long chain polymer molecules, as described above. The properties of such fibres differ significantly from those of natural fibres, and some of these will be detailed in the next section.

The physical properties of materials

CONCEPTS TO SUPPORT KEY STAGE 1

For young children, the classification of materials will tend to be based on direct sensory experience of a range of objects. The 'properties' which they investigate may not therefore be those which engineers or materials scientists would use. In describing any object or material, a young child is unlikely to differentiate between descriptions of 'scientific' properties such as strength, stiffness etc., general characteristics such as flexibility and buoyancy, or specific attributes such as colour and shape.

An understanding of the distinction between properties, characteristics and attributes of materials may not be important for the early years child (although it may be helpful for the teacher). What *is* important is that children should have the opportunity to examine and explore a wide range of common materials with which they may come into contact.

As with the identification of animals and plants, the initial investigation of the properties of materials can be based on **similarities** – those features which group materials together, and **differences** – those features which separate the groups. Some of the 'properties' questions which may be asked about objects made of different materials are listed below. Some will relate to similarities and differences. Others may lead to a description of the characteristics of particular objects or materials. All of them however, help to build an experiential awareness of the materials under investigation. Where appropriate, the property or characteristic implicit in the question is added in brackets (it is not suggested, of course, that these properties would be identified and named in scientific terms for Key Stage 1 children).

Questions about objects and materials

With reference to a particular object or material, is it:

- heavy or light? (density)
- rough or smooth? (texture)
- shiny or dull? (reflectivity, thermal (heat) conductivity, insulation)
- bendy or stiff? (flexibility)
- hard or soft? (hardness)
- large or small? (size is not a property, but coupled with 'heavy or light'?, can help to build an awareness of density).

In addition:

- what shape is it? (characteristic of a particular object, but not a property)
- does it feel cold or warm? (again, not a property, but this question can help with an awareness of heat absorption or insulation)
- does it float or sink? (buoyancy)
- can we scratch a mark on it? (hardness)
- does it make a mark on paper? (hardness)
- is it squashy, can we mould or press it into shapes? (malleability)
- can we see through it? (opaque, translucent, transparent)
- can we pour it? (liquid or loose granular solid)
- can we press it into a smaller shape? (compressibility)
- is it bouncy, stretchy? (elasticity)
- does it attract metals? (magnetic)
- can we smell or taste it? (it goes without saying that the smelling, and particularly the tasting, of unknown materials, should be carefully planned and supervised. Smell and taste may be characteristic of certain materials – perfumes and food for example. They are not however, properties in the scientific sense of the term.)
- what is it made of?

The sorting and grouping of unknown materials and objects using these simple questions will allow for discussion and increasing awareness of the major properties of materials, and of the way in which these properties are exploited in the design and manufacture of everyday objects – rubber bands, paper clips, polythene bags, and so on.

<table>
<tr><td>

CONCEPTS TO SUPPORT KEY STAGE 2

Properties and characteristics of materials

</td><td>

Materials can be investigated and classified according to a variety of properties and characteristics. The properties can be measured as the materials react to a variety of influences, and they include:

</td></tr>
</table>

- **mechanical** properties such as **hardness, strength, elasticity, toughness, stiffness**;
- **thermal** properties like **conductivity** (how well or poorly a material will conduct heat);
- **electrical** properties like **conductivity** (how well or poorly a material will conduct electricity);
- **chemical** properties like **reactivity** and **solubility**;
- **optical** properties like **transparency, reflectivity, refractivity**;
- **magnetic** properties.

Some of the most important properties of materials for consideration here include **density, hardness, strength, elasticity, stiffness (and flexibility), toughness, compressibility, thermal and electrical conductivity, and magnetic properties**. Some of the chemical properties of materials will be explored in Key Idea 3.3 below.

Density

It is usually easy to characterize materials as 'heavy' or 'light', and these descriptions are an intuitive measure of the density of the materials concerned.

$$\textbf{density} = \frac{\text{mass}}{\text{volume}} \text{ (expressed as kg/m}^3\text{, or g/cm}^3\text{)}$$

In practical terms, the density of an object, or of a sample of material, is a measure of the mass of the object (the amount of matter in it) expressed in grams, compared to its volume (the amount of space it takes up) expressed in cubic centimetres.

A useful idea is to imagine a fixed volume (1 litre, for example) of a number of different materials, and to consider how different their masses would be. One litre of pure water has a mass of one kilogram – the density of water is therefore 1 g/cm^3 (1,000 grams/1,000 cubic centimetres). One litre of lead however, has a mass of about 11,340 grams, and the density of lead would therefore be 11.3 g/cm^3. Lead is 11.3 times denser than water. Similarly, one litre of aluminium has a mass of 2,700 grams, and therefore a density of 2.7 g/cm^3.

In addition to a feeling for relative heaviness or lightness, the density of a material also gives an indication of whether or not a sample of the material would float or sink. Materials with a density lower than that of water, i.e. less than 1.0 g/cm^3, will float on water. Those with a density greater than 1.0 g/cm^3 will sink. Interesting investigations can be performed with materials that are 'just floaters' or 'just sinkers'. If an uncooked egg is placed in a container of fresh water it will sink. The density of the egg will be about 1.1 g/cm^3. If enough salt is dissolved into the water, the density of the solution will increase until eventually it is higher than that of the egg, and the egg will float to the surface of the solution. This increased density of salt water is also part of the explanation for people feeling that they 'float better' in the sea than in fresh water.

A similar experiment can also be performed with 'centicubes', which are commonly available as a mathematics resource, and which are made of a plastic material which has a density just greater than 1 g/cm^3. Centicubes are therefore 'just sinkers' in fresh water, but will float to the surface once the density of the water has been increased by the addition of a sufficient quantity of salt.

Hardness

The **hardness** of a material is a measure of its resistance to permanent or plastic deformation by scratching or indentation. It is an important factor in materials which have to resist wear or abrasion – moving parts in machinery for example – and frequently needs to be considered along with the strength of materials. Hardness is measured on a scale (Moh's scale) of 1 (talc) to 10 (diamond). Relative hardness can be demonstrated by investigating which materials can be scratched by a finger nail (hardness 2.5), an iron nail (hardness 4), a steel nail (hardness 6) and (if possible) a piece of quartz (hardness 7).

Strength

The **strength** of a material is the extent to which it can withstand an applied force or load (**stress**) without breaking. The load is expressed in terms of

Fig. 3.4 *Examples of compressive, tensile and shear forces*

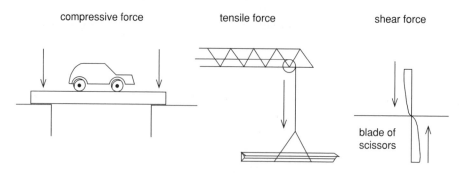

compressive force   tensile force   shear force

blade of scissors

force per unit area (newtons per square metre N/m^2), and can be in the form of:

- **compression force**, as applied to the piers of a bridge, or a roof support;
- **tensile or stretching force**, as applied to a guitar string, tow rope or crane cable;
- **shear force**, as applied by scissors, or when materials are torn (see Fig. 3.4).

Materials are therefore described as having compressive, tensile or shear strength.

Materials which can withstand high compression loading include cast iron, stone and brick, hence the common use of brick for building purposes. Cast iron, stone and brick however, are brittle, and break if subjected to high tension. If a building is to be designed which will resist tensile strain – in an earthquake-prone area for example – steel, which has high tensile strength, would be a more suitable building material.

Elasticity

Almost all materials will stretch to some extent when a tensile force is applied to them, and the increase in length on loading, compared to the original length of the material, is known as **strain**.

The **elasticity** of a material is the extent to which it can regain its original shape or size following deformation (stretching or compression) by the application of a force. Robert Hooke (1635–1703) was the English scientist who first realized that increasing force, applied as a series of increasing loads, will result in a material extending proportionally. In simple terms, the change in length (extension) of a material is proportional to the applied load – **strain** is proportional to **stress**.

This can easily be seen in the classroom by hanging masses (weights) onto a rubber band and measuring the 'stretch' as each mass is added. In general, the 'stretch' or extension of the rubber band is directly proportional to the load added. A graph of the results should be a straight line passing through the origin. Up to a certain point, the removal of the applied load results in the rubber band regaining its original shape and size, and this tendency of materials to return to their original shape and size when stress is removed, is known as elasticity.

As increased loading continues, a point is reached when the rubber band

Fig. 3.5 Stress/strain curves for a variety of materials in tension

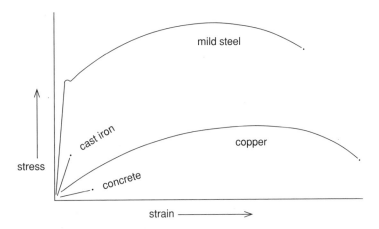

will no longer return to its original shape and size on removal of the load, and permanent deformation has occurred. The rubber band is said to have exceeded its **elastic limit** or **yield stress**, beyond which the rubber is suffering plastic deformation – it is being stretched irreversibly.

Eventually, at maximum stress, the material reaches its breaking point – its **ultimate tensile strength** – and failure or fracture rapidly follows. This sequence is illustrated for a variety of materials in Fig. 3.5.

What can we learn about the materials from their stress/strain diagrams?

■ **Mild steel** has little elasticity, but has the highest yield stress of all the samples; is fairly ductile, i.e. has a large range over which it can sustain plastic deformation, and has the highest ultimate tensile strength.

■ **Cast iron** is brittle – it has the least elasticity of the four samples, and has no ability to sustain plastic deformation, although its tensile strength is higher than that of concrete.

■ **Copper** has little elasticity but is the most ductile of the four samples. It has an ultimate tensile strength less than half that of mild steel.

■ **Concrete** has little elasticity, and the lowest tensile strength of the four samples.

Whilst rubber is the obvious 'elastic' material, metals too are elastic (a spring can be substituted for the rubber band in the above simple investigation), as, to a lesser extent, are plastics and wood. The elasticity or springiness in a metal can be shown in the classroom by investigating a bulldog clip or a paper clip.

Stiffness (and flexibility)

The part of the stress/strain curve (see Fig. 3.5) which relates to elastic (reversible) deformation gives an indication of the **stiffness**, and therefore the flexibility, of the material. Stiffness is the resistance of the material to elastic deformation, and this resistance, or lack of it, results in the characteristic flexibility or rigidity of different materials.

A material with high stiffness will be brittle, will tend to be rigid, and will shatter suddenly under the effect of a load beyond its elastic limit. Glass and ceramics are example of brittle materials which are rigid and have little or no flexibility – they are more likely to fracture than stretch. Conversely, rubber and some plastics can easily be extended under tension and are said to have low stiffness, and hence, high flexibility.

Toughness

The part of the stress/strain curve which relates to plastic deformation gives a good indication of the ability of a material to change shape under load without breaking, and this is a reflection of its **toughness**. Materials which can absorb high tensile forces exhibit two further properties. They are said to be **ductile** if they can be elongated – metals can be drawn out into wires for example, or **malleable** if they can be pressed, bent or beaten into shape – playdough, plasticene, copper pipe, or wrought iron for example. Again, the unbending of paper clips in the classroom will enable children to experience malleable metal at first hand.

This area gives us a good example of the difficulties of misunderstanding which can occur when a commonly used word with a generally understood everyday meaning also has a specific scientific meaning which is different. In the examples given above, playdough, plasticene, copper pipe and wrought iron exhibit plastic properties in the sense that a force applied to them can change their shape permanently. They are not made of plastic however, nor do they exhibit all of the properties of plastics. Some plastics, such as the nylon used in climbing ropes, demonstrate elastic properties, whilst others, such as perspex, are brittle and prone to shatter. Clear understanding of the terms involved, helped by a clear explanation of which of the meanings is being used in any particular context – do we mean plastic the *material*, or plastic the *property*? – and a careful use of language, will help to avoid confusion.

Compressibility

All materials have some ability to be compressed into a smaller space, although the compression of solids and liquids is usually too small to be obvious. The gases however, can easily be compressed, and this characteristic can readily be experienced by attempting to work a bicycle pump when the outlet hole is held closed with a thumb or finger. The 'springiness' felt in the plunger is a result of the air in the barrel of the pump being compressed by the washer. Practical applications of this characteristic are considered in the next section (The uses of materials).

Thermal and electrical conductivity

Thermal conductivity is a measure of the extent to which heat energy can be transferred through a material. Metals are good thermal conductors, whilst plastics and natural materials conduct heat poorly. It is important to remember that conduction of heat can result in a rise or fall in temperature. This property of materials can be illustrated by comparing the temperature of the handles of metal and plastic teaspoons after a short period of immersion in a hot liquid.

The higher temperature of the metal spoon is a measure of the high thermal conductivity of the metal. Conversely, outdoors in winter, metal objects 'feel' colder than those made of wood or other natural materials.

As with heat, **electrical conductivity** is a measure of the ease with which an electrical current can move in a material. Again, metals are good **conductors** of electricity – for commercial purposes, copper and silver have the highest conductivities. Plastics and natural materials are poor conductors, and those materials which oppose or resist the passage of an electrical current are known as **insulators**, and are said to have high resistivity.

The following table summarizes some properties of a variety of common materials.

Material	Density (g/cm^3)	Tensile strength (MN/m^2)	Thermal cond. (W/m/°C)	Electrical resistivity (10^{-8}ohms m)
copper	8.96	215	385	1.67
gold	19.30	125	296	2.3
iron	7.87	210	80	9.71
aluminium	2.70	80	201	2.65
tin	7.30	25	65	12.8
steel	7.86	690	63	12.0
brick	2.30	5	0.6	10^{10} ohms m
concrete	2.40	5	0.1	–
glass	2.50	100	1.0	10^5 ohms m
nylon	1.15	70	0.25	10^{16} ohms m
water	1.00			
polythene	0.92	13	0.2	10^{16} ohms m
rubber	0.91	17	0.15	–
softwood	0.60	100 (with grain)	0.15	–

What does the table tell us about the materials listed? As has already been described, those materials which have a **density** greater than 1.0 g/cm^3 will sink in water, whilst those with densities lower than 1.0 g/cm^3 will float.

The **tensile strength** of the materials is expressed in terms of the maximum force which a sample of the material can sustain under tension (the units are mega-newtons per square metre). Perhaps not surprisingly, the harder metals (steel, copper and iron) demonstrate the highest tensile strengths, with glass and softwood performing better under tension than aluminium, tin, the ceramics and the plastics.

Thermal conductivity is expressed in terms of the efficiency with which heat can be transferred along a sample of the material (the units are Watts per metre per Celsius degree). In this case, copper, gold and aluminium are the best conductors of heat, and the ceramics, plastics and softwood are the poorest.

The **electrical conductivity** of the materials may be inferred by looking at their **resistivity**. Resistivity is a measure of the extent to which the materials impede or resist the passage of an electric current (the units are ohm metres), so a material with a high resistivity will be a poor conductor of electricity, and vice versa. It is easy to see from the table that metals in general, and copper in particular, are good conductors of electricity, (because they have low resistivities) in comparison with the various non-metallic materials, with their high resistivities and correspondingly low conductivities.

Magnetic properties

Some materials have the property to attract iron, a property known as magnetism. Lodestone, an iron oxide, has natural magnetic properties (and reputedly was first discovered near Magnesia in ancient Greece), and other magnetic materials include iron, cobalt and nickel, and alloys of these metals such as steel, alnico (an **al**loy of **ni**ckel and **co**balt) and nichrome. In addition to pure metal magnets, some modern materials have incorporated magnetic metals into ceramics and plastics.

The property of magnetism is a function of the atomic structure of the metals concerned. It is believed that the atoms of ferro-magnetic materials are aligned in the same direction in very small areas (0.01 to 1.0 mm in diameter) known as domains. When brought into close contact with a magnet, the domains also align themselves in the same direction in such a way as to reinforce the overall effect, and magnetism is produced. In non-magnetic materials the domains remain randomly oriented, cancelling out any overall magnetic effect.

It is difficult to provide a definition of magnetism, other than on an operational level – in other words it is easier to explain what magnets do, than what they are.

Some operational characteristics of magnets and magnetism include:

- magnets attract other magnetic materials;
- this attraction may occur from a distance;
- it may occur through other, non-magnetic, materials;
- every magnet has two areas (poles) which produce a stronger force of attraction than other areas;
- a magnet has a north-seeking (north) and a south-seeking (south) pole;
- a freely suspended magnet will come to rest with the north pole pointing northwards;
- unlike poles, i.e. N–S, attract; like poles, i.e. N–N, or S–S, repel;
- the region around a magnet, in which its magnetic force acts, is known as a magnetic field;
- temporary magnets can be made by bringing iron into close contact with a magnet, by stroking a piece of iron with another magnet, or by inducing magnetism with an electric current (see section 4);
- permanent magnets can be made by repeating the above processes with steel;
- heating or hammering a magnet will reduce its magnetism.

Composite materials

These are materials which are formed to realize or exploit the properties of two or more other materials. Examples include:

- bone, which combines the flexibility of protein with the strength of calcium phosphate;
- reinforced concrete, which combines the compressive strength of concrete with the tensile strength of steel;
- glass reinforced plastic (fibreglass), which combines the bonding property of polymer resins (the plastic) with the flexibility of woven glass cloth or fibrous mat.

Other combinations include electric cable, which uses the conductivity of the copper wire core, and the insulation of the plastic outer covering, and the technique of lamination which increases the strength of materials by bonding together a number of layers. Plywood is an example of a laminate made from natural materials, and sailboards are composite laminates of a number of plastic products including polystyrene, woven polyester cloth and polyester resin.

The characteristics of the main groups of materials

Whilst there are always exceptions to any large-scale groupings, it is possible to characterize the main groups of materials in terms of their general properties.

Metals are dense materials which are strong, hard, tough, ductile and malleable. They are excellent conductors of heat and electricity and have high melting points. Some metals have magnetic properties. Some are easily corroded.

Ceramics and glass are materials of low to medium density. They are resistant to abrasion, have compressive strength and good insulating properties. They have high melting or softening points and are resistant to corrosion. They are brittle and weak in tension.

Plastics are low density materials which have low strength and hardness and high flexibility. They are easily moulded and are good insulators. They are highly resistant to corrosion but have low melting points.

Wood is a low density natural material which, because of the arrangement of the lignin strengthened fibres, has fairly good strength in tension and stiffness 'along the grain', coupled with shear strength 'across the grain'. It has high flexibility and is a good insulator. Wood is susceptible to decay and to destruction by fire.

Fabrics are highly flexible and have fairly good strength in tension. They are good insulators, but have poor resistance to abrasion. Natural fibre fabrics are susceptible to decay and destruction by fire. Synthetic fibres may melt and give off toxic fumes if 'overheated' – this sometimes occurs when synthetic fabrics are being ironed at too high a temperature setting.

The uses of materials

Fitness for purpose

The objects, structures, and articles which are made for human use or consumption, usually have a particular purpose or function. It is rare for an object to be 'completely useless', and as a result of the demands which will be made on the object or structure, the materials of which it is made will have been chosen for their ability to 'do the job'.

The uses to which materials are put, will reflect the exploitation of their properties. A simple and familiar example might be to consider the materials commonly found in houses and the ways in which these materials are used.

Material	Property	Household example
Metals	strength	structural components e.g. rolled steel joists
	malleability	water pipes
	thermal conductivity	radiators, saucepans, oven
	electrical conductivity	core of electrical cables
	hardness	drill bits, hammer heads
Ceramics	strength (compression)	brickwork, concrete, paving slabs
	heat resistance	ovenware
	abrasion resistance	china, crockery
Glass	thermal insulation	loft, cavity wall insulation
	transparency	windows
Plastics	flexibility	moulded items e.g. mixing, washing up bowls
	electrical insulation	sheathing of electrical cables
	thermal insulation	saucepan handles
	lightness and strength	construction; window frames
Wood	lightness and strength	construction; doors, window frames, furniture
Fabrics	flexibility, insulation	curtains, furnishings, clothing

Sometimes of course, a particular 'job' can be done by more than one type of material. A plate can be made of china, glass, plastic or paper, but the way in which it can be used will be limited by the properties of the material concerned. 'Ovenware' china and hardened 'Pyrex' glass plates can be used in an oven, but are more likely than plastic plates to break if dropped. Conversely, plastic plates, whilst being lighter and almost unbreakable, will scratch more easily than glass or china, and cannot be used in the oven. Paper plates whilst having very few of the properties of those made from china, glass or plastic, have been designed as disposable items, and with the 'convenience' of the users in mind.

Similarly, clothes made from synthetic fibres will tend to be longer lasting because they are more resistant to abrasion than those made from natural fibres. They are also stronger because of the length of the fibres from which they are made. This is because the strength of natural fibres is limited by the length of the fibres available from the plant or animal concerned. Synthetic fibres can be spun to any length, and this results in an increased strength for a given diameter of yarn. In spite of the greater strength and durability of clothes made from synthetic fibres, there are still many people who prefer the softer 'feel' (and the absorbency) of clothes made from natural fibres.

Continuing the 'fitness for purpose' concept from the previous section, a further development is the idea that some materials demonstrate more than one property in their production and use for particular situations. An example of this is provided by the metal strings used on musical instruments such as guitars. Firstly, these strings are produced as a result of the ductile nature of the metals used (often nickel steel, sometimes wound with copper wire). The **toughness** of the steel (see 'properties' above) allows the metal to be drawn out into fine wire. The **tensile strength** of the steel is then employed to allow the string to be tensioned enough to bring it to the required musical pitch. Finally, when the string is plucked, the **elasticity** of the metal allows it to vibrate consistently at the frequency which produces the musical note for which it has been tuned.

Considerations for the choice of materials

The materials which are used in the production of objects and structures are chosen because they exhibit particular properties. There are however, other factors which are taken into account when any articles are produced, particularly on a large scale. Inevitably, the final choice of materials for a product represents a compromise between some or all of these factors. They may include the **cost** of raw materials (and hence the price of the finished product), the possibility of using **alternative materials**, the **availability** of the required materials, the degree of **maintenance** necessary, and the **aesthetic qualities** of the materials concerned.

Cost/price – today, the cost of materials is one of the most significant factors in manufacturing industry. 'Cost no object' projects are rare, and are usually those which involve national security, as in defence procurement, or prestige, as in the exploration of space. Most commercial and industrial operators want to produce at the lowest cost and sell at the highest price, and this mission is what drives the continuing search for alternative materials.

Alternative materials – are those materials which can replace original materials, usually at lower cost, and still exhibit most of the required properties. Everyday examples of this tendency include the large scale substitution of plastic objects for metal ones. In most kitchens for example, metal colanders, sieves, cheese graters and tea strainers have been replaced by plastic versions (although tea strainers are themselves becoming obsolete as leaf tea is superseded by tea bags).

Similarly, the baths in most houses are now made from glass reinforced or high density plastic. In the earlier years of this century they would probably have been made from cast iron (if plumbed in) or galvanized iron ('tin' baths).

As a final example, motorists now sit on fabric (usually synthetic) seat covers rather than the leather seats which characterized cars during the early and middle decades of the century.

Availability – some materials are becoming scarce, and this has increased the need to develop substitutes. The scarcity of large size hardwood timber for construction purposes has led to the development of laminated beams, or the substitution of metal alternatives.

Maintenance – some of the newer materials are less demanding of maintenance than more traditional ones. A good example of the 'maintenance-free' tendency has been the large scale substitution of glass reinforced plastic for wood as a construction material for the leisure boating industry.

Aesthetic qualities – in some cases, materials are chosen for their aesthetic qualities as well as for their properties, cost, availability etc. Examples include decorative articles – jewellery, fabrics – and materials used in sympathy with a particular environment or location – the use of stone rather than brick for buildings in national parks. Appeal is also made to shoppers on the grounds of 'quality' in the marketing of furniture made from solid wood rather than from veneered chipboard.

A materials case study: drinks containers

Many of the issues raised above can be addressed simply in the classroom by a study of the wide variety of drinks containers available today. Containers can be found which are made from metal, ceramic, glass, plastic and paper. The properties of the materials from which the containers are made can be investigated, and the limitations of each discussed and tested. Some of the characteristics, design features and limitations are listed below:

Alloy drink can – light (aluminium alloy has a density of $2.7g/cm^3$), strong in compression (with care it is possible to stand on the top of an empty drink can), designed to stack easily and be recyclable, but not reusable. Malleable – it is easy to buckle an aluminium can by hand.

China mug or cup – the traditional hot drink container? Keeps drinks hot, resists abrasion during washing up. Strong but breakable.

Glass – the traditional cold drink container? An important factor may be the visibility of the contents of the glass – particularly in social situations! Breakable, possibility of injury.

High density plastic (melamine) mug or cup – light, strong, keeps drinks hot. Virtually unbreakable, but liable to abrasion damage (possible health hazard as bacteria can collect in surface scratches).

Enamel mug – light, unbreakable. Hot drinks lose heat quickly. Now almost replaced by plastic versions.

Thermoplastic cup – very light (and sometimes unstable), thin, and disposable. Rapid, and sometimes uncomfortable heat transfer to user's hand. Hot drinks lose heat quickly. Disposable and non-biodegradable, so sometimes the cause of litter problems. Splits easily. Not designed for reuse.

Expanded polystyrene cup – light, good insulation (hot drinks and no burned fingers). Disposable and non-biodegradable. Not designed for reuse.

Paper cup – very light, cheap, disposable but biodegradable. Not designed for reuse.

The particulate nature of matter

Although this concept is not part of the curriculum for primary schools, and some of the ideas involved are difficult (though by no means impossible) for children to grasp, an understanding of the nature of matter is helpful for teachers, particularly in terms of an explanation of the way in which materials behave.

The kinetic theory

At the heart of the explanation of the nature of matter is the kinetic theory. This assumes that all matter is made of particles, and that these particles are in constant motion. The particles concerned are very small, and may be atoms of an element, or molecules of a compound (see below). It has been estimated that molecules of a light oil are two millionths of a millimetre (2×10^{-6} mm) in diameter, and are therefore well below the resolution of ordinary light microscopes.

The states of matter: solid, liquid and gas

The concepts of solid, liquid and gas *are* part of the Key Stage 2 curriculum, and whilst children may well recognize and differentiate them in operational terms, the kinetic theory of matter also allows teachers to understand their properties in particle terms.

In a **solid** material, strong forces of attraction hold the particles close together in a tightly packed and rigid lattice-like formation. Particle movement is confined to vibration in a fixed position. This accounts for the density of solids, and the fact that a solid has a **fixed shape and volume**. A useful mental model might be to imagine apples packed in layers in a box as representing the particles in a solid material.

In a **liquid**, the forces of attraction between the particles are weaker than in a solid. The particles are therefore more widely spaced, and are able to move more freely around each other. A liquid will therefore be less dense than a solid, will have a **fixed volume, but not a fixed shape** (although it will take up the shape of the bottom of a container into which it is poured). A mental model for the particles in a liquid might be the movement of marbles in a bag, or of balls in a 'ball pool'.

In a **gas**, the particles are widely spaced and are moving independently of each other at high speed (500 metres per second) and at random. A gas will therefore have a very low density – about 1,000 times less dense than a liquid – and will have **no fixed volume or shape**. A mental model for the particles in a gas might be the 'flying balls' inside the National Lottery number dispenser!

Changes of state

When a solid is heated, the heat energy transferred causes the particles in the solid to vibrate more rapidly. In doing so, they move apart, causing the solid to expand. If enough heat energy is transferred, the particles vibrate rapidly

Fig. 3.6 *The states of matter and changes of state*

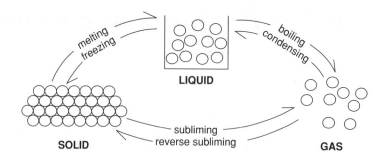

enough to break free from their fixed positions in the lattice, and they are able to move around each other. At this point (the melting point) **the solid melts and becomes a liquid**.

Note – water is unique in that it is **less dense** as a solid at 0°C than it is as a liquid (it is at its densest at 4°C), and that is why ice floats on water.

Similarly, if heat energy is transferred to a liquid, the particles will move more and more rapidly until eventually, particles are moving so fast that they are able to escape from the liquid as gas. The escape of gas particles from the surface of a liquid is known as **evaporation**, and the temperature at which gas bubbles escape from the body (rather than the surface) of the liquid is known as the **boiling point**.

Conversely, if heat energy is transferred out of a gas, the particles begin to slow down until they no longer move independently of each other, but become loosely bonded together so that they move around each other. At this stage the gas has **condensed** to form a liquid. The process is a reversal of evaporation, and the temperature at which a gas condenses will be the same as the boiling point of the liquid form of the same material.

To continue the process, if heat energy is transferred out of a liquid, the particles will slow down until they are unable to move around each other, and can only vibrate in a fixed position. The material contracts in size and the liquid becomes a solid at a temperature known as the **freezing point**. As with the above case, the freezing point (liquid to solid) for a material will be the same as the melting point (solid to liquid).

A small number of substances change state directly from solid to gas and vice versa. This process is known as **sublimation** (and reverse sublimation). Carbon dioxide, a solid at −70°C, sublimates to form carbon dioxide gas at normal atmospheric temperatures and pressures. Under some circumstances, and due to a process known as ablation, ice sublimates directly to water vapour, which is a gas.

To use the most common example, on heating, ice (a solid) melts at 0°C to become water (a liquid). On further heating water boils and evaporates at 100°C to become water vapour (a gas). Conversely, on cooling, water vapour condenses at 100°C to become water. On further cooling, water freezes at 0°C to form ice.

Another useful classroom demonstration of the states of matter is that candle wax (solid), melts on heating by a match flame to form liquid wax, which in turn vaporizes to form paraffin vapour (gas) which burns to form the candle flame.

The compression of gas

Because the particles in a gas are moving independently of each other and are relatively widely spaced, it is possible to force them together into a smaller space, a process known as compression. When the particles of a gas are compressed they collide with each other, and with the sides of any container, more frequently. The increased frequency of collisions in the container results in an increase of pressure. As with the simple experiment described above (Key Idea 3.1: Compressibility), this pressure can be felt if a finger or thumb is held over the end of a bicycle pump whilst the plunger is being pushed in.

Similarly, a blown up balloon has had 'extra' air forced into it under pressure. The increased number of air particles, and hence collisions, causes pressure to be exerted on the inside surface of the balloon, and as the inside pressure is greater than the outside (atmospheric) pressure, the balloon is kept in shape by the pressure of the compressed air inside it.

Elements, compounds and mixtures

A substance or material made up of particles which are all of the same kind, and which cannot be broken down into any other substances, is known as an **element**. There are 105 elements, most of which occur naturally in the crust of the Earth, or the atmosphere. Most of the elements are solid metals such as iron (chemical symbol, Fe), zinc (Zn) copper (Cu), and lead (Pb) – mercury (Hg) is a liquid metal, and carbon (C) is a non-metallic solid. Some elements are gases such as hydrogen (H), oxygen (O), nitrogen (N) and chlorine (Cl).

When two or more elements combine together chemically, a new substance known as a **compound** is formed. A compound is characterized by the specific proportions of each constituent element which it contains, and is a different material, with different properties from any of them. In order to retrieve the original elements in a compound (in some cases a difficult process) a chemical reaction is necessary. Simple examples of compounds would include common salt – sodium chloride – (NaCl), water (H_2O), and carbon dioxide (CO_2). An example of a compound made from three elements is chalk – calcium carbonate – $CaCO_3$ (calcium, carbon and oxygen).

When two or more substances are combined together without a chemical reaction taking place, a **mixture** is formed. In contrast to compounds, mixtures do not form new substances, they can contain any proportion of constituents, they have similar properties to those of the original constituents, and they can usually be separated into their component ingredients. Mixtures can be made of elements – alloys are solid mixtures of metallic elements, air is a mixture of gaseous elements – or of compounds – emulsion paint is a mixture of water, pigments, and compounds which speed up the curing and drying process; sea water is a mixture of water and dissolved salts; petrol is a mixture of compounds of hydrogen and carbon (hydrocarbons).

The structure of atoms

The behaviour of solids, liquids and gases can be explained in terms of kinetic theory and the particulate nature of matter. But what are these particles like?

The basic units of matter are known as **atoms**. Under normal conditions of temperature and pressure, atoms cannot be broken down into simpler or smaller particles (this is possible of course, but lies in the realms of nuclear physics).

An atom is thought to contain:

Fig. 3.7 The structure
of a carbon atom

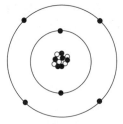

the nucleus of a carbon atom
contains:
6 protons and 6 neutrons.

6 electrons orbit the nucleus – 2 in
the inner shell, and 4 in the
second shell

Fig. 3.8 Periodic table
entries for carbon and
copper

| 12 |
| C |
| **Carbon** |
| 6 |

carbon atoms have:
6 neutrons + 6 protons
(mass number = 12)
6 electrons

| 64 |
| **Cu** |
| **Copper** |
| 29 |

copper atoms have:
35 neutrons + 29 protons
(mass number = 64)
29 electrons

■ a **nucleus** composed of **protons** (positively charged) and **neutrons** (no charge)
■ **electrons** (negatively charged) orbiting the nucleus at high speed

The atom is electrically neutral, and this state is achieved because there are always the same number of (positive) protons in the nucleus as there are (negative) electrons surrounding it (see Fig. 3.7). Almost all the mass (the amount of matter) in an atom is contained in the protons and neutrons of the nucleus. It is thought that electrons have a mass nearly two thousand times less than protons and neutrons, so that their contribution to the total mass of an atom is negligible.

Although conventional diagrams show the electron shells as being relatively close to the nucleus, it has been suggested that this is not the case. Using a greatly enlarged scale for the size of an atom (the diameter of an atom is estimated at one five-millionth of a millimetre), if the nucleus at the centre of the atom was one centimetre in diameter, the closest electron shell would be one kilometre away! In other words, almost all the 'content' of an atom is empty space.

The periodic table Each of the elements has a characteristic number of protons (and therefore electrons), and neutrons, and the conventional way of describing these details is by listing them in the periodic table. Each entry in the table consists of the name and chemical symbol of the element concerned, together with two numbers, one corresponding to the total number of protons and neutrons in the nucleus (the mass number) and the other to the number of protons (the atomic number). This is illustrated in Fig. 3.8 for carbon and copper.

Although beyond the scope of this book, reference to a copy of the periodic table will allow the reader to admire the beautiful simplicity of the arrangement. Basically, the elements are differentiated by the numbers of electrons which surround their nuclei, and these can be found by reference to the atomic number, as there are always the same number of electrons as protons in an atom. Each successive element in the table can be seen to have one more electron (and hence one more proton) than the preceding element. So phosphorus, with 15 electrons surrounding the nucleus of each atom, is placed before sulphur, with 16 electrons.

A feature of the periodic table is that elements are arranged in such a way as to place those with similar properties in the same vertical column or **group**. The position of an element in the group is an indication of its reactivity. For example, those elements in group I, the alkali metals, react on contact with water. The least reactive is lithium, followed by sodium, potassium, rubidium and caesium, which generates enormous explosive force immediately on contact with water.

All the elements to the left of the stepped line are metals, and the transition elements are also known as the heavy metals. Those to the right of the line are metalloids (elements such as silicon, with some properties similar to those of metals), non-metals, or gases. The lines (or **periods**) in which the elements are arranged also correspond to the number of electrons in each shell surrounding the nucleus, and the significance of this is explained in the next section.

Some elements have more than one kind of atom, and the explanation for this lies with the number of neutrons in the nucleus. Carbon atoms for example, usually have 6 protons and 6 neutrons in their nuclei, and the atomic mass of 'normal' carbon is 12. Some carbon atoms however, have 6 protons (this is invariable – if the proton number changed, the element would not be carbon) and 8 neutrons. These alternative atoms are known as **isotopes**, and C-14 is the radioactive isotope of carbon. Because the decay rate of the isotope is predictable and measurable, C-14 is very useful in dating any remains which contain carbon.

Carbon also demonstrates another feature of some elements, namely that they can exist in a number of different physical forms, known as **allotropes**. Two well-known allotropes of carbon are graphite and diamond, and a newly discovered allotrope of the same element (with a spherical molecular structure) has been given the name of Buckminsterfullerene.

Atomic bonding The behaviour of all materials, substances and matter (including living matter) can be explained in terms of the nature of the bonding between atoms, and between groups of atoms known as molecules, and the transfer of energy between them by the movement of electrons.

The negatively charged electrons spinning round atomic nuclei are held in layers or 'shells' depending on their energy levels and the degree of attraction to the positively charged protons in the nucleus. Each shell can hold a fixed maximum number of electrons – the four shells closest to the nucleus can hold a maximum of 2, 8, 8 and 18 electrons respectively. Each electron shell corresponds to a line (or period) of the periodic table, and the shells of successive elements in the table 'fill up' with electrons in sequence. So, an atom of carbon (atomic number 6) will have 6 electrons orbiting the nucleus, 2 in the inner

Fig. 3.9 Electron
diagrams of some
common elements

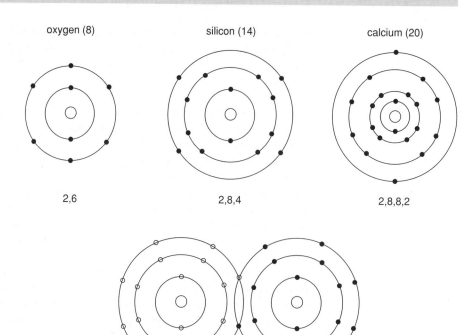

Fig. 3.10 Covalent
bonding: a chlorine
molecule

shell and 4 in the next shell. An atom of silicon (atomic number 14) will have
14 electrons orbiting its nucleus, 2 in the inner shell, 8 in the next shell and
4 in its outer shell (see Fig. 3.9).

During chemical reactions the tendency is for the electrons in the outer
shells of atoms to form stable bonds with those of other atoms. The most
common types of bonding are ionic, covalent and metallic.

Ionic bonding occurs when electrons from the outer shell of atoms of a
metallic element are transferred to the outer shell of atoms of a non-metallic
element. A common example of this transfer is in the formation of sodium
chloride. Sodium atoms have 11 electrons arranged 2, 8, 1 in the first three
shells. Chlorine atoms have 17 electrons arranged 2, 8, 7. The transfer of the
single electron from the outer shell of the sodium atom (resulting in a positively charged sodium ion, Na^+) to the outer shell of the chlorine atom (resulting
in a negatively charged chlorine ion, Cl^-) bonds the ions together with a strong
electrostatic charge. The result is a cubic lattice of alternating sodium and
chlorine ions, visible as crystalline salt.

Covalent bonding occurs when electrons are shared between atoms. In
the previous example, the chlorine atoms, 2, 8, 7 will tend to combine with
other atoms to form a stable outer shell. If each of two chlorine atoms shares
one outer shell electron, the effect is to stabilize the outer shell, and a chlorine
molecule results.

In Fig. 3.10 the electrons of one atom have been depicted as 'solid' to
distinguish them from those of the other atom. The outer shell of each of the
chlorine atoms has seven electrons in it. When two chlorine atoms combine
to form a molecule, one electron from each of the outer shells is 'shared' in

a covalent bond between the atoms, creating a stable arrangement which holds the atoms together.

Similarly, compounds can be formed with covalent bonds. In water, the molecules are formed with strong covalent bonds between the hydrogen and oxygen atoms, but weak bonds between the molecules allow them to move around each other, thus demonstrating the properties of a liquid. Similarly, the giant covalent structures of the loosely linked long chain polymer molecules of plastics and rubber are able, up to a point, to stretch and then return to their original shape – clearly the basis of elasticity.

Materials with covalent structures tend to be poor conductors of heat and electricity, as there are few 'free' electrons to effect the energy transfers necessary.

Finally, **metallic bonding** consists of a densely packed lattice of positively charged metal ions (atoms which have lost or 'given up' one or more electrons from their outer shells) surrounded, and held tightly in place, by a 'sea' of those electrons. The very strong forces of attraction between the ions and the 'free' electrons result in the properties of metals – strength, hardness, and toughness, whilst the 'sea' of electrons accounts for the high thermal and electrical conductivity of metals. Also, the atoms in the tightly packed lattice of a metal are able to 'slip' in layers across each other, and it is this feature which gives metals their malleability.

Changing materials

Materials can be changed, and these changes can be permanent or reversible

Simple changes in the shape of objects are brought about by the application of forces, and the nature of the change in shape will be a function of the properties of the materials of which the objects are made (see above, Key Idea 3.1: The Physical Properties of Materials).

Change in shape

Squashing – objects which can be squashed will usually behave in one of two ways:

- they will return to their original shape once the applied squashing force is removed. Example: squashing a rubber ball, a football, a balloon. The materials are exhibiting the property of stiffness, and have not been loaded beyond their elastic limits;
- they will remain in their 'new' shape once the applied squashing force is removed. Example: moulding or shaping playdough or plasticene. The materials have been loaded beyond their elastic limits, but are now exhibiting the property of toughness (malleability, the ability to sustain plastic deformation).

Bending – similarly, objects which are bent will either:

- return to their original shape once the applied bending force is removed. Example: bending a plastic or wooden ruler. Again, the materials are demonstrating the property of stiffness (hence elasticity);
- remain in their 'new' shape once the applied bending force is removed. Example: bending pipe cleaners or thin metal tube; folding paper. The materials are demonstrating the property of toughness (malleability, the ability to sustain plastic deformation);
- Fracture, if the elastic limit is exceeded with brittle materials, or the maximum tensile strength is exceeded with malleable materials.

Twisting – this process is usually achieved by applying a turning action (torque) to an object, for example a ruler, a block of plasticene or playdough, or a 'twist' of paper. An object held in this state is said to be under torsion. Again, the objects will either:

- return to their original shape (exhibiting stiffness);
- remain twisted (exhibiting toughness);
- fracture (either at the elastic limit, or at the maximum tensile strength of the materials concerned).

Stretching – objects which are stretched, for example rubber bands, metal springs and wire, 'rolls' of plasticene, cotton and wool fibres, fishing line, will usually lengthen, then either:

- return to their original length (exhibiting stiffness);
- remain 'stretched' (exhibiting toughness – ductility);
- fracture (as above).

It is interesting for children to be able to investigate the nature of materials whose shape is changed, as they do not all behave in the neatly predictable ways described above. If a crisp packet is 'screwed up' – squashed and bent – it will begin to regain its original shape, but will never 'uncurl' completely. This shows that even when materials are taken beyond their elastic limits, some residual elasticity remains.

It is relatively easy to discover that the physical processes which cause changes in shape, do not result in any change in mass. 'Before and after' weighings will readily show that the mass of the material has remained constant even though its shape may have changed due to the application of force.

Heating and cooling everyday materials

The effects of changes in temperature on materials can be explained in terms of the states of matter and changes of state (see Key Idea 3.2: The States of Matter).

It is important for young children to realize that sometimes the effects of heating or cooling materials can be easily reversed, and sometimes changes occur which are difficult to reverse – in practical terms they are permanent. Examples from the everyday life of children would include the heating and cooling of water, milk, chocolate, candle wax, cake mixture, clay, and matchwood.

Water – boils (eventually) when heated. Steam is a cloud of minute water droplets at or near 100°C. The gas which evaporates from boiling water is water vapour and is invisible. When cooled, water vapour condenses to form water droplets. All of these processes can be easily demonstrated in a classroom (with care) by boiling water in a kettle, and then holding a suitable surface (a pyrex plate is ideal) in the plume of steam. Condensation occurs almost immediately, and the water droplets which run down the plate can be collected in a suitable container.

When cooled below 0°C, water freezes to form ice (making 'lollies' in the school 'fridge). Uniquely, ice (the solid) is less dense than water, and floats. When heated, the ice melts to form water. The heating and cooling processes are reversible.

Milk – also boils on heating (sometimes 'boiling over'). When frozen, milk separates out into water- and fat-based components and these can clearly be seen as two different layers in the frozen milk.

Chocolate – a solid, melts when heated (either in a warm hand or a pan!). It is interesting to see what happens when a chocolate bar is broken up into small pieces before being heated, in comparison to one which is heated as a single large piece (the small pieces melt more quickly because of a larger surface area exposed to heat transfer). If allowed to cool, the chocolate will reconstitute, but will not resume its former shape. So the process is reversible, but sometimes young children tend to think that the cooled-down chocolate is 'not the same' as the original, because of its different appearance and shape.

Candle wax – a candle, (made of paraffin wax) melts when heated or lit. The liquid wax vaporises to form a gas, which burns as a flame (the brightness of the flame is as a result of white hot particles of carbon). When the candle is blown out, and cooling begins, the vapour disperses and liquid wax solidifies. In one sense then, the process is reversible (although the vapour is not condensed to form liquid wax). In another sense however, a permanent change has occurred because the wax (a fuel) has been used up in the burning process – the candle 'burns down'.

Cake mixture – to begin with, it is interesting to notice the changes which take place to the consistency and colour of the ingredients of a cake during the mixing process. When the mixture is heated (baked) in an oven, irreversible chemical changes take place. The liquid mixture solidifies and increases in volume as carbon dioxide gas, produced during the baking process, is trapped in bubbles in the mix. The resulting cake, when cooled, is a fused matrix of the original ingredients, which cannot be reconstituted in their previous form. It has usually increased in size.

Clay – when clay is heated to very high temperatures in a kiln, the constituent minerals fuse to form a ceramic material. An irreversible chemical reaction has taken place and a new compound has formed from a mixture of other compounds. Some modelling clays are plastics-based polymers, and will harden at much lower (oven) temperatures.

Matchwood splint – if a splint, or paper twist, is heated by a match or other flame, the wood or paper will burn (carbon from the organic material combines with oxygen in the air to form carbon dioxide gas). As with the candle, the flame is composed partly of incandescent particles of carbon and partly of unburnt gas. The change in the wood is permanent, as it cannot be reconstituted in its original form.

One of the less obvious outcomes of heating everyday materials is the extent to which they expand. This can be seen outdoors where, on hot days, concrete road surfaces expand and squeeze out the tarmac filler placed between road sections. Many steel bridges have carriageways which are mounted on rollers at one end in order to allow for expansion of the metal during hot weather. The metal will regain its original length when temperatures return to normal. Railway lines are laid with gaps between adjacent rails to allow for expansion during hot weather. In exceptional circumstances, even this precaution is not enough to prevent the rails from buckling in the heat.

CONCEPTS TO SUPPORT KEY STAGE 2

Mixtures, as explained in Key Idea 3.2 (Elements, Compounds and Mixtures), are derived when two or more substances are combined together without a chemical reaction taking place. In many cases, the original substances can be separated out by simple physical procedures which, in effect, reverse the mixing process.

Separating mixtures

Using the 'solid, liquid, gas' classification of substances, there are nine different types of mixtures. They are described here, with examples, and where appropriate, an explanation of a simple separating system.

Solid-in-solid (particles) – e.g. dried soil, sand and gravel; can be separated by **sieving**. Stones can be removed from topsoil with a sieve, before planting a garden or laying a lawn. The basic principle of a sieve is that large particles are trapped by a mesh, whilst small particles pass through the gaps – even a garden rake is a form of sieve.

Although solid particles of different sizes can be separated by sieving, it may not always be appropriate to do so. The traditional (but perhaps contrived) 'salt and sand' and 'sand and iron filings' mixtures are best separated by other means (although it is arguable as to why anyone might want to mix them in the first place!).

Solid-in-liquid – some solids can be **dissolved** in liquids – salt, or sugar, in water for example, to form a **solution**. What happens is that the crystalline salt or sugar breaks down into particles so small that they cannot be seen, and these then become dispersed evenly in the water, weakly bonded to the water molecules.

A solid in solution **(solute)** can be recovered from a liquid **(solvent)** by causing the solvent to evaporate. This can be achieved by heating the solution until the solvent has been removed by **evaporation**. What has happened is that the additional heat energy has caused the loosening of the bonds between the salt or sugar crystals and the water molecules, which 'escape' from the solution as gaseous water vapour (this process can take place without heat, but takes much longer to complete). The original solute is recovered, once again in crystalline form.

There is a limit to the mass of solid that can dissolve in a given amount of liquid, and this limit is different for different solids. At the point at which no more of a particular solid will dissolve into a given amount of a liquid, a saturated solution has been produced. A key factor in this process is the temperature of the solvent. The amount of a solid which will dissolve in a given amount of liquid will increase with increasing temperature, and the solubility curves for different solids are characteristic for a range of temperatures (see Fig. 3.11). Gases show the opposite tendency, and as temperature rises, less gas will dissolve in a given mass of solvent.

The *mass* of a solute which will dissolve in a solvent is affected by the temperature of the solvent. The *speed* at which a soluble substance will dissolve is also affected by the size of the grains or pieces of the substance. The smaller the pieces, the faster the substance will dissolve. This is because as volume decreases, relative surface area increases, and the effect can be demonstrated easily by noting the time taken to dissolve a variety of different sizes of sugar pieces in a fixed volume of water at a constant temperature. For example, four different grain 'sizes' could be derived from: a whole sugar cube; a cube broken into pieces; a cube crushed into granules; and a cube ground into powder.

If the solid will not dissolve in a liquid, a **suspension** results. The best classroom example is muddy water – shake up some soil and water in a jar. Even after many hours (sometimes days) small particles will remain suspended

Fig. 3.11 *The solubility curves of two different compounds*

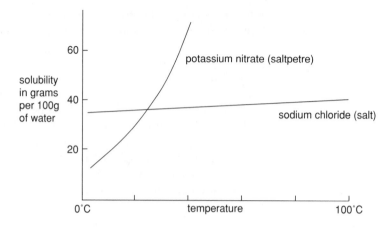

in the water (a useful subjective test is how clearly small print can be read through the suspension).

Undissolved solid particles can be separated from the liquid by **filtering** (filtration). The mixture of solid particles in a liquid is poured into a funnel containing filter paper or other material which will 'trap' the larger particles (gravel is used in some parts of water filtration plants). As with sieving, the principle is that larger particles (the **residue**) are trapped by the 'mesh' of the filter paper, whilst the liquid (the **filtrate**) passes through. Everyday examples of this process would include the making of filter coffee (where the filtrate is the required product) and the 'straining' of peas or cabbage from the water in which the cooking took place – in this case the residue is the required material.

A useful classroom example would be the separation of milk solids from liquid, using muslin or similar cloths, during the making of cream cheese. Similarly, sand or soil can be separated from water by filtering the mixture through filter or blotting paper, or kitchen roll.

Solid-in-gas – e.g. smoke particles in the air, technically an **aerosol**, can also be removed by **filtration**. This occurs commercially during the 'scrubbing' of air in industrial processes before its return to the atmosphere. An everyday example of this process in action would be the dirt which accumulates on curtains. The 'dirt' consists of small solid particles trapped by the weave of the cloth.

Liquid-in-solid – e.g. butter, a **solid emulsion** – water droplets in a fat, can be separated by 'boiling off' the water (a process used in some types of cooking).

Liquid-in-liquid – such a mixture is known as an **emulsion**, e.g. a vinegar and oil-based salad dressing. The constituents can most easily be separated by allowing the components of the emulsion to separate into 'layers' – the less dense component will 'float' on top of the denser component – and then by carefully pouring off the top layer.

If the mixture of liquids is a solution, e.g. alcohol and water, or petroleum, separation can be achieved by **distillation**. The basic process involves heating the mixture until one of the constituents reaches boiling point. The evaporated gas is drawn off the mixture, condensed and collected separately. This process is repeated a number of times during the 'fractional distillation' of crude oil, as the basic raw material consists of a mixture of a number of different products (fractions) with different boiling points.

Liquid-in-gas – e.g. mist or cloud – fine water droplets suspended in the air, again, technically an **aerosol**. In Gibraltar, an outcrop of limestone rock with a serious water supply problem, water is collected from the damp easterly wind (the Levanter) which streams over the top of the rock, by means of large vertical screens of nylon fabric, down which the condensed droplets run into concrete catchments and reservoirs.

Gas-in-solid – e.g. expanded polystyrene, is an example of a **solid foam**. Although the air does not mix with the plastic, a chemical reaction has occurred during the curing of the product, and separation of the components of the mixture is impossible in practical terms.

Gas-in-liquid – may take the form of a solution, e.g. oxygenated water in fish tank, or a **foam**, e.g. shaving foam – a mixture of soap products and a propellant gas.

Gas-in-gas – e.g. air – which is a mixture of gases (see Key Idea 3.1: Natural Materials from the Physical Environment). The separation of the individual gases is an industrial process which involves the liquefaction of air (which occurs at about −200˚C), followed by fractional distillation.

Changing materials   The processes which cause changes in substances or materials can include physical and chemical reactions.

Physical changes

Physical changes include those which cause a change in shape (**mechanical changes**), a change in state (**heating and cooling**), or a physical **mixing** of substances or materials.

Mechanical changes

The squashing, bending, twisting, stretching, etc., of solid materials (see above, Change in shape), occur as the materials respond to applied force. The resulting change will reflect the properties of the materials concerned. If the material is deformed within its elastic limit (a function of its stiffness, see Key Idea 3.1: Stiffness), the mechanical change will be reversible. If the elastic limit is exceeded by the applied load, plastic deformation will take place and the change will be irreversible.

The **heating and cooling** of many simple materials can cause reversible changes in state. These include melting, boiling, evaporation, condensing, freezing (or solidifying) and they have already been described in detail above (see Key Idea 3.2: Changes of State). The heating and cooling of water can be used to demonstrate the conservation of mass, i.e. that the mass of water will remain the same after a change of state. The careful freezing of a known

mass (not volume) of water should result in an equal mass of ice, and melting of that ice should restore the original mass of water.

The **mixing** of materials is a process which can often be reversed (see above, Separating Mixtures), and simple mixtures can usually be separated by sieving, filtering, or by the evaporation of the solvent from a solution to recover the solute.

The making of a solution is another good way to demonstrate the conservation of mass. If 30 grams of salt is dissolved into 100 grams of water, 130 grams of salt solution will result. It is not easy to demonstrate the conservation of mass during the reversal of the process because of the practical difficulty involved in collecting all the evaporated water vapour and condensing it.

Chemical reactions and heat energy

During many chemical reactions, the bonds which exist between particles (atoms or molecules) of the substances involved (elements or compounds) are broken and reformed as new compounds are produced. If the total energy of the product is less than that of the original constituents, a release of energy accompanies the reaction. This energy release is commonly in the form of heat (which can be felt for example, when plaster of Paris is mixed with water and allowed to 'set'), and this type of reaction is known as **exothermic** (literally, heat out).

Conversely, in some reactions, energy is needed to form the resultant compound, and this energy may be absorbed from the surrounding medium. A good example of this type of **endothermic** (heat in) reaction occurs when lemonade (citric acid) and bicarbonate of soda (sodium bicarbonate) are mixed. If the temperature of the lemonade is noted before the sodium bicarbonate is added, it will be noticed that a drop in temperature of up to 5°C can occur once the sodium bicarbonate is stirred into the solution. The drop in temperature of the solution represents the transfer of heat energy needed to cause the breakdown of the molecular bonding (and the release of carbon dioxide gas). The effervescence which occurs when these two compounds are mixed, is the basis for the 'fizziness' of sherbet.

Most of these types of reaction are not easily reversible.

Changes involving oxygen

Many chemical reactions which are important in everyday life involve the use of oxygen from the atmosphere in a process known as oxidation. Two common examples are burning and rusting.

The **burning** (or combustion) of a fuel in the presence of oxygen results in the production of carbon dioxide, water, and the liberation of a large amount of energy. What has happened during this process is that the carbon from the fuel (usually a hydrocarbon) is oxidized to form carbon dioxide, and hydrogen from the fuel combines with oxygen to form water. The energy released by the breaking of the carbon bonds during the reaction is transferred in a number of ways.

Imagine a car starting up. The fuel (petrol or diesel) is burnt in the cylinders, in the presence of oxygen. The reaction is so rapid as to be explosive, and the energy released in the reaction can be transferred in the following ways:

productive energy:

- through the gears and clutch to make the car move forward – mechanical energy;
- through the dynamo to power the electrical circuits – electrical energy – hence:
  - light energy;
  - sound energy (horn);
  - magnetic energy (central locking system);
  - heat energy (heating system).

unproductive energy (transferred in an unusable form):

- heat;
- sound (engine noise).

The chemical reactions are also traceable to the production of carbon dioxide (and carbon monoxide) as a component of the exhaust gases, and the water produced during the combustion of fuel can often be seen dripping from the exhaust pipe of a recently started car, or as the 'steam' coming from an exhaust pipe on a cold morning.

The original materials burnt as fuels cannot be recovered after combustion. The process is not reversible in any practical sense at all (coal, oil, and natural gas are examples of fossil fuels; wood, charcoal and peat are present day examples).

Another form of oxidation occurs when **rusting** takes place. Iron is oxidized in the presence of water to form hydrated iron oxide (rust). The process is a slow and corrosive one which causes millions of pounds worth of damage every year. Whilst the process is reversible in chemical terms, it is not practicable to do so – a rusted iron component could not be reconstituted in its original form. The solution is to slow down or prevent rusting by excluding oxygen (air) and water from the metal. This can be done by coating the iron with paint, a layer of tin, or of zinc (a process known as galvanizing), or by alloying the iron with chromium to make stainless steel.

An interesting classroom investigation into the rates and prevention of rusting can be set up by placing iron nails in containers as follows:

- nails alone (control)
- nails dampened with water
- nails under water
- nails under boiled water (some oxygen removed)
- as each of above, but nails smeared with vaseline, painted or oiled.

The results will speak for themselves!

Finally, it is worth remembering that **cellular respiration** is a form of oxidation. The 'fuel' in this case takes the form of energy rich organic molecules (carbohydrates) stored in the tissues of living organisms, and the oxygen is delivered to the tissues by the process of breathing. As with the combustion of fossil fuels, the products of this oxidation process are carbon dioxide and water, with an accompanying release of energy. Details of the process are given in Section 2 (see Key Idea 2.2: The Cardio-vascular System; Respiration).

The rock cycle

The main classification of rocks – into **igneous, sedimentary** and **metamorphic** types – is based on the way in which the rocks are formed.

Igneous rocks

Igneous rocks are formed by the cooling of molten magma which wells up from deep beneath the Earth's surface. In some places the magma remains below the surface and cools slowly (**intrusive** igneous rock), whilst in others it is forced to the surface and erupts as volcanic ash and lava (**extrusive** igneous rock).

The magma is a melted mixture of rock forming minerals (mainly silicates), and as cooling proceeds, the individual minerals crystallize out and become solid at different temperatures. The crystalline nature of igneous rocks is a characteristic feature, and a sample of such a rock looks rather like a fully interlocking three-dimensional jigsaw.

If cooling has been slow because the magma has solidified deep below the surface, the resulting intrusive rock will usually be dark in colour, fairly dense, and its crystals will be large and obvious, as in granite, for example. If however, the magma has been thrown out of the Earth during a volcanic eruption, it will have cooled rapidly and the resulting extrusive rock will usually be pale in colour, less dense, and its crystals will usually be too small to be seen with the naked eye, as in pumice or volcanic ash.

In addition to obvious surface features formed from extrusive igneous rocks (such as volcanoes, ash cones and lava flows), intrusive igneous rocks are occasionally visible in the landscape as a result of the removal of the original surface layers by erosion. Examples of intrusive features which have been excavated by erosion in the UK include the columnar basalt of the Giant's Causeway in County Antrim in Northern Ireland (the same outcrop incidentally, as the columnar structures of Fingal's Cave on the island of Staffa in the Hebrides), and the outcrops of the Great Whin Sill in the north-east of England – at Hadrian's Wall, High Force waterfall, and the Farne Islands for example. Fig. 3.12 summarizes the main features formed from igneous intrusive and extrusive rocks.

Sedimentary rocks

The rocks of the Earth's crust are continuously being eroded away. That is to say, they are broken down into small fragments by the process of weathering (frost-shattering, mechanical or chemical weathering), and then removed from their original sites by the transport of the weathered debris (by rivers, glaciers, the wind, or the sea). A useful 'formula' is that:

erosion = (is a result of) weathering + transport

Fig. 3.12 Features
formed by igneous rocks

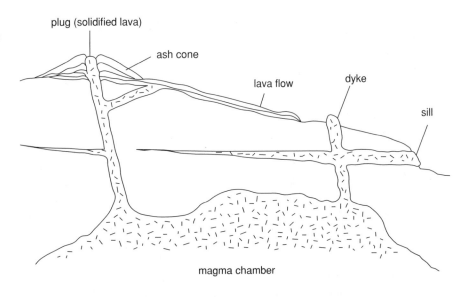

Fig. 3.13 The
*deposition of
sedimentary rocks*

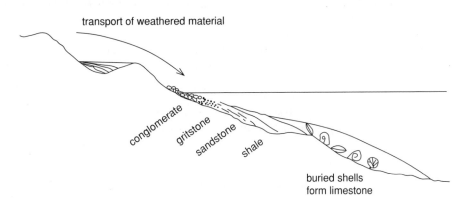

Eventually the eroded fragments of the original rocks are deposited, usually under water, in thick layers (or strata). These layers of sediment eventually become compressed into rocks by the weight of water and other sediments above them. The resulting sedimentary rocks will therefore be characterized by the nature of the sediments from which they were formed.

Sedimentary rocks are therefore characteristically formed from small particles of weathered rocks and minerals which are bound together by a related matrix substance (rather like currants in a fruit cake). If the sediment is soft it is often possible to scrape away the particles, and a look through a hand lens will usually confirm that the rock is not formed from interlocking crystals.

In sites where sediments may be deposited (where a fast-flowing river enters a lake, for example) the heaviest particles are usually deposited first, followed by a graded sequence of particle sizes, with the finest particles being deposited furthest out in the lake. This is summarized in the following table and in Fig. 3.13.

Sediment	(becomes)	Sedimentary rock
gravel		conglomerate
coarse sand		gritstone
sand		sandstone
mud		mudstone
silt		shale
calcium shells		limestone
silica shells		flint, chert
salts		rock salt, gypsum
plant fossils		peat, coal, bitumen

Metamorphic rocks

Metamorphic (literally, 'change shape') rocks are formed when an original rock type (which may be igneous, sedimentary or metamorphic) is altered by the effect of heat or pressure, or both. This heat or pressure is easily generated in unstable areas of the Earth's crust where volcanic or earthquake activity is common.

Examples of **heat** metamorphism:

- **igneous rocks** become **gneiss** (broadly banded) or **schist** (narrowly banded);
- **limestone** becomes **marble**;
- **sandstone** becomes **quartzite**.

As an example of **pressure** metamorphism:

- **shale** becomes **slate**.

It is possible to imagine a long-term rock cycle as follows: Following a **mountain building** period, and the uplift of parts of the Earth's surface, possibly by buckling of the crust associated with the movement of continental plates, **erosion** begins, followed by the **deposition** under water of transported sediments. These sediments are compressed to form sedimentary rocks, which eventually fill the basins between former continental masses. When the continental masses move towards each other, again as a result of **crustal movement**, folding and buckling of the sediments results in the formation of **new fold mountains** and the process begins again.

Fig. 3.14a represents two continental land masses separated by an ocean basin. Over many millions of years the surfaces of the land masses are lowered by erosion, and the weathered debris is transported into the ocean, eventually to become sedimentary rock strata (layers) of great thickness (Fig. 3.14b).

Finally, when the two land masses are forced towards each other, the sediments in the ocean basin are buckled and uplifted to form fold mountains, as in Fig. 3.14c. It is thought for example, that the Mediterranean basin may be the remains of a large trench which filled with sediments transported from what are now Europe and Africa, and then suffered uplift when the African

Fig. 3.14   *The rock cycle*

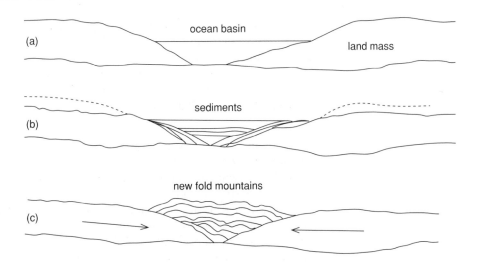

plate moved against the Scandinavian shield, resulting in the formation of the present-day Alps.

Soil formation and characteristics

The rocks which make up the foundations of the present day landscape are often not visible as outcrops at all. This is because they lie beneath a layer of soil. As was pointed out in Key Idea 3.2, soil is the valuable natural material on which plant life (and therefore all animal life) depends.

Soil is a mixture of four main ingredients:

- weathered particles of bedrock;
- decaying organic matter (humus);
- water;
- air.

The larger particles of weathered rock tend to be at depth, and the largest concentration of humus is near the surface of the soil. It is the decay of the organic matter which recycles the nutrients on which the plant cover depends. The gaps between the particles of soil will be filled with air near to the surface, and water at a greater depth.

The nature of the soil in any particular place will be governed by a number of factors, including:

- the **type of bedrock** – a sandstone will tend to form a well drained, gritty, **sandy** soil, usually light brown in colour. A shale or mudstone will cause a poorly drained, blue-grey, sticky **clay** soil to develop. A well balanced mixture of sand and clay will give rise to a rich brown **loam** soil, whilst chalk or limestone will produce a thin dark soil which tends to support grassland;
- the **climate** of the locality – areas with heavy rainfall will tend to develop waterlogged or poorly drained acid soils, whilst those with less rainfall will give rise to better drained loams;
- the **flatness** or **steepness** of the slope – flat areas produce impeded drainage

and waterlogged soils, whilst on steep slopes, soil creep will cause the soils at the bottom of the slope to be thicker than those at the top;

■ the **length of time** since the bedrock was exposed to weathering – the most mature soils are those which have been undisturbed for longest. Those areas most recently exposed to weathering (such as areas of bare rock exposed by the melting of glacier ice) will give rise to the thinnest 'skeletal' soils.

A useful and simple test for soil type is to take a small amount of soil in the hand, then try to roll it into a spindle. A clay soil will roll into thin spindles, a sandy soil will form poor or crumbly spindles, and a loam soil will be 'in between' these two types.

Similarly, if soils are placed in pots and 'watered', the speed at which the water disappears will be an indication of the permeability of the soil. A clay soil will be relatively impermeable – the water will take a long time to disappear. A sandy soil will have good permeability and the water will 'drain away' quickly. Once again, a loam soil will be 'in between' the other two examples.

The water cycle

All living things depend on water for their survival. In addition to the part it plays in essential life processes, people also use water (among other things) for transport, industrial processes, sanitation and recreation.

There is a finite amount of water on the planet, and the small amount which is readily available is recycled over long periods of time. It is said that the water, which today wells up into the Roman baths in the city of Bath, fell as rain on the Mendip Hills 30,000 years ago. The proportion of the Earth's water supply which is available to living things is very small, as the following details show:

- 70% of the Earth's surface is covered by water;
- 97% of that water is salty, 3% is fresh;
- Of the fresh water, up to 85% exists in the form of ice;
- So only 15% of 3%, i.e. 0.45%, of the Earth's water blanket is freely available at or near the Earth's surface, and circulates in what is known as the water cycle.

In simple terms, the water cycle proceeds as follows:

- fresh water from the atmosphere falls onto the Earth's land surface as **precipitation** (rain, hail, sleet, snow, and in some areas fog and mist);
- some of this water seeps into the ground, some runs off the surface, eventually to collect in streams, rivers, lakes and the sea;
- some ground water is drawn up into plants, and eventually returns to the atmosphere as water vapour (a gas) by a process known as **transpiration**. This involves the diffusion of water vapour out of the tissue of the plant leaves through small pores known as stomata. To see evidence of this process, seal a polythene bag over a growing plant for a short while – the inside of the bag will soon be covered with water droplets which have condensed from the water vapour transpired by the plant. Very large volumes of water are returned to the atmosphere by this process. It is said that a large oak tree transpires the equivalent of 360 litres of water per hour on a sunny day!;
- some surface water returns to the atmosphere by **evaporation** (see Key Idea 3.2: Changes of State) from the surface of rivers, ponds and lakes, and the sea. This process can be rapid even at normal atmospheric temperatures. To observe this, draw a chalk line round a shallow playground puddle and return to it regularly to compare the newly dried area as the puddle shrinks;
- the cycle is completed when water droplets, visible as clouds, form by the **condensation** of water vapour in the atmosphere. Eventually coalescing droplets grow to a size large enough to fall from the sky as rain, hail, sleet or snow, depending on the prevailing weather conditions.

A diagram of the water cycle can be found at Fig. 2.29.

Materials and their properties: National Curriculum coverage

Below is listed each of the component parts of the relevant programme of study of science in the National Curriculum (SCAA, 1995). In the bracket below each component the relevant Key Idea is shown, together with the section heading(s) in the book where further specific details may be found.

KEY STAGE 1

Pupils should be taught:

1. Grouping materials

a to use their senses to explore and recognize the similarities and differences between materials;
   (KEY IDEA 3.1: The physical properties of materials)
b to sort materials into groups on the basis of their simple properties, including texture, appearance, transparency and whether they are magnetic or non-magnetic;
   (KEY IDEA 3.1: The physical properties of materials)
c to recognize and name common types of material, e.g. metal, plastic, wood, paper, rock, and to know that some of these materials are found naturally;
   (KEY IDEA 3.1: Natural and manufactured materials)
d that many materials, e.g. glass, wood, wool, have a variety of uses;
   (KEY IDEA 3.1: Fitness for purpose)
e that materials are chosen for specific uses, e.g. glass for windows, wool for clothing, on the basis of their properties.
   (KEY IDEA 3.1: Fitness for purpose)

2. Changing materials

a that objects made from some materials can be changed in shape by processes including squashing, bending, twisting and stretching;
   (KEY IDEA 3.3: Change in shape)
b to describe the way some everyday materials, e.g. water, chocolate, bread, clay, change when they are heated or cooled.
   (KEY IDEA 3.3: Heating and cooling everyday materials)

KEY STAGE 2

Pupils should be taught:

1. Grouping and classifying materials

a to compare everyday materials, e.g. wood, rock, iron, aluminium, paper, polythene, on the basis of their properties, including hardness, strength, flexibility and magnetic behaviour, and to relate these properties to everyday uses of the materials;
   (KEY IDEA 3.1: The physical properties of materials)
b that some materials are better thermal insulators than others;
c that some materials are better electrical conductors than others;
   (KEY IDEA 3.1: The physical properties of materials)

d to describe and group rocks and soils on the basis of characteristics, including appearance, texture and permeability;
(KEY IDEA 3.4: The rock cycle)

e to recognize the differences between solids, liquids and gases, in terms of ease of flow and maintenance of shape and volume.
(KEY IDEA 3.2: The states of matter: Solid, liquid and gas)

2. Changing materials

a that mixing materials, e.g. adding salt to water, can cause them to change;

b that, heating and cooling materials, e.g. water, clay, dough, can cause them to change, and that temperature is a measure of how hot or cold they are;

c that some changes can be reversed and some cannot;

d that dissolving, melting, boiling, condensing, freezing and evaporating are changes that can be reversed;

e about the water cycle and the part played by evaporation and condensation;
(KEY IDEA 3.5: The water cycle)

f that the changes that occur when most materials, e.g. wood, wax, natural gas, are burned are not reversible.
(a–d, and f, KEY IDEA 3.3: Changing materials)

3. Separating mixtures of materials

a that solid particles of different sizes, e.g. those in soils, can be separated by sieving;

b that some solids, e.g. salt, sugar, dissolve in water to give solutions but some, e.g. sand, chalk, do not;

c that insoluble solids can be separated from liquids by filtering;

d that solids that have dissolved can be recovered by evaporating the liquid from the solution;

e that there is a limit to the mass of solid that can dissolve in a given amount of water, and that this limit is different for different solids.
(all KEY IDEA 3.3: Separating mixtures)

Physical processes

SOME KEY IDEAS IN PHYSICAL SCIENCE

4.1 *Sources and forms of energy: Energy is derived from a variety of sources, exists in a variety of forms, and can be stored, released and transferred**

4.2 *Forces: Forces can make things start to move, can make moving things speed up, slow down, change direction or stop, and can make things change their shape*

4.3 *The Earth and beyond*

---

* Please note that Key Idea 4.1 has been subdivided into three sections for easy reference: The primary sources of energy, Forms of energy, Light, Sound.

Sources and forms of energy

Energy is derived from a variety of sources, exists in a variety of forms, and can be stored, released and transferred

Introduction Almost all of the physical interactions in the Universe can be explained in terms of the transfer of energy. What follows is an attempt to describe in a logical sequence, the sources and forms of energy which affect all our lives. Some of the concepts explored are not *directly* concerned with the science National Curriculum at Key Stages 1 and 2. The hope however, is that the knowledge and understanding implicit in the concepts outlined below may be seen by teachers as being of value, not as optional background information, but as basic to a deeper understanding of the processes of physical science. As usual, where a concept directly supports an NC requirement, this is indicated in the text.

Some definitions Terms like energy, work, power, force (and forces) and pressure, often cause confusion to people who may not have had the opportunity to study physics in any depth (and sometimes even then!).

Many of these terms describe interconnecting processes, and some of the confusion results from their interchangeable use in everyday speech. The next section will attempt to define some of these terms in scientific language, whilst at the same time setting them into everyday contexts in which they are more easily understandable.

To start with, **energy** is the **capacity to perform work**. To put it the other way round, for any work to be done – the boiling of a kettle, the moving of a pile of bricks, the synthesis of a protein molecule – energy is required. Energy is measured in terms of work done, and the unit of measurement is the **joule** (J).

Mechanical work is done when a force moves an object through a measured distance. **Work** (in joules) = **force** (in newtons) × **distance** moved in the direction of the force (in metres).

A possible cause of confusion here is the use of the same unit of measurement, the joule, for a number of apparently different processes. For example, the joule is used to measure the quantity of energy produced during a chemical reaction which liberates heat, e.g.:

12 g of carbon burnt completely in the presence of oxygen will liberate 393.5 kJ of energy (kJ = kilojoule).

The joule can also be used to measure the amount of mechanical work done, e.g.:

when a force of 1 newton moves something through a distance of 1 metre, 1 joule of work is done.

Although these examples may seem to refer to widely differing processes, what is being measured in both cases is the energy produced by, or causing, the particular effect.

Power is defined as the amount of **work done, or of energy transformed** (joules) **per second** and is measured in watts (W). So a 60 watt light bulb when lit, is transforming 60 joules of energy (or doing 60 joules of work) per second.

The primary sources of energy

Bonding within and between atoms and molecules

The ultimate source of energy in the Universe is that which exists in the bonding between the particles in the atom, and in the bonds between the atoms and molecules of all matter. All of the known sources and forms of energy can eventually be traced back to the attraction and repulsion of atomic and molecular particles. These forces of attraction and repulsion are thought to be of four basic kinds: the strong nuclear, weak nuclear, electromagnetic, and gravitational forces.

A fundamental principle of science which relates to energy is the **law of conservation of energy**. Basically this states that energy can be converted from one form to another but cannot be created or destroyed. What is believed to happen is that energy is not 'used up' by a system, but is transferred or converted into other forms of energy. So the energy released by the combustion of petrol fuel in a car is converted into heat, sound, mechanical movement, electricity (which is then used as a further energy supply), and so on. None of the original energy derived from the breaking of the hydrocarbon bonds in the fuel is 'lost', but it can all be accounted for, at least theoretically, in terms of energy transfer or conversion.

Modern versions of this principle would extend the law to include mass as well as energy. Albert Einstein, with the famous equation $e = mc^2$, showed that mass and energy were theoretically inter-convertible (e = energy, m = mass, c = the speed of light, a constant).

It is now known that when matter releases its energy, a small loss of mass results. In normal chemical reactions the rate of conversion of mass to energy is so small that it is difficult to measure accurately. In nuclear reactions however, so much energy is released that the change in mass is large enough to be measurable.

The effects of the bonding forces within and between atoms and molecules can be classified in terms of a variety of primary energy sources, resulting in a range of further sources of transferable energy:

- **bonding within atoms (strong nuclear force)** gives rise to **nuclear energy;**
- **bonding and transfer between atoms and molecules (weak nuclear, and electromagnetic forces)** gives rise directly to **chemical, electromagnetic and strain energy;**

- **gravity (the force of attraction between masses)** gives rise to **potential and kinetic energy.**

Two further ideas are worth noting:

- **the vibration of atoms and molecules of matter, intensified by the transfer of energy from other sources**, gives rise to **heat and light energy;**
- some of the energy derived from these sources can be transferred or transmitted by **waves.**

One such 'family' of waves is that which relates to the electromagnetic spectrum, where energy transferred from electrons is transmitted in wave form. Another example is that of **sound**, where the mechanical energy of a vibrating material is also transferred in wave form.

Forms of energy

The following sections provide further detail on the nature and characteristics of the forms of energy listed above.

Nuclear energy

The bonds which hold together the nuclear particles of matter involve very large amounts of energy. It is said, for example, that if it were possible to convert (and conserve) all the nuclear energy in just one gram of matter, it would keep a 1,000 watt light bulb burning for 2,850 years!

In some cases, this energy is released slowly, and in small amounts, under natural conditions (as in radioactive decay). In others, very large amounts of energy are released rapidly by the deliberate splitting (or fission) of atomic nuclei.

Radioactive decay

Some elements have isotopes (see Key Idea 3.2: The Periodic Table) which are relatively unstable, and which lose atomic particles at a given and measurable rate under natural conditions. Such isotopes are said to emit radiation, and to be radioactive. In emitting the atomic particles, the radioactive isotopes are said to decay, and the rate of decay is measured as the half-life, i.e. the time taken for half of a given mass of the isotope to decay.

In decaying, an isotope may:

- lose positively charged particles from the atomic nuclei (alpha particles). Because of the resulting loss of atomic mass, this has the effect of converting the original element into one which is placed earlier in the periodic table. An example of alpha-decay is the natural decay of uranium, which through a number of conversions, eventually decays to form lead.
- lose negatively charged electrons (beta particles). This occurs as the result of a nuclear neutron becoming a proton, and the effect is to move the element 'up' the periodic table. An example of beta-decay is the decay of carbon-14 to nitrogen, a process which takes many thousands of years, and which is used in the accurate dating of organic remains.
- emit, as high energy electromagnetic waves, the highly penetrating (and therefore potentially damaging) gamma rays, which have no electric charge.

Nuclear fission

When an atom of the radioactive isotope uranium-235 is bombarded by neutrons, it is possible for the atomic nucleus to absorb one of the 'incoming' neutrons. The resultant, and highly unstable uranium-236 nucleus tends to split (hence nuclear fission) forming the nuclei of two new elements – barium and krypton for example – whilst at the same time releasing two or three high energy neutrons, and a large amount of energy (300 billion joules). If this process is controlled so that one of the released neutrons itself bombards and is absorbed by another uranium-235 nucleus, a chain reaction results which can produce large amounts of energy, converted as heat.

This is exactly what happens inside a nuclear reactor. Naturally occurring uranium contains about 99.3% of stable uranium-238, and 0.7% of radioactive uranium-235, a mixture which will not sustain a chain reaction. U-235 can be enriched however, so that the fuel rods in a nuclear reactor contain 97% of U-238 and 3% of U-235. These fuel rods are sheathed in graphite to slow down the movement of the bombarding neutrons, thereby increasing the chances of absorption of neutrons by the U-235 nuclei. In addition, rods of boron steel can be lowered into the reactor to absorb neutrons if the reaction is proceeding too fast.

In a conventional, gas-cooled nuclear reactor, the heat produced by the fission reaction is absorbed by carbon dioxide gas which is pumped through the reactor. This gas, at 400°C, is then passed through water boilers, producing steam, which is then used to turn turbines to generate electricity, as in a conventional fossil fuel fired power station.

If the neutron bombardment were unchecked, the rate of absorption of neutrons were not moderated by boron steel, and the uranium fuel were all of the U-235 type, then an uncontrolled nuclear explosion would occur, and this is the basis of the 'atom bomb'.

Nuclear fusion

When atomic nuclei join together (fusion), even more energy is liberated than during the fission process. In the natural universe this process is happening in the Sun (and indeed, in all other stars). Nuclei of 'heavy' hydrogen (known as deuterium), collide and combine in conditions of high temperature and pressure, forming helium nuclei and releasing large amounts of energy. The burning of the Sun is, in effect, an uncontrolled nuclear explosion. It has been calculated that the Sun is converting 4.2 million tonnes of mass into energy *every second*. When considering that the conversion of *one gram* of mass results in the production of 300 billion joules, the power of the Sun as a producer of energy is placed into clear focus.

A present day scientific controversy concerns claims made in the late 1980s, that nuclear fusion had been achieved under 'cold' conditions, i.e. involving normal laboratory glassware. Researchers claimed that significant amounts of heat had been generated during the electrolysis of deuterium oxide (heavy water). Their claim was that this heat generation could not be explained simply in terms of an exothermic reaction (see Key Idea 3.3: Chemical Reactions and Heat Energy), and may therefore have occurred as a result of nuclear fusion. The potential industrial and commercial significance of this claim is obvious, but other workers have refuted the claim, stating that the experiment has been unrepeatable to date, and the controversy continues.

Whether derived from fission or fusion, the energy contained in the atomic nucleus can be released and transferred into other forms. In peaceful applications this usually involves the use of the heat of the reaction to generate electricity for industrial or domestic purposes. A more 'strategic' role for nuclear power is the use of the resultant electricity to drive surface ships and submarines, or to generate the massively destructive force of a nuclear explosion.

It is perhaps appropriate to use these latter examples in order to reflect on the ethical, moral, social and political implications of, and the dilemmas which almost always result from, the application of scientific knowledge. There are no easy answers, but surely we should all continue to ask questions of the decision-makers?

CONCEPTS TO SUPPORT KEY STAGE 2

Chemical energy

As outlined in Key Idea 3.3 (Chemical Reactions and Heat Energy), energy is released when the bonds between the atoms and molecules of compounds are broken during chemical reactions, and the total energy of the products of the reaction is less than that of the original substances.

This release of chemical energy is most commonly seen during reactions which involve oxidation (the burning, or combustion, of substances in the presence of oxygen). Those substances which readily give up their energy when burnt, and particularly those which contain carbon, can be used as fuels, i.e. as convenient sources of energy. Examples would include:

- the burning of renewable natural fuels such as wood and charcoal to release energy in the form of heat and/or light (sound is also generated, but is, in the context of heat generation, a 'waste' of energy);
- the combustion of 'fossil fuels' such as coal, oil and natural gas for the same purposes;
- the respiration by plants and animals of the energy-rich organic compounds derived from food in order to provide energy for life processes.

In any of the above examples, the basic 'chemistry' of the reaction is that compounds of carbon and hydrogen (hydrocarbons in the case of natural and fossil fuels, carbohydrates in the case of plant and animal tissues), react with oxygen from the air to produce carbon dioxide, water, and energy. The chemical formula for the burning of natural gas (methane) is:

$$CH_4 \quad + \quad 2O_2 \text{------burning---------} CO_2 \quad + \quad 2H_2O \quad + \quad \text{energy}$$

methane   oxygen   carbon   water   heat
                                        dioxide

The formula for the cellular respiration of glucose is:

$$C_6H_{12}O_6 \quad + \quad 6O_2 \text{-----respiration--------} 6CO_2 \quad + \quad 6H_2O \quad + \quad \text{energy (chemical bonding)}$$

glucose   oxygen   carbon   water   energy
                                         dioxide

The basic requirement of most fuels is that they should be efficient in the production of heat which can be converted to other forms of energy. In some cases this heat energy is transferred to light by the increased vibration of the molecules of the substances involved in the reaction. An example would be the burning of candles made of paraffin wax, where the heat produced is locally intense enough to cause the particles of carbon to glow white hot – hence the light of the candle flame.

The heat produced by the burning of fuels may also be used:

- directly, to heat water for the production of steam for industrial processes, or to heat other substances, e.g. in the smelting of metals, or for domestic use (for cooking in areas dependent on renewable fuel sources) or for central heating;
- for conversion into electricity for industrial and domestic use (see below).

In the case of some fuels, the speed of reaction is so rapid as to be explosive. This property has been used effectively (although not particularly efficiently) in the development of the internal combustion engine. The explosive power of the energy release which takes place inside the cylinders of a car engine when an air/petrol mixture burns, is converted into the mechanical energy of movement, electromagnetic energy for the ignition system, windscreen wipers, central locking system etc., heat, light and sound.

Long-term energy transfer

In terms of the Earth, the ultimate source of usable energy is the Sun, our nearest star. It is the Sun which provides us with radiant energy in the form of light and heat, and it has been doing so for a long time – modern estimates put the age of the Sun at 6 billion years, and that of the Earth at 4.6 billion years.

It is interesting to track the sequence of energy transfers which would have taken place during the geological formation of fossil fuels and their subsequent recovery and combustion in modern times.

- the nuclei of deuterium atoms in the Sun collided and combined to form helium nuclei, with an accompanying release of (nuclear) energy;
- some of this energy would transfer to the Earth in the form of solar radiation of heat and light;
- green plants would use the light (electromagnetic) energy from the Sun to synthesize carbohydrates (chemical energy);
- during the Carboniferous period of geological time (between 350 and 270 million years ago) some of the green plants were preserved without decaying in shallow marshes or lagoons (a modern-day equivalent would be a peat bog);
- other plants (in particular marine algae) would have been eaten by aquatic animals whose remains themselves were preserved by a covering of sediments on the ocean floor;
- over spans of geological time, the preserved plants became coal and the preserved animals turned into oil, with an accompanying production of natural gas (hence, **fossil** fuels). The original carbohydrates present in the preserved plant and animal tissues were fossilized as hydrocarbons;
- as the fossil fuels have been recovered and burned in modern times, the chemical energy, which has been 'locked' into the bonding of the hydrocarbon compounds for up to 350 million years, has been released and transferred for the benefit of present day people, but with the consequent problem of the disposal of waste products.

In the case of coal ash, disposal is often in landfill sites or out at sea. If nuclear waste products are considered also, the problem is two-fold. Firstly because of the need to make highly radioactive materials safe, and secondly, to ensure the security of materials with obvious military significance – another example of the interface between science, society at large, and the decision-makers.

With reference to the carbon dioxide produced as a result of the burning of fossil fuels, the commonest response of the industrialized nations has been simply to discharge it directly into the atmosphere.

In addition to the possibility of global warming as a result of this increase in the amount of carbon dioxide in the atmosphere (see Key Idea 2.6: The carbon cycle), one of the important points to remember about the consumption of fossil fuels is that they are non-renewable (at least in terms of human time spans). The modern-day consumption of fossil fuels represents a 'cashing-in' of energy which was 'banked' millions of years ago. It is, in effect, a once-and-for-all process, and should therefore be a cause for concern. Although coal reserves are extensive (if unpopular), supplies of oil and natural gas may well run out over the next 50 years or so, and this will have a serious impact on transport systems and policies worldwide.

Renewable (i.e. non-chemical and non-nuclear) forms of energy may well assume increasing importance in future years as supplies of fossil fuels decline. Those forms already in use include:

- solar energy, where the radiant heat energy from the Sun is converted directly into electricity in 'solar cells';
- tidal energy, where the kinetic energy of moving water is converted into electricity at tidal barrages;
- wind energy, where the kinetic energy of air moving from high to low pressure areas in the atmosphere is converted into electricity at 'wind farms';
- hydro-electricity, where the kinetic energy of falling water is converted into electric power.

In addition, the direct conversion of the motion of sea waves has been used experimentally to generate electricity, but it is unlikely that this will ever become fully commercially viable as an alternative energy source.

Electricity As has been described above, much of the energy released from within and between atoms and molecules, as well as the kinetic energy derived from molecular motion (tidal, wind, wave and hydro-energy) is converted into electricity. This is because electricity is a convenient form of energy which can be transported relatively easily (along cables or power lines) and can itself be converted into other forms of energy such as heat, light and sound.

The following sections will deal with the nature of electricity and its behaviour in simple circuits, the generation of electricity, and static electricity.

What is electricity?

At its simplest, an electric current is a flow of electrons. In order for an electric current to flow in a simple circuit, two requirements are necessary:

- a source of chemical energy;
- a continuous loop of a conducting material which will allow the transfer of that energy.

The source of chemical energy most commonly used in primary schools is the electric cell (a group of cells forms a battery). Batteries are relatively safe because they produce small amounts of electricity and cause a 'one-way' electron flow – they are said to produce a 'direct current' as opposed to the 'alternating current' and high power of the mains electricity supply. Modern batteries are 'dry', i.e. their chemical constituents are often in solid or gel forms, and are commonly encased in metal or strong card. Each will have two terminals or connection points, a positive terminal (the anode) and a negative terminal (the cathode).

The chemical reaction which takes place in the battery produces an excess of electrons at one pole of the battery, and since electrons have a negative electrical charge, this pole is the negative terminal or cathode. Similarly, there is a net positive charge at the other pole of the battery, and this is the positive terminal or anode. If the two terminals of the battery are connected to a continuous loop (or circuit) of materials which will allow the transfer of those electrons (electrical conductors), the difference in electrical potential between the two battery terminals will cause the electrons to 'flow' through the material, as a current of electricity, from the negative pole (the cathode) to the positive pole (the anode) of the battery.

Note: there is a possibility of confusion here. Although it is now known that the flow of electrons in an electric circuit is from the negative to the positive pole of a battery, the current is traditionally depicted in circuit diagrams as flowing from the positive to the negative pole, and this is termed the 'conventional' current.

The most effective electrical conductors are metals, in particular copper and silver (see Key Idea 3.1: Electrical Conductivity), and graphite (an allotrope of carbon).

Electricity in simple circuits

There are three important variables which relate to electrical circuits: current, voltage and resistance.

The electric **current** in a circuit – the flow of electrons – can be measured as the quantity of charge passing any particular point in the circuit in a given time. The unit of electrical charge is known as the coulomb (which is the charge on 6×10^{18} electrons), and when one coulomb of charge flows in one second, the current is said to be **one ampere** (or 1 amp or 1A). In conventional form:

charge in coulombs (Q) = current in amperes (I) × time (t): Q = It

and current in amps (I) = charge flowing in coulombs (Q) per second (t): I = Q/t

A useful mental model for this effect is to imagine the *rate of flow* of water in a pipe. The current (of water) flowing through a pipe, in litres per second for example, could be measured by finding the total volume which passed a given point in a particular time, and then dividing that volume by the time of flow in seconds. This would be directly analogous to finding the current in an electrical circuit by dividing the total charge by the time over which the charge was measured, i.e. I = Q/t. Similarly, the total volume of flow of water through a pipe could be calculated by multiplying the current in litres per second, by the total time of flow in seconds. This would be analogous to Q = It.

What are the factors which affect the current – the rate of flow – of electrons in a simple electric circuit? Firstly, for the current of electrons to flow at all, there must be a difference in electrical potential between different parts of the circuit. This **potential difference** is measured in volts, and a potential difference of **one volt** (V) between two points will allow **one joule** of work to be done **per coulomb of electric charge** passing between the points. The voltage of a battery is therefore a measure of the amount of energy it can provide, and is a function of the transfer of energy from the chemical constituents of the battery to the conducting materials of the circuit. A 12 volt battery will therefore transfer twice as much energy (12 joules per coulomb) as a 6 volt battery.

To continue the water analogy, if an electric current can be represented by the *rate of flow* of water in a pipe, the voltage would correspond to the water *pressure*. This, in a closed circuit such as a central heating system for example, would be governed by the size and power of the water pump, (or in an electrical circuit, by the battery).

The second factor affecting the rate of flow of electrons in a circuit is the **resistance** of the materials in the circuit. Some materials, even though they allow the passage of electrons, i.e. they are conductors of electricity, nevertheless can slow down or impede electron transfer. Such materials are known as resistors, and their resistant properties are measured in ohms. A resistance of **one ohm** will need a voltage of one volt to drive a current of one amp through it. Using the water analogy once more, the resistance of different materials (or components) in an electrical circuit can be compared to pipes of different *diameter* through which water must pass in a closed system – the smaller the diameter of the pipe, the greater the resistance to the flow of water.

So the flow of electrons (the current) in an electrical circuit is related to the potential difference (the voltage) and the resistance of the circuit materials, just as the flow of water through pipes is related to the water pressure and the diameter of the pipes in the system.

These relationships have been summarized in the form of a law, known as Ohm's law, which states that the current flowing in a circuit is proportional to the potential difference (the voltage), providing the temperature of the conductor remains constant.

The formulae which derive from Ohm's law can be rewritten in three different ways, in order to isolate each of the variables in turn:

$$\text{current (I)} = \frac{\text{voltage (V)}}{\text{resistance (R)}}: \qquad I = \frac{V}{R}$$

$$\text{voltage (V)} = \text{current (I)} \times \text{resistance (R)}: \quad V = IR$$

$$\text{resistance (R)} = \frac{\text{voltage (V)}}{\text{current (I)}}: \qquad R = \frac{V}{I}$$

Fig. 4.1 *Series and parallel circuits*

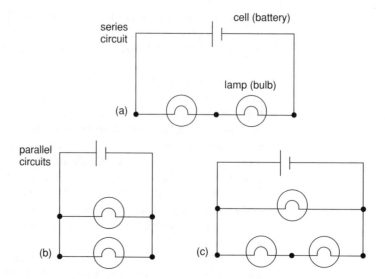

and can be used to begin to understand the behaviour of components in simple electrical circuits.

There are two types of simple circuits:

- **series** circuits, where component parts are connected 'end to end', and there is only one possible route along which the electric current may flow;
- **parallel** circuits, where one or more components may be connected 'side by side', so that there is more than one route along which the electric current may flow.

Series circuits

In a series circuit, (Fig. 4.1a) as there is only one possible route for the flow of electrons:

- the current will be the same at any point in the circuit, and it can be measured by connecting an ammeter into the circuit, in series;
- the voltage will vary at different points in the circuit, will be 'shared out' between the components in the circuit, depending on their resistance, and can be measured by connecting a voltmeter across any part of the circuit, in parallel;
- the total resistance of the circuit will be the sum of the resistances of all the circuit components.

What does this mean in practice? Using a simple example, and referring to Fig. 4.2a, if a battery is delivering 6 volts, and a lamp has a resistance of 6 ohms, using Ohm's law (and ignoring the resistance of the connecting wires):

$$\text{current (in amps)} = \frac{\text{voltage (in volts)}}{\text{resistance (in ohms)}}$$

$$I = \frac{V}{R} = \frac{6}{6} = 1 \text{ amp}$$

so a current of 1 amp is flowing in the circuit. If another lamp were added to the circuit, in series (as in Fig. 4.2b), the voltage would remain at 6 volts, but

Fig. 4.2 *Changing*
effects in series circuits

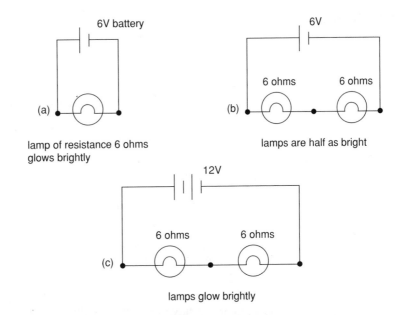

(a) lamp of resistance 6 ohms
glows brightly

(b) lamps are half as bright

(c) lamps glow brightly

the resistance would have been increased to 12 ohms (sum of resistances = 6 + 6). The current would then be:

$$I = \frac{V}{R} = \frac{6}{12} = 0.5 \text{ amps}$$

As a result of the reduction in current to 0.5 amps, the two lamps in this circuit would be glowing less brightly than the single one in the previous circuit. If the two lamps in Fig. 4.2b were required to glow at the same brightness as the single one in 4.2a, the voltage in the circuit would need to be increased to 12 volts, in order to return the current to 1 amp (as in Fig. 4.2c):

$$I = \frac{V}{R} = \frac{12}{12} = 1 \text{ amp}$$

The current in a series circuit can therefore be raised by increasing the voltage, or lowered by increasing the resistance (by adding more components).

Parallel circuits

In a simple parallel circuit however, (Fig. 4.1b) there are alternative routes for the flow of electrons, and the current will flow along both. This results in a very different effect when two electric lamps are connected in parallel.

The total resistance in a parallel circuit is calculated from the reciprocal values of the individual resistances, e.g.:

$$\frac{1}{R(\text{total})} = \frac{1}{R1} + \frac{1}{R2} \text{ etc.}$$

So, in Fig. 4.3, the **total resistance of the circuit** is calculated from:

$$\frac{1}{R} = \frac{1}{6} + \frac{1}{6} = \frac{2}{6}$$

Fig. 4.3 The effect of resistance in a parallel circuit

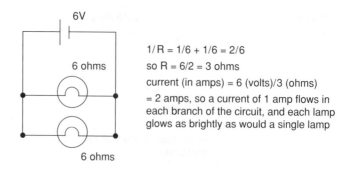

1/R = 1/6 + 1/6 = 2/6

so R = 6/2 = 3 ohms

current (in amps) = 6 (volts)/3 (ohms)

= 2 amps, so a current of 1 amp flows in each branch of the circuit, and each lamp glows as brightly as would a single lamp

If $\dfrac{1}{R} = \dfrac{2}{6}$ then $\mathbf{R} = \dfrac{6}{2} = \mathbf{3\ ohms}$

Again, from Ohm's law: current (in amps) $= \dfrac{\text{voltage (in volts)}}{\text{resistance (in ohms)}}$

$= \dfrac{6\ \text{volts}}{3\ \text{ohms}}$

so the current flowing in the parallel circuit in Fig. 4.3 = **2 amps**.

Since the current of two amps divides equally between the two routes of the circuit in Fig. 4.3, (because they both present the same resistance) it follows that 1 amp is flowing along each route, and both lamps will be as bright as the single lamp in the series circuit in Fig. 4.2a.

If the aim in designing a circuit were to be able to add extra lamps whilst maintaining their brightness, then a parallel circuit would be ideal for the purpose. However, this approach is not without cost of course, and in this case the life of the battery is greatly shortened by the connection of components in parallel.

If the resistances of the 'branch' routes in a parallel circuit are different, more current will flow along the 'easier' route. This means that in a parallel circuit, the route which presents the least resistance to the flow of electrons, i.e. the route containing the components with the lower resistance, will have a higher current passing along it than the route which presents the higher resistance. But whichever way the current 'divides' at the junction in a parallel circuit, the sum of the currents which flow along the 'branches' of the circuit will always be equal to the current entering (or leaving) the junction. So, in the example in Fig. 4.1c, if a 3 amp current were flowing in the circuit, 2 amps would flow through the branch with the single lamp, and 1 amp through the branch with two lamps. When the two routes join, the total current of 3 amps is restored.

Switches

In some cases, the components (lamps, bells and buzzers, motors and so on) which are connected into an electrical circuit are not required to function continuously. Rather than disconnect the battery each time the current is to be cut off, an alternative is to use switches of various kinds. A switch is simply a device which will 'make and break' a circuit. Usually, when a switch is closed, the circuit is 'made', i.e. there is a continuous loop of conducting material

Fig. 4.4 *A simple circuit and its corresponding circuit diagram*

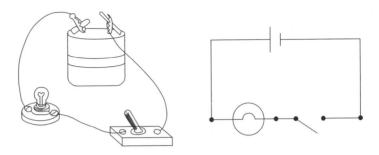

connected to the electricity supply, and current can flow. Conversely, when the switch is open, the circuit, and hence the supply, is interrupted.

In addition to normal switches which stay in a fixed position until deliberately changed, there are spring-loaded switches for bell pushes, pressure-sensitive switches for burglar alarms, light-sensitive switches for street or security lighting, temperature-sensitive switches for heating (or cooling) systems, tilt switches which make a circuit when an object is moved, and so on!

Circuit diagrams

The layout of an electrical circuit can be drawn as a picture, or, using conventional symbols, as a circuit diagram. The basic information needed when 'converting' a circuit into a diagram includes the **number and type of components** in the circuit, the **order** in which they are connected and the **number and voltage of the batteries** included in the circuit. Fig. 4.4 shows a drawing of a simple circuit and its corresponding circuit diagram. The conventional symbols for components commonly used in simple circuits can be found in the Appendix.

Work and power in electrical circuits

The energy of the electrons flowing in a current in an electric circuit can be transferred to the electrical appliances in the circuit, and the outcomes can be measured in terms of the **work done**. In the element of an electric fire or kettle, the energy is largely transferred as heat. In an electric bell, the energy is transferred as mechanical energy, transported as wave energy, and heard as sound. In the filament of an electric lamp, the high resistance of the material to the passage of current causes the molecules to vibrate at such a rate that both heat and light energy are released.

Overall, the work done, in joules, is measured as voltage × charge, and since the charge = current × time:

work done = voltage × current × time = $V \times I \times t$

Since **power** is defined as work done per unit time (see Definitions, above), power, in watts (W) in an electrical circuit, is defined as:

potential difference (voltage) × current = VI

This simple equation allows us to discover some interesting insights into the running of electrical appliances. For example, what current would flow through a light bulb rated at 240V, 60W? And what would be the resistance of the filament?

133

Since W = VI, i.e. 60 = 240 × I (current),

the **current** (I) taken by the lamp is $\dfrac{60}{240}$ = **0.25 amps**

And from Ohm's law, resistance = $\dfrac{\text{voltage}}{\text{current}}$

so the **resistance** of the filament = $\dfrac{240}{0.25}$ = **960 ohms**

Using the same formulae for an electric iron rated at 240V, 1,000W, we find that the iron takes a current of 4.16 amps, and has a resistance of 57.69 ohms.

Finally, the 'unit' of electricity in terms of domestic supply, is the kilowatt hour (k Wh), i.e. the electrical energy which would do 1,000 joules of work per second, supplied for an hour. If we know the unit cost of electricity, and this information is usually included in electricity bills, we can calculate the running costs of our electrical appliances. How much does it cost to boil a kettle; how much to leave a light on overnight; how much to bake a fruit cake; and how much to watch a TV news bulletin? How much cheaper is it to cook a jacket potato in a microwave oven than in a conventional oven (leaving aside the issue of the difference in texture resulting from the two different cooking methods)? (The cost of 1 unit of electricity at the time of writing is 7.76 pence. 1 unit of electricity is a kilowatt hour, i.e. 1,000 watts × 3,600 seconds = 3,600,000 joules)

- a **kettle** rated at 2,000 watts, takes **4 minutes to boil**, so it does:

  2,000 (watts) × 4 (minutes) × 60 (seconds) = 480,000 joules of work

  Cost = $\dfrac{480,000}{3,600,000}$ × 7.76 = **1.03 pence**

- a **lamp** rated at 60 watts, **left on overnight** (say **8 hours**), does:

  60 (watts) × 8 (hours) × 60 (minutes) × 60 (seconds) = 1,728,000 joules of work

  Cost = $\dfrac{1,728,000}{3,600,000}$ × 7.76 = **3.72 pence**

- an **oven** rated at 3,000 watts is used for **2 hours** to **bake a fruit cake**. It does:

  3,000 × 2 × 60 × 60 = 21,600,000 joules of work

  Cost = $\dfrac{21,600,000}{3,600,000}$ × 7.76 = **46.56 pence**

- a **14-inch colour TV** rated at 60 watts is **switched on for 30 minutes** during a news bulletin.

  It does 60 × 30 × 60 = 108,000 joules of work

  Cost = $\dfrac{108,000}{3,600,000}$ × 7.76 = **0.23 pence**

- a **microwave oven**, rated at 600 watts, takes **6 minutes** to **cook a jacket potato**.

It does 600 × 6 × 60 = 216,000 joules of work

Cost of 'microwaving' a potato = $\dfrac{216,000}{3,600,000}$ × 7.76 = **0.46 pence**

- a **conventional oven**, rated at 3,000 watts, takes **1 hour** to **bake** the same **potato**.

It does 3,000 × 60 × 60 = 10,800,000 joules of work

Cost of 'oven baking' a jacket potato = $\dfrac{10,800,000}{3,600,000}$ × 7.76

= **23.28 pence**

(Whilst it is unlikely that an oven would be used to bake a single potato, the simple cost comparison is a convincing demonstration of the effect of the lower power output of microwave ovens!)

The generation of electricity

Electricity supply from batteries has advantages and drawbacks. The advantages, particularly from a primary school perspective, include:

- the relative safety of low voltages and direct current;
- the convenience and portability of small units;
- the 'storage' of electricity in battery form;
- the ready availability of batteries.

The earliest batteries were produced in 1800 by the Italian physicist Allesandro Volta. He stacked alternating discs of copper, zinc, and cardboard soaked in salt water, to form a 'Voltaic pile' from which an electric current could be drawn. Such batteries were large and cumbersome and above all, expensive.

Even today, the major disadvantages of battery electricity are the costs involved (compare the price of the cheapest battery with the cost of boiling a kettle (see above) using mains supply), and the very factors which make it safest for primary school use – the availability of low voltages and direct current. For large scale industrial and domestic use, other ways of generating electricity are needed, and these depend on converting the kinetic energy of motion into electricity.

As long ago as the 1830s, Michael Faraday had discovered that an electromotive force (in effect, a voltage) was induced into a conductor which was moved across the lines of force of a magnet. Faraday's first 'dynamo' featured a large copper disc which could be rotated between the poles of a horseshoe magnet. When the disc was turning, electricity was 'generated' and could be drawn off by means of contact points. Eventually, this process was refined so that a coil of insulated wire wound round an armature was made to spin rapidly inside a ring of powerful magnets, or, as in the case of modern electricity generating stations, the magnets are made to spin inside fixed coils.

This process of electromagnetic induction is the basis of all modern electricity

Fig. 4.5 *Stages in the generation of electricity*

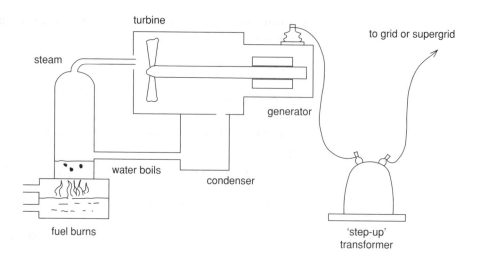

generation. The differences in each of the systems relate mainly to the means by which the magnets fixed onto the armatures are made to spin inside the coils in the generators, and these different methods are now summarized.

In **nuclear power stations**, the heat energy released by the fission of nuclear fuel (enriched uranium) is transferred to carbon dioxide gas which circulates in the reactor. The hot gas is piped from the reactors to water boilers where it is used to produce 'superheated' steam at 400°C. At this stage the process becomes similar to that of a 'conventional' or thermal power station, as the steam is used to drive steam turbines, turning heat energy into rotary mechanical energy – the kinetic energy of motion. The turbines are linked to the generators, whose rotating shafts 'produce' electricity by electromagnetic induction (see above, Nuclear Energy).

Conventional or **thermal power stations** generate heat by the combustion of fossil fuels (coal, oil and natural gas). This heat energy is used to turn water into steam, which is used to turn turbines, which are linked to the generators, as before (see Fig. 4.5).

Hydroelectric power stations use the kinetic energy of falling water to drive turbines directly, and the generator magnets are attached to the drive shaft of the turbines.

Steam turbines (and hence the connected generators) rotate at high speeds – about 3,000 revolutions per minute (rpm) – generating electricity at 11,000–25,000 volts. Hydroelectric turbines spin more slowly – at about 400 rpm, but the outcome is similar to that of steam turbines because larger numbers of magnets are fixed to the hydrogenerator shafts. The generated voltage is then 'stepped up' by transformers to 275,000 or 400,000 volts before transmission from the generating station via the grid or supergrid system of overhead cables. The transmission at high voltage (and low current) minimizes the power loss caused by the heating of the cables. At or near the point of use, the voltage is 'stepped down' to whatever value is needed for industrial use (10,000–40,000 volts), or to the 240 volts used in domestic supply in the U.K.

Electricity, as a form of energy, exemplifies Key Idea 4.1. It can be:

- stored (in battery form), and hence transported in small amounts and released at will;
- released during generation by the conversion of other forms of energy, or controlled and released by switching in circuits;
- transferred geographically by transmission lines to its point of use, or converted into other forms of energy as required.

In terms of convenience, availability, control and application and cleanliness (at least at the point of use) it is easy to understand the widespread use of electricity in the modern world. The implications of the costs of electricity generation, in terms of consumption of non-renewable resources and pollution of the bio-physical environment, should not, and ultimately cannot, be ignored.

Static electricity   Perhaps the easiest (and cheapest) way to see the effects of electricity in the classroom is to investigate the accumulation of charged particles on materials with insulating properties. The charged particles result from the displacement of electrons from the atoms of the insulating material, and this displacement is often achieved by the collision of atoms brought about by friction – when the insulating material is rubbed against another insulator, for example. Because the materials are not conductors, the accumulated charges cannot 'flow' in the form of current electricity, but are 'static', and remain in place on the charged object until they either leak away to the air or the earth, or are deliberately discharged by contact with a conducting material. Some examples of the effects of static electricity are as follows:

- vinyl records can become charged with static electricity. The excess of negatively charged particles on the vinyl attracts small positively charged items such as dust particles and small fabric fibres ('fluff') to the record, and these particles will need to be removed if sound quality is not to be affected;
- an inflated balloon can be charged with static electricity by rubbing it against woollen cloth – a sweater or cardigan, for example. The 'charged' balloon can then be placed carefully against a wall, and the attraction between the charged particles on the balloon and the oppositely charged particles on the wall, will allow the balloon to 'hang' against the wall for a short time until the static charge 'leaks' away;
- clothing made from synthetic fibres – nylon or terylene for example, can become charged with static electricity, particularly in dry conditions (when there is less chance of the charge 'leaking' away through a damp atmosphere). The removal of such clothing sometimes results in the discharge of the static electricity, with accompanying sparks (visible if the clothing is removed in the dark) and crackling sounds. The sparks occur because collision between electrons and air molecules during the discharge causes light to be emitted as a form of radiation, and the crackling sounds are heard when air is expanded by the heat of the discharge, and then is rapidly replaced by cooler air rushing to fill the partial vacuum thus caused;
- the same process is at work during a thunderstorm. Static electricity builds up in the clouds when air and water molecules are brought into violent

collision by pressure differences in the atmosphere. The electric charge, often at very high voltage, discharges to earth, or from cloud to cloud, as lightning. The energy of the discharge is converted to light as a 'flash' of lightning, and the heat of the discharge expands the air in its immediate vicinity so rapidly that the warmed air is replaced at supersonic speed – a thunderclap is caused by air breaking the sound barrier!;

■ if a tap is turned on so that the flow of water is controlled as a thin, but constant, 'thread', and a suitably charged object (such as a plastic pen which has been rubbed against a woollen garment sleeve, for example) is brought close to, but not touching, the stream of water, the stream of water will 'bend' towards the charged object. This is because the charged particles on the plastic pen attract the oppositely charged poles of the water molecules, 'pulling' them towards the pen;

■ finally, a moving car collects charged particles by friction with the air through which it passes, and in dry conditions, these remain as a static charge on the vehicle. Under these conditions, the particles may be discharged by a person touching the outside of the car once it has stopped moving. The static electricity is, in effect, 'earthed' through the person, and the discharge is felt as an uncomfortable 'shock'.

The electromagnetic spectrum

The energy derived from the bonding within and between atoms and molecules can be transferred in a number of ways – by chain reaction, by transfer through a material without the material moving (as in heat conduction), or by transfer through a moving medium (as in heat convection, or wind energy).

In some cases however, the vibration of electrons in materials causes the formation of rapidly vibrating electrical and magnetic fields, and the energy present in these electromagnetic fields is transmitted in wave form without the presence of a material medium. In other words, electromagnetic energy can travel in wave form through a vacuum (such as space) – a process known as electromagnetic radiation.

The 'family' of waves by which such energy is transmitted is known as the electromagnetic spectrum, which includes radio waves, microwaves, infra-red rays, visible light, ultraviolet rays, X-rays and gamma rays. All of the waves in the electromagnetic spectrum travel at the same velocity through space – 300,000 kilometres per second, i.e. 3×10^8 m/s. What causes the variations in the properties of the different waves is their wavelength, i.e. the distance between successive wave crests, and their frequency, i.e. the number of waves passing a fixed point per second.

Since the velocity is the same for each of the wave types, and velocity = wavelength × frequency, it follows that the wavelengths and frequencies will be related. The longer the wavelength, the lower the frequency, and the shorter the wavelength, the higher the frequency. This is shown in Fig. 4.6. Note that in each case, the product of wavelength and frequency is equal to 3×10^8 m/s.

Radio waves are the longest of the electromagnetic waves, ranging from 10,000 m to less than 10 m in length. They 'carry' electrical impulses generated from sound energy which can be superimposed on the wave forms, and then be decoded at a receiving station to reproduce the original signal.

Fig. 4.6 *The electromagnetic spectrum*

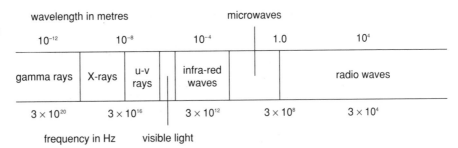

Fig. 4.7 *The six colours of the rainbow*

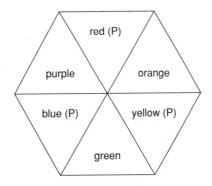

when two primary colours (P) are mixed, the intervening colour results

Microwaves, at a wavelength of 1 m, are absorbed by water molecules, which themselves vibrate at an increased rate, i.e. their temperature rises, and this effect is the basis of microwave cookery.

It is **infra-red radiation** which accounts for the transfer of heat energy from the Sun, across the intervening 93 million miles of space, to the Earth's surface (60% of solar radiation is in the form of heat). The heat absorbed by the Earth's surface is then transferred to the atmosphere, and it is this heat which causes temperature (and hence pressure) differences in the atmosphere, and which therefore drives the 'weather machine'. Infra-red rays have wavelengths between 1 mm (10^{-3} m) and 1 micron (1 thousandth of a millimetre – 10^{-6} m).

Visible light is also a form of electromagnetic radiation. It ranges in frequency from red light (at about 0.8 microns – 8×10^{-7} m) to violet light (at about 0.4 microns – 4×10^{-7} m). An interesting thought is that there are actually only *six* colours in the well-known 'rainbow' of light. Sir Isaac Newton, who investigated the splitting of a source of white light by using a prism, in addition to being a brilliant scientist, was also an alchemist, and seven was a lucky number. It is tempting to imagine that the great man 'saw' seven colours in his rainbow, even though it is a matter of judgment as to how far the blue end of the spectrum divides into the three colours of blue, indigo and violet.

A glance at a colour wheel confirms the six-colour theory (in my opinion!). The three primary colours mix in pairs to form three secondary colours, and these are the six which are present in the rainbow – red, orange, yellow, green, blue, and purple (see Fig. 4.7).

Ultraviolet light, at wavelengths from 0.4 microns (4×10^{-7} m) down to 0.01 microns (10^{-8} m) is a significant component of sunlight, and one which stimulates the production of vitamin D in humans, and which causes 'tanning' by the production of the pigment melanin in the skin. It may also be a cause of the increasing incidence of reported cases of melanoma (skin cancer), as humans are exposed to increasing levels of ultraviolet light at the Earth's surface, as a result of the thinning of the upper atmosphere ozone layer.

X-rays, with wavelengths from 0.01 microns (10^{-8} m) down to 0.00001 micron (10^{-12} m) are absorbed by solid matter, but can penetrate soft tissue. Their application in medical science is well-known, as they allow practitioners to 'see' the state of the bones and teeth 'inside' a living person. If a radioactive tracer is used, as in a 'barium meal' or by the injection of an isotope into the blood stream, the outline of soft tissues can also be photographed and monitored. The absorption of X-rays displaces electrons in the absorbing tissue, so prolonged exposure to X-rays can cause tissue damage.

Gamma rays range in wavelength from 0.00001 micron (10^{-12} m) down to less than one thousand millionth of a micron (10^{-16} m), (dimensions on so small a scale are inconceivable in real terms). These rays are associated with radioactivity. They are known to be emitted by radioactive substances, and they are able to penetrate materials, including metals, to a considerable degree. They are difficult to screen and deflect, and their penetrative properties represent a serious hazard to human health.

Strain energy   Materials which have elastic properties (see Key Idea 3.1: Elasticity; Stiffness (and Flexibility)) are able to change their shape following the application of a load, and recover their original shape when the load is removed. This property is essentially a result of the atomic and molecular bonding of the materials concerned, and of the behaviour of the molecules when loaded.

What happens with elastic materials is that the structure of the molecular bonding becomes distorted, but not destroyed, by the application of a load. When the load is removed, the molecular structures resume their original shape. In some cases, as in the 'uncurling' of a crumpled crisp packet, or the 'unwinding' of a clock spring, this process of returning to original shape and size is a slow one. In other cases, as in the 'twanging' of a rubber band, the process is rapid and powerful.

The property of elasticity thus allows the energy of atomic and molecular bonding to be transferred as the kinetic energy of mechanical motion, and this in turn allows a force to be applied by the material during the process of returning to its original shape (for the effect of forces, see Key Idea 4.2, below).

The 'elastic' (or strain) energy inherent in elastic materials has been used in a wide variety of applications, some of which are listed below. Strain energy is available in:

■ rubber – for 'bands', engine mountings, car tyres;
■ metals – for springs – coil springs in forcemeters, suspension units and clockwork toys, leaf springs, lock mechanisms, bulldog clips;
■ glassfibre – for archery bows, diving boards, vaulting poles;
■ plastic foams – for soft furnishings;
■ fabrics – for 'stretchy' clothing (e.g. lycra), trampoline beds.

Potential and kinetic energy

All of the forms of energy described so far have their origins in the bonding within atoms (nuclear energy), or in the bonding and transfer between atoms and molecules (chemical, electromagnetic and strain energy).

In order to understand the concept of potential energy it is necessary to have some understanding of the concept of gravity. This concept will be dealt with more fully in Key Idea 4.2 (Forces), but a brief introduction is appropriate here.

In simple terms, gravity is the force of attraction between masses. All objects are made up of matter, and the amount of matter in any given object is said to be its mass, measured in grams. Sir Isaac Newton was the first person to theorize that any two objects would be attracted towards each other by virtue of their masses, and that the strength of the force of attraction – the gravitational force – would depend on the masses of the two objects and their distance apart.

The (relatively) large mass of the Earth thus exerts an attraction – a 'pull' – on smaller objects in its near vicinity. Any object close to the Earth's surface will be 'pulled' towards the centre of the Earth – its centre of mass – by the gravitational force which exists between the Earth and the object. It is this tendency for objects to 'fall' to Earth under the 'pull' of gravity which gives rise to the linked concepts of potential and kinetic energy.

Potential energy

The energy which an object possesses by virtue of its position, is known as its **potential energy**. If the object is not moving, no work is being done, nor is any energy being converted. However, if the object has been raised to its present position, work has been done on the object (work = force × distance moved in the direction of the force), and it has gained potential energy, i.e. it has the potential to do work by virtue of its position. The greater the mass of the object, and the height it has been raised above the surface, the greater is the work which has been done on it, and therefore the greater is its potential energy. Examples of 'objects' having potential energy would include the head of a pile-driver which is poised for release, a skier at the top of a hill, a child (or adult!) at the top of a fairground helter-skelter, a glider at the top of a winch wire, or a 'head' of water in a hydro-electric scheme reservoir. Each of these 'objects' has the potential for doing work, based on the position to which they have been raised above the surface of the Earth.

Kinetic energy

This is the energy which an object possesses by virtue of its motion. In each of the above examples, once the object is released, and begins to move towards the Earth's surface, accelerated by the force of gravity, it possesses an increasing amount of kinetic energy. This energy, in the form of motion, would enable work to be done if any of the objects were involved in a collision (as in the pile-driver, or the reservoir water 'hitting' the hydro-electric turbine blades). As the kinetic energy of the falling object increases, its potential energy decreases proportionally.

Not all kinetic energy is developed as a result of gravitational attraction. Any object in motion is said to possess kinetic energy. The motion may result from the conversion of other forms of energy, for example:

- chemical energy derived from the combustion of a fossil fuel is converted into kinetic energy in a car engine. This kinetic energy is transferred through mechanical linkages – clutch, gears, drive shafts – to the motion of the whole vehicle;
- chemical energy from the respiration of food is transferred through a person's muscles and bones (levers) into kinetic energy when a supermarket trolley is pushed along or a bicycle is pedalled;
- electrical energy is converted into kinetic energy in an electric motor, when a current passing through a coil of wire placed in a magnetic field causes the coil to rotate.

Kinetic energy is also important at the atomic and molecular level. It is the motion of molecules, for example in a gas, which creates the gas pressure (see Key Idea 3.2: The Compression of Gas). As more and more molecules of gas are forced into a fixed space, the number of collisions between molecules increases. These collisions result in a more intense 'bombardment' of the sides of the container by gas molecules. This in turn is measurable as an increase of gas pressure (pressure is force per unit area), as in the inflation of a balloon or a car tyre.

Finally, the kinetic energy (the motion) of atoms and molecules can be increased by the transfer of energy released from nuclear or chemical reactions. This increase in kinetic energy transfers as thermal (heat) energy, and this is the subject of the next section (see also Key Idea 3.2: Changes of State).

Heat and temperature

Heat energy is a function of the vibration of the atoms and molecules of which substances are made. As has already been described, the states of matter can be visualized in terms of the vibration of their constituent atoms or molecules, and changes of state in substances are brought about by the transfer, into and out of the substances, of heat energy in the form of atomic or molecular motion (see Key Idea 3.2: The States of Matter; Changes of State). Increases in motion, and therefore increases in the amount of thermal energy transferred into substances, give rise to:

- changes in state via melting, boiling and evaporation;
- the expansion of heated substances;
- the burning of fuels, and the cellular respiration of carbohydrates in living cells.

All of these processes are described in Key Idea 3.3: Heating and Cooling Everyday Materials; Changing Materials: Chemical reactions and heat energy; Changes involving oxygen.

The difference between heat and temperature

Heat is the total amount of thermal energy contained in a given amount of material, and is measured in joules. Temperature is a measure of the intensity of heat – of how hot something is – and is measured in degrees Celsius (°C). On the Celsius scale, 0° is the freezing point, and 100° is the boiling point, of pure water. Some examples might make the distinction clearer:

- Two litres of water at 20°C will hold twice as much heat as one litre of water at 20°C. Although the water is at the same temperature in each case, there will be twice as many molecular collisions in two litres of water than in one litre (because there are twice as many molecules) – the total quantity of heat in two litres of water will therefore be double that which is present in one litre.
- There will be more heat in a bath full of tepid water than there will be in a match flame. Although the temperature of the match flame will be much higher than that of the bath water, the total molecular movement will be greater in the large volume of bath water than in the small amount of fuel which burns to form the match flame.
- In some cases, it is possible to transfer heat into a substance without raising its temperature. Under conditions of atmospheric pressure, water heated to a temperature of 100°C, will boil. If more heat is transferred into the water, it continues to boil (eventually boiling away as water vapour) without any rise in its temperature.

Heat transfer

In general, there is a tendency towards equilibrium in the physical world. Just as atmospheric pressure tends to 'even out', with high pressure air flowing towards low pressure, and water 'seeks to find its own level', flowing from high to low ground, so heat will tend to flow from areas of higher temperature towards areas of lower temperature. In other words, there is a tendency for the energy of molecular vibration to disperse itself evenly through the materials of the physical environment.

Heat can be transferred in three ways – by conduction, convection and radiation.

Conduction is the transfer of heat energy through a solid material, either by the movement of free electrons, or by the collision of the molecules of which the material is made. 'Free electron' conduction is more rapid, and is typical of those materials, such as metals, which have good thermal conductivity. 'Collision' conduction is slower, and typical of poor conductors of heat. A simple demonstration of good and poor heat conductivity is to place a metal and a wooden spoon into a container of hot water. After a short time the metal spoon handle is hot to the touch, because of the rapid conduction of heat along the handle. The wooden spoon however, stays cool to the touch, as wood is a poor conductor of heat.

Convection is the transfer of heat by means of the movement of a locally heated fluid substance (usually air or water). As a fluid is heated in a particular locality, the heating causes expansion, which in turn causes a lowering of density. The less dense warm fluid begins to rise, and is replaced by cooler, denser fluid from below. Eventually, convection currents are set up which allow for a continuous flow of heat upwards from the source. Examples of systems which use convection currents for heat transfer are:

- electric convector heaters warm the air at one place in a room, and the resulting convection currents transport the heat around the room;
- domestic hot water systems depend on convection currents to transfer heat

from an immersion heater (similar to the 'element' in an electric kettle) to the rest of the water in the hot tank.

It is easy to demonstrate the 'updraught' part of a convection current by hanging a piece of light material, or a cut-out spiral, above a convector heater. The movement of the hanging material will clearly provide evidence for the existence of rising currents of warm air.

Radiation is the transfer of heat without the presence of a material medium, by means of electromagnetic waves (see above, The Electromagnetic Spectrum). Heat radiation can be felt as the 'glow' from a fire or radiator, or as the heat from the Sun. It is interesting to remember that most domestic 'radiators', such as those found in central heating systems, in addition to *radiating* heat energy, will also warm a room by *convection*.

Light   In some nuclear, atomic and molecular reactions, large amounts of energy are produced and some of this energy is emitted by the vibrating particles in the form of light. As has already been described (see above, The Electromagnetic Spectrum), light energy is a form of radiation which is transmitted by electromagnetic waves. These waves are generated by changes in electrical and magnetic field strength and as such, can travel through the vacuum of space. In this respect, light waves differ significantly from other forms of wave energy such as sound or ocean waves, both of which need a medium or material to 'wave' in. Sound and ocean waves transmit energy through the oscillation of particles – of gases, liquids or solids in the case of sound, and of water in the case of ocean waves. Light energy however, is transmitted by the oscillation of electromagnetic fields, and therefore needs no material medium through which to travel.

For the purposes of this book, the behaviour of light **waves** can explain each of the concepts which will be explored (and certainly those of the science National Curriculum). The story is not as simple as that however, and it is important to note that not all of the effects of light can be explained in terms of wave behaviour. In some cases – photosynthesis for example – light behaves as if it were made of particles (photons), with different amounts of energy attached to each parcel (or quantum) of light of a particular wavelength. Suffice it to say that current explanations of the behaviour of light invoke a particle/wave theory which accepts the possibility that light conforms to wave theory on some occasions and to particle theory on others.

CONCEPTS TO SUPPORT KEY STAGE 1

Sources of light

There are a number of different sources of light, all of which have one thing in common – light sources transfer energy into the increased vibration of atoms and molecules such that the vibrating particles (which may be electrons, atoms or molecules) firstly emit heat by radiation, followed by light, as energy levels increase and particles vibrate even faster. Some examples of light sources, and their energy conversions include:

■ the Sun – the energy released by nuclear fusion (see above) is converted into radiant heat and (sun)light. The light from the Sun supplies us with our 'daylight' and the light energy which enables the process of photosynthesis to take place in green plants (see Key Idea 2.2: Plant nutrition – photosynthesis);

- electric lamps (bulbs) – electrical energy is passed as a current through the thin wire filament (often made from tungsten) of a light bulb. The electrical resistance of the filament is high, and this resistivity increases the collisions between molecules in the material, causing both heat and light to be emitted. Most light bulbs contain an inert gas (usually argon), because if air were used the hot filament would react with the oxygen in the air, and would 'burn' away;
- flourescent tubes – electrical energy is used to excite the molecules of mercury vapour (mixed with an inert gas) inside a glass tube, producing ultraviolet radiation. The u/v radiation causes a 'phosphor' coating on the inside of the tube to emit a fluorescent glow. Fluorescent tube lights produce less heat, and therefore consume less power, than incandescent bulbs (a 40 watt tube will produce the same light intensity as a 150 watt bulb).
- a candle – chemical energy released by the burning of a fuel (paraffin wax, a hydrocarbon) causes heating, and the particles of carbon from the fuel become 'white hot', hence the light of the candle flame;

The 'heat then light' sequence is related to the energy levels of the materials involved. As energy levels increase, causing particles to vibrate at ever increasing speeds, the light produced has a colour which matches the frequency of vibration relative to the electromagnetic spectrum. Since red light has the lowest frequency of visible light, and blue light the highest, we would expect that the light emitted by a material which was experiencing increasing energy transfer – which was heating up – would appear to change in a pattern which worked through the spectrum of visible light from red to blue. This is, in effect, what happens. Imagine a blacksmith heating a bar of steel. First it glows a dull red, then orange, then yellow, and eventually it appears to be blue-white and white hot. A similar effect, deliberately restricted by design to the red end of the spectrum, is demonstrated by an electric fire which has just been switched on. Radiant heat from the electric element is felt before the fire begins to 'glow' red, then orange – the 'glow' of the electric element is, of course, a light source.

It is important to remember that all light sources **emit** light – they 'give it out' as a form of radiant energy. There is sometimes confusion in the minds of young children who think that any bright light, such as that *reflected* from a pale coloured wall or a mirror, is a light source, and care is needed to distinguish the differences in such cases.

Light and seeing At a simple level, and without going into explanations involving light rays entering the eye, it is possible to show that we need light in order to see. A simple device (a 'light and dark' box) can be used, or the process can be investigated as a 'thought experiment' (although the real experience is always more convincing!).

If a box is constructed as in Fig. 4.8 (a shoe box is ideal as a basis) it can be used to compare the two experiences of looking at a picture or an object with and without light.

If an observer looks through the small 'peephole' when the shutter is closed, it will be difficult, if not impossible, to see anything of the picture at the end of the box. If the shutter is opened, allowing light to fall on the picture, it

Fig. 4.8 A 'light and dark' box

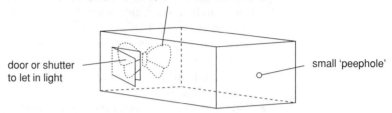

brightly coloured picture attached to 'end wall' of box

door or shutter to let in light

small 'peephole'

immediately becomes visible through the peephole. The without/with light difference is obvious, and should be a convincing demonstration that light needs to fall on objects in order for us to be able to see them.

Light and dark

From the simple experiment described above, it should be possible to extend understanding into other, and similar situations in the real world.

- What is it like inside the box when there is no light getting in? It is dark in the box.
- What happens when the daylight is poor or very dim? We cannot see very well.
- What happens when the daylight goes altogether? It is dark and we cannot see at all (or – we have to switch on other lights to be able to see).
- What happens when we close our eyes so that no light can get into them? We cannot see anything at all.

From these and similar questions, based initially on the light and dark box, it is possible to progress towards an awareness that when there is no light, it will be dark and we will not be able to see anything.

CONCEPTS TO SUPPORT KEY STAGE 2

The behaviour of waves

If a piece of rope (such as a skipping rope) is fixed at one end, held loosely at the other, and the 'held' end moved sharply up and down, a 'wave form' develops and seems to move along the rope towards the fixed end (see Fig. 4.9). The same effect can be seen if one end of a coiled spring such as a 'slinky' is waved from side to side on a table.

What is happening in this process is that energy from the moving hand and arm is transmitted along the rope through the wave form. This energy can be felt as a jerk if the fixed end is held in a hand and a single 'wave' imparted to the rope. It is important to notice that the rope does not go anywhere – what happens is that the *wave form* moves along the rope, at right angles to the vibrations of the rope, carrying its energy with it. Because the wave front advances at right angles to the direction of vibration, these waves are known as 'transverse' waves. This transfer of energy by means of a wave form is also the process which causes a whip to 'crack'. Energy imparted to the whip handle travels in wave form along the whip until it reaches the end. It is said that the whip end moves faster than the speed of sound, and that the crack heard is the sound barrier being broken! The main features of waves are outlined in Fig. 4.10.

The speed at which a wave travels is a product of its wavelength (the

Fig. 4.9 Making wave forms with a skipping rope

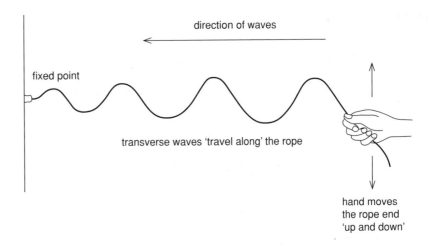

Fig. 4.10 The main features of wave forms

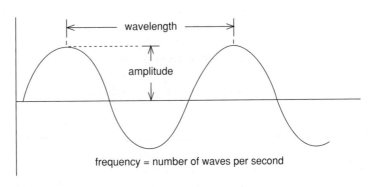

distance in metres between two successive wave crests) and its frequency (the number of 'waves' passing a point per second, measured as Hertz, or Hz), hence,

speed (in metres per second) = wavelength × frequency

The amplitude, or size, of a wave (the height from its crest to its undisturbed position) is a measure of its energy – the larger the amplitude, the greater the energy contained by the wave.

Light waves   Light waves, along with all the other waves represented in the electromagnetic spectrum (see above) travel at a constant speed of 3×10^8 metres (300,000 kilometres) per second in a vacuum (and at almost the same speed in air). As can be seen from Fig. 4.6, the constant speed is maintained because the wavelengths of light shorten as the frequency increases.

Red light, with the longest wavelength of about 0.75 of one millionth of a metre (0.75 microns, or 0.75×10^{-6} m), has a frequency of 4×10^{14} Hz, so its speed will be:

$(0.75 \times 10^{-6}) \times (4 \times 10^{14})$ m/s $= 3 \times 10^8$ m/s

Blue light, with the shortest wavelength of about 0.4 of one millionth of a metre (0.4 microns, or 0.4×10^{-6} m), has the correspondingly higher frequency of 7.5×10^{14} Hz, and its speed will be:

Fig. 4.11 *The straight line experiment*

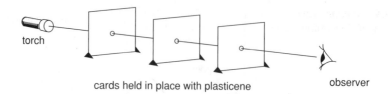

torch

cards held in place with plasticene   observer

$(0.4 \times 10^{-6}) \times (7.5 \times 10^{14})$ m/s = 3×10^8 m/s

(Note: speed is measured as distance travelled per unit time, e.g. 30 metres per second,

and **average (mean) speed** is: $\dfrac{\text{total distance travelled}}{\text{total time taken}}$

Velocity is speed in a particular direction, and when an object is travelling at uniform velocity, both its speed and direction remain unchanged.)

Light **waves**, along with other transverse waves like ocean waves, behave in certain predictable ways, and this behaviour gives rise to certain effects. Light emitted from a radiating source (like the Sun) travels away from it in straight lines in all directions and may, on reaching an object, be **absorbed** or **reflected** by, or **transmitted** through, the material of which the object is made.

Straight line travel

Light (often produced as narrow 'beams' or 'rays' by the appropriate masking of a light source) can easily be shown to travel in straight lines. If light rays were 'curved' we would be able to see round corners! A more convincing practical investigation is to set up the simple experiment shown in Fig. 4.11. When the holes in all three cards are in line, the light from the torch, travelling in a straight line, is visible. As soon as one card is displaced so that the holes are no longer in a straight line, the light cannot be seen.

The reflection and absorption of light

When light reaches an object, some of it 'bounces off' (is reflected away from) the surface of the object. Almost all objects which are not themselves light sources, reflect some of the light which falls on them, and the reflected light is 'scattered' in all directions from the reflecting surface. Some of this reflected light enters our eyes, enabling us to see the reflecting objects. Nerve endings in our eyes are stimulated by the light reflected by the surfaces of objects and people which surround us, and the received messages are transmitted to the brain, which interprets the information and 'sees' the objects concerned (see Key Idea 2.2: The Nervous System).

If the reflecting object is flat, i.e. if it has a plane surface, and is particularly shiny, almost all of the light falling on it will be reflected, producing clear images of the objects nearby. This effect provides the basis for mirrors. If the reflecting surface is not flat, as in a metal dish or a spoon bowl, the resulting images will have distorted shapes.

Light which falls onto a flat surface at a particular angle, will be reflected from it at an equal angle, and it is this effect which causes the accurate (and 'reversed') reflection of the mirror image. This effect can be shown clearly with a mirror and four pins. Set up a mirror on a pinboard as shown in Fig. 4.12.

Fig. 4.12 *Angles of incidence and reflection*

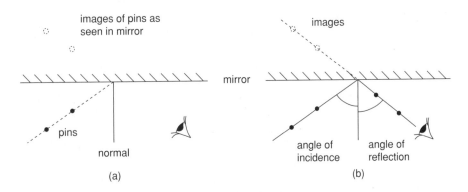

Draw a line at right angles to the mirror surface (the 'normal' line) and position two pins so that they line up with the point where the normal line meets the mirror (Fig. 4.12a). Now place two more pins so that they appear to line up with the images of the first two pins as seen in the mirror (Fig. 4.12b). When the pin holes (representing the track of the light rays reflected from the pins) are later joined up with a pencil line, it will be discovered that the angle of incidence is equal to the angle of reflection.

The reversing of an image can easily be investigated by looking at familiar objects, or the written word, in a mirror. The image appears to be the 'wrong way round' (lateral inversion), but not upside down.

It is important to remember that during the day, light from the Sun 'bathes' the objects on which it falls. There is sometimes a tendency for children to visualize sunlight as existing as single lines (possibly because of the frequent representation of light as 'rays'), and this can cause confusion.

We see the objects around us because they reflect light from their surfaces, and some of this reflected light enters our eyes. We see them *in colour* because objects and surfaces absorb some wavelengths of light and reflect other wavelengths, and it is these reflected wavelengths which give objects their colour. For example, when sunlight falls on the leaves of plants, the blue and red wavelengths are absorbed by the chlorophyll pigments (and are used in the process of photosynthesis), and the green wavelengths are reflected, which is why we see plant leaves as being of a green colour. Objects which absorb all the light which falls on them, and therefore do not reflect light of any colour, are seen as black objects.

An interesting thought experiment relating to this concept is as follows:- if you were in a completely dark, totally enclosed room, the walls of which consisted of 100% non-reflecting black surfaces, and the atmosphere of which was completely pure and dust-free, what would you see if you switched on a torch in the room? (answer at the end of the section).

Shadows Objects or surfaces which reflect or absorb all of the light which falls on them (in other words, will not allow light to pass through them), are said to be opaque. If light falls onto an object directly, and from a bright source, and all of the light is reflected from or absorbed by the object, there will be an area 'behind' the object (relative to the light source) where less light is falling, and this area will be seen as a darker outline – a shadow of the object. This can easily be shown by bringing any object close to the wall of a brightly lit room.

The shadow of the object will be obvious, and will be sharper edged and darker, the closer the object is to the wall. As the object is moved away from the wall and is no longer 'shading' it so closely, more reflected light can reach the wall from other surfaces, and the shadowed area appears to go 'fuzzy', is less distinct, and becomes less dark.

The shadows which are darkest and have the 'sharpest' edges are those 'cast' by objects which are in direct sunlight, or in the light emitted from a powerful source like an overhead projector (which is actually designed to focus and project onto a screen the shadows cast by areas of darker pigment – the writing or print – on OHT slides).

On a cloudy day, when light from the Sun is diffused and scattered by the water droplets in the clouds, shadows are far less pronounced or are absent because the light appears to be coming 'from everywhere' rather than directly from a single source. Indoors, however, where less light is available, even the scattered light of a cloudy day may be bright enough to produce shadows – daylight coming through the windows acts as a bright source in a relatively dark room.

Transmission

Some of the light which reaches an object may not be reflected or absorbed, but may be transmitted through the object, and objects which will allow the passage of light are said to be either translucent or transparent. A translucent material will allow the passage of some light, but the light is so scattered that no clear images are transmitted through the material. Tissue paper and 'frosted' glass are examples of translucent materials. A transparent material is one which transmits most of the light which reaches it, allowing more or less clear visibility of objects which are viewed through it. Glass, polythene and water are all materials which can be transparent in their 'clear' forms, although it is possible to turn any potentially transparent material opaque by the addition of pigments which will reflect and absorb light of different wavelengths. This concept is a deliberate design feature of 'sunglasses' for example, where glass or plastic lenses are deliberately pigmented so that the amount of light entering the eyes is reduced.

It is important to remember that no material will allow the transmission of all available light, as some of the light energy will be absorbed during its passage through the material. It is said that window glass transmits about 80% of incident light, and anyone who has used increasing powers of microscope or telescope lenses will be aware of the dimness of image provided by higher power lenses – a dimness caused by the absorption of much of the light by the lens materials themselves.

Refraction

When light, travelling through air, enters a more dense material such as water or glass, it slows down (fractionally) and its direction is changed by its passage through such material, a process known as refraction. The investigation of this property led Sir Isaac Newton to conduct what is seen as one of the most famous experiments in the history of science. In a darkened room, Newton allowed sunlight, restricted to a narrow beam by a gap in the curtain, to fall on a triangular glass prism. The 'white' sunlight was broken up into its constituent components of coloured light – the spectrum – as the light was refracted through the glass of the prism (see above, The Electromagnetic Spectrum).

Fig. 4.13 The refraction
of light

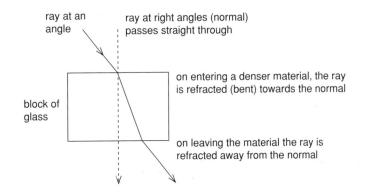

Fig. 4.14 The appearing
coin 'trick'

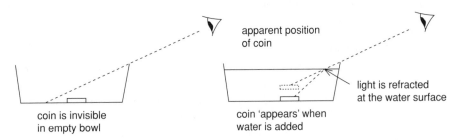

Light which is travelling between transparent materials of different densities will usually behave as follows:

- light falling at right angles onto the surface of a denser (transparent) material will pass straight through the material;
- light falling at an angle, and travelling into a denser material, will be refracted towards the normal, i.e. a line at a right angle to the surface of the material;
- light leaving a dense material will be refracted away from the normal.

These effects are summarized diagrammatically in Fig. 4.13.

An understanding of the behaviour of light, and of its refraction during passage through glass, has allowed for the development of the branch of science known as optics. Using lenses of appropriate shapes, light can be bent so that images of objects can be focused and magnified (a highly beneficial outcome for all those people who need reading glasses, or who use binoculars or telescopes to 'bring distant objects closer').

In another everyday context, the refraction of light at a water surface causes an apparent shallowing, such that underwater objects appear to be in a different position from their actual location. An excellent demonstration of this effect is provided by a washing up bowl (or other suitable opaque container), a coin, and some water. Place a coin in an empty washing up bowl so that it is just out of sight below the rim of the bowl. Without moving the viewing position, slowly add water to the bowl and the coin will begin to appear above the rim. Fig. 4.14 shows what is happening. Light reflected from the surface of the penny is refracted at the water surface so that the previously invisible coin can be seen (although the image of the coin appears at a shallower depth than its actual position).

Answer to the 'torch in the black room' thought experiment:- *you would see nothing*. The black walls would absorb all the light which fell on them, and there would be no 'beam' of torchlight visible because there would be no particles in the atmosphere to reflect the torchlight back to your eyes.

Sound

CONCEPTS TO
SUPPORT KEY
STAGES 1 AND 2

Sound waves

Sound, like light, is a form of energy which is transmitted by waves, but sound differs from light in a number of fundamental ways.

Firstly, sound is generated as a result of mechanical vibration. Any object which is emitting a sound will be vibrating. Sound can be made therefore, by any means which will cause an object (or objects) to vibrate mechanically – by striking, plucking or blowing, for example.

Obvious (and visible) examples of objects which vibrate and produce a sound include a cymbal, the rim of which can be seen to be vibrating when struck, or a guitar string, which can be seen to vibrate when plucked, and felt to vibrate when touched lightly with a finger. Other sounds which can be 'felt' as well as heard include the sounds emitted by a loudspeaker (the 'cone' of the loudspeaker, or its fabric covering can be felt to vibrate), or the human voice box (the larynx), which can be felt vibrating if fingers are lightly placed against the throat whilst talking or singing.

An interesting activity is to consider exactly *what* is vibrating when musical instruments make a sound. Here are some examples:

- stringed instruments: (violin, viola, cello, bass; guitar, mandolin, lute, harp; piano, harpsichord, spinet; dulcimer), where the vibrating components are plucked, strummed, bowed or hammered strings.

Woodwind instruments include:

- 'blown' tubes: (flute, piccolo, fife, recorder family, ocarina), where the vibration is started by air which is blown over a sharp edge at or near the mouthpiece;
- single reed instruments: (clarinet, saxophone family), where a single reed is made to vibrate by air blown across it 'end on';
- double reed instruments: (oboe, cor anglais, bassoon; bagpipes), where a double reed vibrates in the same manner;
- brass instruments: (trumpet, trombone, euphonium, tuba), where the vibrating components are the player's pursed lips (children find great enjoyment from learning that basically, brass players are blowing 'raspberries' into their instruments!);
- percussion instruments: (drum family), where a membrane (the drumskin) is vibrating;
- pitched percussion instruments: (xylophone, glockenspiel, marimba; chime bars, tubular bells), where the vibrating component is the material of which the instrument is made.

In many cases, it is the nature of the original vibration (plucked string, blown tube, double reed, etc.) which gives the instrument its own characteristic sound quality. The sound of an oboe is unmistakably different from that of a clarinet,

Fig. 4.15 *The movement of molecules in a sound wave*

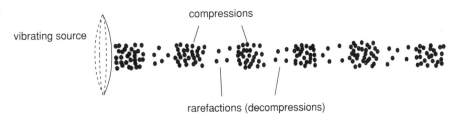

Secondly, the waves which transmit sound energy need a material medium through which to travel – there must be some form of matter between the source of the vibration and the recipient. Sound can therefore travel through air and other gases, through water and other liquids, through solid materials, but *not* through a vacuum. The loudest explosion imaginable in space would be inaudible on Earth, as there is no intervening material medium through which the sound of the explosion could travel.

Thirdly, and unlike light and ocean (transverse) waves, where the direction of the vibration or oscillation is at right angles to the direction of wave travel, the vibrations in **sound waves** are forwards and backwards in the direction of wave travel, and the waves are therefore said to be **longitudinal**. What happens is that the vibrating sound source causes alternate compressions and rarefactions (decompressions) in the molecules of the transmitting material, and these travel outwards from the sound source as waves. Once again, a 'slinky' can provide a good visual simulation of how a sound wave travels. Each neighbouring loop of the slinky represents a molecule of air, or water, or some solid material, and if the slinky is laid on a table with one end fixed, and the other end is moved sharply towards the fixed point, a local compression 'wave' will pass along the spring. If the sharp movement is repeated so as to simulate a vibrating sound source, the transmission of the waves along the spring becomes clearly visible. Figure 4.15 gives an impression of the nature of a sound wave passing through a material.

Note: there is a possible cause of confusion here. As has been described, sound waves are formed from alternate compressions and rarefactions of molecules in the transmission material, and the resultant vibration is forwards and backwards in the direction of wave travel. Sound waves are usually drawn however, using the typical 'sine curve' wave form used to describe light and ocean waves (see Figs. 4.10 and 4.18), where the vibration is at right angles to the direction of movement of the wave front. Whilst such diagrams allow us to understand the relationships between wavelength, frequency, amplitude and so on, it is important to remember that the wave form depicted does not simulate the appearance or travel of a sound wave.

The speed of sound

Since the materials of the transmission media vary in density, i.e. in the 'closeness together' of their constituent molecules, sound travels at different speeds, and

153

Fig. 4.16 *Investigating reflected sound*

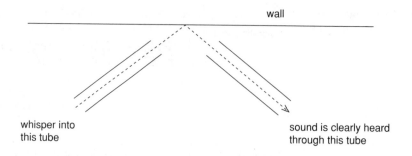

wall

whisper into
this tube

sound is clearly heard
through this tube

at different energy levels, through different materials. In general terms, the denser the material, the faster and more effectively sound will travel through it. As an example, sound travels at 331 metres per second in air at 0°C (nearly 1 million times slower than light!), and at 1,400 metres per second through water. Similarly, sound is transmitted more effectively by a liquid or a solid, than by a gas. The old 'tracking' device of listening for approaching footfalls by placing an ear to the ground, worked because of the more effective transmission of sound through solid ground than through the air. This can be demonstrated easily in a classroom by asking someone to place an ear against a wall, whilst someone a distance away gently scratches the same wall with a finger nail. The 'scratching' sound will be clearly heard when listening with an ear against the wall, but may well be inaudible through the air.

In order for sound to be heard, some form of 'receiver' is necessary, which can pick up the vibrations of the sound waves and translate them into understandable signals. In humans this receiver is the eardrum, or tympanic membrane (see also Key Idea 2.2: The ear). Sound waves are gathered by the outer ear and funnelled down the ear canal to the eardrum, which then vibrates 'in phase' (resonates) at the same frequency as the incoming waves. The sound energy is then transferred via the eardrum and the ear ossicles (three small bones, see Fig. 2.9) into waves in a liquid (the perilymph) in the inner ear, and these vibrations are 'sensed' by hair cells in the coiled tube (the cochlea), and sent as impulses via the auditory nerve, to the brain, which 'hears' the sound.

FURTHER CONCEPTS TO SUPPORT KEY STAGE 2

As with light and ocean waves, sound waves, when reaching an object, may be reflected and/or absorbed by the object, or transmitted through it.

The reflection of sound

When sound waves reach a solid object made of dense and rigid material, such as a wall or a rock face, most of the waves are reflected away from the surface of the material. If the 'hearer' is in a position to receive these reflected waves, they will be heard as an echo of the original sound. The reflected waves behave in the same way as light waves in that their reflected angle is equal to their angle of incidence (their incoming angle). This effect can be investigated by speaking quietly into a tube (a kitchen roll inner is ideal) held at an angle close to a wall. The speech can be heard most clearly through a similar tube held at a similar 'reflected' angle close by (see Fig. 4.16).

The absorption of sound

Some materials, notably those which are flexible and soft, such as fabrics, polystyrene, and some soft fibrous materials, absorb sound energy, so that it is neither reflected back into the medium through which it has travelled, nor transmitted through the medium at which it has arrived. The vibration of the sound waves is prevented from travelling further, and very little sound is therefore heard beyond the absorbing surface. The use of soft, energy absorbent materials is the basis for soundproofing. Areas which need to be soundproofed are lined with such materials in order to prevent or restrict the transmission of sound waves beyond the specified area. A simple 'amateur' soundproofing effect can be achieved through the use of card fibre egg boxes, which are effective for two reasons. Firstly, the cardboard material absorbs sound energy, and secondly, the design of the egg boxes maximizes the surface area over which sound can be absorbed. Heavy curtains, thick carpets, and soft furnishings all have similar effects.

The transmission of sound

This has already been described above, but it is worth noting that sound waves which can only be transmitted through some form of material, travel faster as they transfer to denser materials. This is exactly opposite to the behaviour of light waves which are slowed down by passage through a denser medium.

Pitch

The pitch of a sound, in musical terms, relates to the frequency of vibration of the sound source. The higher the frequency, the higher the note heard, and vice versa. As a guide, humans can hear in a frequency range from about 20 Hz (20 vibrations per second) up to about 18,000 Hz (the 'middle C' note on a piano is produced by a string vibrating 256 times per second, i.e. at a frequency of 256 Hz). It is well known that the range of audible frequencies decreases with increasing age – high frequencies in particular become inaudible to older people. An experiment conducted recently showed that 40–50 year old people were rarely able to hear frequencies above 13,000 Hz.

How can the pitch of a musical note be changed? By varying:

- the length of the vibrating column of air, as with the slide of a trombone, the valves of a trumpet, or the holes in a clarinet or oboe;
- the thickness, length or tension of a string – the strings of a double bass are thicker and longer than those of a violin, and the notes produced are correspondingly lower. Increasing tension on strings of the same length and thickness will result in notes of higher pitch. Similarly, fretting or stopping a given string effectively shortens its length and increases the frequency (and therefore the pitch) of the resulting note;
- the mass of a struck object, as in the increasing size of xylophone or marimba bars, or of tuning forks. This can be seen clearly in the graph below, which shows that the pitch of the note of a tuning fork is related to its mass – the higher the mass, the lower the note – an inversely proportional relationship (see Fig. 4.17).

In the cases described above, the shortening of the air column or the string, or the lowering of the mass of the struck object, will increase the frequency of vibration, and this will cause a rise in pitch of the notes heard. Conversely, longer air columns and strings, or more massive struck objects will decrease the frequency of vibration, and deeper notes will be heard.

In musical terms, a doubling of frequency results in the raising of the pitch of a note by one octave. So, the 'middle C' note of the piano has a frequency of

Fig. 4.17 *The relationship between the mass and frequency (pitch) of tuning forks*

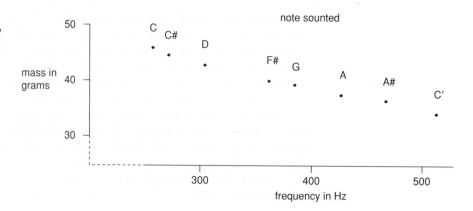

Fig. 4.18 *Sound waves – pitch and loudness*

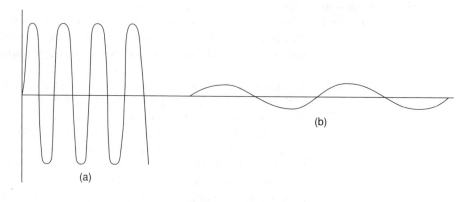

256 Hz, the 'C' note which is one octave above middle C has a frequency of 512 Hz, and the 'C' note which is two octaves above middle C has a frequency of 1,024 Hz.

Loudness The loudness of a sound is a function of the amplitude of the wave form. A wave's amplitude is the height from its crest to its undisturbed position, and the greater the amplitude, the more energy is carried by the wave. Sound waves of large amplitude will have been produced by vigorously vibrating sources, so the greater the amplitude of the sound waves, the louder the sound will be. To use a previous orchestral example, a double bass will usually sound louder than a violin because the vibrations produced by the strings of the bass have a greater amplitude (are larger) than those of the violin.

Fig. 4.18a shows the wave form of a loud (large amplitude) high pitched (high frequency) sound, and Fig. 4.18b shows a soft (small amplitude) low pitched (low frequency) sound.

Forces

Forces can make things start to move, can make moving things speed up, slow down, change direction or stop, and can make things change their shape

Introduction

Some of the difficulties which children (and adults) have with understanding forces and their effects are because:

- forces themselves cannot be seen (although their effects can);
- some forces cannot be felt;
- some of the explanations of forces and their effects appear to contradict a 'common-sense' view of the way in which the world works – for example, why should a small object fall to the ground at the same speed as a large object, when both are released from the same height at the same time? (see below!);
- we may have limited personal experience of some of the common effects of forces in everyday life – for example, we are all affected by gravity, but how many people can really say that they are *conscious* of the 'pull' of gravity – when we lose our balance, we fall over, we do not feel as if we are pulled;
- any simple 'earthbound' consideration of the forces acting on moving objects is complicated by the effects of gravity, friction and air resistance (see below).

Key Idea 4.1, relating to energy, has hopefully demonstrated some of the inter-relationships between such concepts as energy, work and power. The present section will introduce some of the concepts which relate to forces and their effects, and will show how and where they interact with energy, work and power.

CONCEPTS TO SUPPORT KEY STAGES 1 AND 2

In everyday terms, a force is a push or a pull, and it is sometimes helpful to make a mental substitution of the words 'push' or 'pull' whenever the term 'force' is encountered. This will be done in the text in the early part of the present section so that readers can decide on its usefulness (or otherwise).

Some definitions

To revise the definitions from Key Idea 4.1, energy is the capacity or ability to perform work, and work is done (in mechanical terms) when a force (a push or pull) is applied to (or acts on) an object, causing it to move – remember:

work done (or energy transformed) = force (a push or pull) × distance moved in the direction of the force (push or pull).

So forces (pushes and pulls) are involved whenever work is done or when any object moves, and two simple, but very important ideas which help with an understanding of forces are that:

- forces act on (or are applied to) objects – they do not exist 'in' or 'on' objects, nor do objects 'use up' or 'run out of' force;
- forces cause objects to accelerate (change their velocity) – either from being stationary to moving, or from moving at a constant speed to moving at an increased or a lower speed (a deceleration is seen as negative acceleration), or by a change of direction (velocity is speed in a particular direction, so if that direction changes, the velocity has changed, and this constitutes an acceleration).

In the next section the following definitions may also be useful:

- **speed**, in m/s, is the **distance travelled/time taken**, e.g. the speed of sound in air is 331 metres per second;
- **velocity**, in m/s or kph (kilometres per hour), is **speed** (distance travelled/ time taken) **in a particular direction**, e.g. the car was travelling westwards at 90 kilometres per hour;
- **acceleration**, in m/s^2, is **change in velocity/time taken for this change**, e.g. a car is advertised as being capable of accelerating from 0–90 kilometres per hour in 7.5 seconds;
- **mass**, in grams (or kilograms), is the **amount of matter** in an object.

The effects of forces: the laws of motion

Sir Isaac Newton was the first person to systematically study the effect of forces (pushes and pulls) on the movement of objects, and his three 'laws of motion' still enable us to predict the behaviour of moving objects in the everyday world. An annotated version of Newton's laws of motion is as follows:

The first law of motion

Every object continues in a state of rest (remains stationary) or of uniform motion (constant speed) in a straight line, unless acted on by a force or forces.

What are the implications of the first law of motion in everyday terms?

The first part of the law, relating to stationary objects, is not difficult to visualize. A stationary object will remain stationary unless and until it is acted on by a force or forces. So when a force is applied to, or acts on, a stationary object, the object will begin to move. For example, imagine a brick lying on the ground (there are forces acting on the brick, but these forces are 'balanced' – see below). The brick will remain motionless on the ground until someone picks it up. In picking it up, the person is applying a force, a 'pull', to the brick (they can also feel the 'pull' of gravity on the brick), and it begins to move as it is lifted off the ground. Similarly, a line of stationary railway trucks will begin to move when a locomotive applies a force by pushing or pulling them to a new location, or a ball can be made to move through the air by the force applied to it (the push) from the throwers arm and hand.

In the time during which the force is applied, the object undergoes acceleration, i.e. a change in velocity, from zero velocity (stationary) to a final velocity which will depend on the size of the force applied to the object, the length of time during which the force is applied, and the mass of the object. Once the force is no longer acting on the object, i.e. the brick has been lifted to its required height, the trucks have attained their required speed, and the ball leaves the thrower's hand, acceleration (but not necessarily movement) stops.

The second part of the law, relating to objects which are moving at a constant speed in a straight line, is not so easy to imagine in everyday terms. According to Newton, objects which are moving in a straight line at a constant speed will continue in that state until forces act on them which will change that state. In practice, such continuous straight-line movement at a constant speed without the application of other forces, is possible only in conditions of zero gravity in a vacuum, i.e. in deep space. Under such conditions, Newton theorized, an object which is moving at a constant speed in a straight line will continue to do so for ever, unless it is acted on by a force.

Perhaps the closest we can get to seeing this effect in action is to consider a space probe heading for a distant planet. Once the probe has been started on its journey, and has escaped the gravitational 'pull' of the Earth, it will continue in straight line motion at a constant speed until forces are applied to it (usually by the firing of rocket motors) to change its direction of travel, to slow it down or speed it up.

The interiors of spacecraft have proved to be excellent laboratories for experimenting on the theory implicit in the first law of motion. A number of TV broadcasts from space have shown astronauts 'placing' objects like pens, spanners, and even globules of water in 'mid-air' inside the spacecraft. The objects appear to 'hang suspended'. In fact, they are simply obeying Newton's first law, and are remaining stationary – staying where they are put – because no forces are acting on them. Similarly, when pushed gently in a particular direction, the objects move in a straight line and at a constant speed (also obeying the first law, and with no forces acting on them), until another force – contact with a hand, or collision with part of the spacecraft, changes their speed or direction of movement.

On Earth, it is practically impossible to study a moving object which has no forces acting on it, as all moving objects are affected by the forces of gravity and friction.'

The best we can do is to consider systems where the effect of friction is minimized – an ice hockey puck sliding across ice for example, or where the forces acting on a moving object effectively cancel each other out, as in an object moving down an incline which has been designed so that the effect of gravity compensates for the effect of friction.

As an earthbound example of the latter case, imagine a cyclist freewheeling at a constant speed in a straight line, down a long, and very gentle gradient (the gradient is necessary to allow the cyclist to freewheel, but is gentle enough for the speed to be constant rather than accelerating, so the effect of friction is minimized). The constant straight line movement would theoretically continue until a force is applied to the object – which in this case is the combined system of the freewheeling cycle and the cyclist. The cyclist can change the constant straight-line movement by applying different forces to the system – by starting to pedal, for example – which would cause an increase in speed (an acceleration), or by putting on the brakes, which would cause a deceleration. External forces could also change the constant straight line movement – the cyclist could be 'blown off course' by the force of the wind (the 'push' being provided by the kinetic energy of air molecules), causing a change of direction, or an extreme case would be the prevention of further forward movement by the contact force of a collision with a solid object – a crash, in other words!

Sometimes the consideration of objects in constant straight-line motion on Earth can result in the apparent contradiction of the first of Newton's laws of motion. This is because, in practice, a number of forces will be acting on any object travelling in a straight line at a constant speed on or near the surface of the Earth. These will include:

■ the 'pull' of the Earth's gravity;
■ the force which tends to resist movement between objects – friction;
■ air resistance (or drag) – a form of friction.

It is the combination of these forces acting on an object moving at constant speed in a straight line, which will slow it down and may eventually cause it to stop. Imagine our cyclist again. If the cyclist were pedalling in a straight line along a horizontal road, and were then to stop pedalling and begin to freewheel, the combined effects of gravity, friction and air resistance would eventually cause the cycle to slow down and stop. As another example, if a person in a supermarket were to stop pushing their shopping trolley, the trolley would also slow down and stop.

This 'slowing down and stopping' effect which occurs to objects when 'pushing' or 'pulling' stops gives rise to one of the most plausible common-sense contradictions to Newton's first law of motion – a contradiction which seems to be borne out by experience. Cyclists instinctively know that they need to keep pedalling steadily in order to maintain a constant speed on a horizontal road, and trolley-pushers know that they must keep pushing steadily in order to keep trolleys moving at a constant speed around the store. Surely then, experience shows that the maintenance of a constant speed needs the application of a constant force? According to Newton's first law however, an object which has no forces (or balanced forces) acting on it will remain at rest or will continue travelling in constant straight line motion, so the cyclist should not need to pedal, nor the trolley-pusher to push, in order to maintain the required constant speed!

There are two effects to bear in mind here. The first is that the slowing down and stopping of the cycle or the trolley *would* be predicted by the first law of motion – gravity, friction and air resistance are the forces which are acting on the moving objects in this case. Secondly, the constant 'push' supplied by the cyclist and the shopper is being used in each case to overcome the opposing forces – the combined effects of gravity, friction and air resistance – in order to maintain a constant speed. If it were possible to relocate the travellers to a hypothetical road or supermarket in deep space, where gravity, friction and air resistance were negligible, the movement of their separate vehicles would be literally, effortless. Once the pedalling or pushing had accelerated the cycle or the trolley to the required speed, no further effort would be necessary as constant straight line motion would have been achieved.

Momentum

If, in Newtonian terms, there is no force acting on an object which is moving at a constant speed, what is it which keeps the object moving? It is the **momentum** of the object, which is a measure of the ease with which the object's motion can be changed. It is defined as:

momentum = mass × velocity

and is measured in kilogram metres per second (kg m/s).

An object with a small mass, e.g. a cycle, moving at a constant speed, will therefore have less momentum, and will be easier to speed up, slow down, deflect (turn) or stop, than will an object of large mass, e.g. a car or a lorry, travelling at the same speed.

An object will continue to accelerate as long as a force is applied to it. A ball, for example, is 'pushed' into the air by the thrower's hand. Once the force is removed, i.e. the ball leaves the thrower's hand, acceleration stops and movement through the air continues because of the momentum imparted to the ball by its mass and velocity. Given that the forces of gravity and friction will eventually slow down and stop the ball, its momentum will keep it moving until another force acts on it to change its motion. That force may be the contact force applied when the ball hits the ground or a catcher's hand (or a pane of glass!).

The first law of motion describes the effect of forces on objects, and consideration of the law allows us to conclude that forces can start things moving (lifting a brick, throwing a ball), can make moving things speed up (pedalling a cycle which had been freewheeling) slow down, or stop (putting on the brakes of a moving cycle), or change direction (being blown off course by the wind).

The second law of motion

The second law of motion describes the relationship between forces, acceleration and the mass of the objects on which the forces are acting.

When a force acts on an object, the resulting acceleration is directly proportional to the force, and inversely proportional to the mass of (the amount of matter in) the object, and the acceleration changes in the direction in which the force acts.

Again, what does this mean in everyday terms?

Put simply, when the force on an object increases, its resultant acceleration will increase proportionally. This can be shown by setting up an experiment as in Fig. 4.19.

In a similar fashion to the 'freewheeling cyclist' described above, the ramp is set up so that the pull of gravity on the trolley will just compensate for the effect of friction, and these two forces effectively cancel each other out.

Before starting the experiment therefore, the ramp should be tilted so that the trolley will just roll down it at a constant speed, i.e. the effect of friction is overcome. It will then be found that as the force pulling the trolley is increased (by adding weights to the end of the string), the acceleration of the trolley, measured as the increasing distance travelled each second, will increase proportionally. The table below shows the (hypothetical) acceleration achieved when a trolley is pulled along the ramp by 100 and 200 gram masses.

Distance travelled	in 1st second	in 2nd second	in 3rd second	total distance travelled in 3 secs
100 g 'pulling' the trolley	1 metre	2 metres	3 metres	6 metres
200 g 'pulling' the trolley	2 metres	4 metres	6 metres	12 metres

Fig. 4.19 Investigating the second law of motion

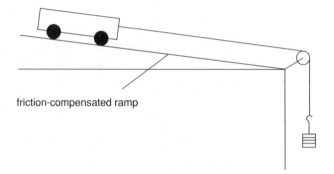

friction-compensated ramp

It can be seen that the trolley when pulled by a 100 g mass accelerates, i.e. increases its velocity, at the rate of 1 metre per second, *every* second, i.e. 1 metre in the 1st second, 1 + 1 m in the 2nd second, 2 + 1 m in the third, and so on. Similarly, the trolley when pulled by a 200 g mass accelerates at 2 metres per second every second (2 m in the 1st second, 2 + 2 m in the 2nd, 4 + 2 m in the 3rd, etc.). Conventionally these values would be written as 1 m/s^2, and 2 m/s^2. This effect can be summarized as:

force is proportional to acceleration, or **F (is proportional to) a**   (1)

and can be easily investigated by dropping a marble into a sand tray from different heights. The force of the impact of the marble in the sand will be proportional to the acceleration due to gravity, and will therefore vary according to the length of time during which the marble falls – the longer the 'falling' time (i.e. the higher the release point), the greater the acceleration. A comparison of the size of the 'craters' left by the marble will confirm this.

Similarly, the force supplied or produced by a moving object will be proportional to its mass. Imagine the start of a snooker game. The cue ball is pushed towards the group of red balls and strikes them, scattering them around the table. What might the result be if the cue ball were to be replaced by a table tennis ball or a sponge rubber ball accelerating at the same rate? In either case, the mass of the replacement cue ball is much smaller than that of the regular cue ball, and the correspondingly smaller force delivered by such small masses would have little impact (literally) on the triangular pack of red balls. This relationship can be summarized as:

force is proportional to mass, or **F (is proportional to) m** (2)

and can also be investigated with a sand tray, but this time by dropping spheres of similar size but different masses, e.g. a pea, a marble, a ball bearing, into the sand from the same height. Again, the larger 'craters' left by spheres of larger mass should confirm the effect.

The two effects described in equations (1) and (2) can be combined as

Force = mass × acceleration, or (**F = ma**) (3)

Conversely, if the force acting on an object remains constant, the acceleration of the object produced by the force will be *inversely* proportional to the mass of the object. In other words, if the mass of the object doubles, the acceleration will be halved, providing the force remains constant. In the trolley experiment shown above, the second law predicts that if the mass of the trolley were 100 g, and it moved 1 metre along the ramp in the 1st second of travel, an increase of mass of the trolley to 200 g would result in it travelling only 0.5 metres in the 1st second, under the effect of the same force – when the mass doubles, the acceleration is halved.

So, acceleration is inversely proportional to mass, or

a (is proportional to) $\dfrac{\mathbf{1}}{\mathbf{m}}$ (4)

and since F (is proportional to) a, (from (1), above)

$\mathbf{a} = \dfrac{\mathbf{F}}{\mathbf{m}}$, a rewritten form of (3) above (5)

Gravity

This last equation can also be exemplified by a consideration of objects falling – being pulled towards the Earth – under the effect of gravity. All finite objects are made of matter, and the amount of matter in an object is known as its mass, measured in grams. There is a force of attraction, known as the gravitational force, between all objects, and again it was Newton who realized that the force of attraction between two objects was a function of the mass and the distance apart of the two objects. The larger the masses of the two objects, and the closer together they are, the greater will be the gravitational attraction between them. Between objects of small mass the gravitational force is so small as to be almost negligible. Objects of larger mass (like the Earth) however, do exert a pull (a gravitational force) on small objects in their vicinity, and it is this pull, continuously exerted by the mass of the Earth, which tends to return any airborne objects to the Earth's surface. In practice of course, this means that objects 'fall' to Earth under the effect of the gravitational force. Although we do not feel the 'pull' of gravity ourselves (partly because our systems have evolved under gravity, so we tend not to notice it), we can feel the effect of gravity every time we lift an object – a heavy bag of shopping,

Fig. 4.20 *Measuring mass and weight*

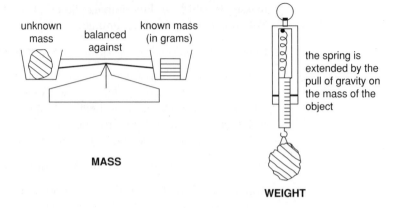

unknown mass

balanced against

known mass (in grams)

the spring is extended by the pull of gravity on the mass of the object

MASS

WEIGHT

for example. The force of gravity is 'pulling' the mass of the shopping back towards the centre of the Earth, and we need to apply a lifting force to overcome its effect. More force is needed to lift a heavy bag of shopping than a light one, because the heavy bag 'weighs' more. What is the difference between mass and weight?

The difference between mass and weight

In simple terms, mass is the amount of matter in an object, and is measured in grams. Under normal circumstances, and as long as it remains intact, an object will always have the same mass, i.e. there will always be the same amount of matter in it. A steel ball bearing will have the same amount of steel in it – its mass will be the same – whether it is on the Earth's surface or on the Moon.

The weight of an object is the force exerted by its mass as a result of the acceleration due to gravity. All objects are being accelerated towards the centre of the Earth by the planet's gravitational force, and the 'pull' of gravity on the mass of an object is known as its weight, measured in newtons (N). A newton is defined as that force which will give an acceleration of 1 m/s^2 to a mass of 1 kilogram.

weight = mass × acceleration due to gravity

A useful idea is to imagine that mass is calculated by comparing an object of unknown mass with standard masses (in grams) using a beam balance or scale (as in the statue of Justice on top of the Old Bailey). Weight is calculated by measuring the pull of gravity on the mass of an object, for example, by measuring the extension of a spring to which the mass has been attached, as in a spring balance or forcemeter, for example (see Fig. 4.20).

A source of confusion here, is that many spring balances are calibrated in grams, rather than newtons, and we talk about objects 'weighing' so many grams. Strictly speaking, objects have a **mass** of so many **grams**, and **weigh** so many **newtons**.

Repeating the commonly used Moon analogy, if an object with a mass of 1 kilogram were weighed using a spring balance on Earth, it would weigh 9.8

newtons (since the acceleration due to the Earth's gravitational force is 9.8 m/s^2, and a newton is defined as that force which will give an acceleration of 1 m/s^2 to a mass of 1 kilogram). If the object were transferred to the Moon, its mass would not change (it would remain at 1 kilogram), but the object would weigh approximately 1.6 newtons, because the Moon, being smaller and less massive, has a gravitational pull which is about one-sixth of that on Earth. The weaker 'pull' of the Moon's gravity on the mass of 1 kilogram would result in a smaller extension of the spring balance, registering as a lower weight.

Falling objects

The force – the 'pull' – of gravity varies – large masses are attracted towards the centre of the Earth with a larger force than are small masses, and that is why large masses weigh more than small ones. However, since as mass increases, acceleration proportionally decreases (a (prop) $\frac{1}{m}$), the overall effect on falling objects on Earth is that the *acceleration* due to gravity is constant. We can use the formulae derived from Newton's second law of motion to explain this behaviour.

From F = m × a, we can derive $a = \dfrac{F}{m}$

Imagine two objects, one of mass 50 kilograms and the other of mass 10 kilograms. At what rate will each of them accelerate if they are both released from the same height above the Earth at the same time?

Using $a = \dfrac{F}{m}$ we find that acceleration $= \dfrac{\text{Force (weight)}}{\text{mass}}$

Since a mass of 1 kilogram weighs 9.8 newtons, the 50 kilogram mass will weigh 490 newtons and will have an acceleration of

$$\frac{490}{50} = 9.8 \,\text{m/s}^2$$

Similarly, the 10 kilogram mass will weigh 98 newtons and will have an acceleration of

$$\frac{98}{10} = 9.8 \,\text{m/s}^2$$

Since both objects have the same rate of acceleration, they will both fall at the same rate and will hit the ground at the same time.

This effect provides a good example of an area in which 'scientific' or 'school' knowledge is apparently contradicted by real world experience or perception. Some children (and some adults) find it hard to understand, and even harder to accept, the constant acceleration due to gravity. There is often an intuitive belief that 'heavier objects should hit the ground first', and even when this is shown to be not the case, through theory or by practical demonstration, people often revert to their private 'belief systems', preferring to accept a common-sense view of the way in which the world works, rather than a scientific view which apparently does not 'stand to reason'.

An object falling through the Earth's atmosphere will not continue to accelerate indefinitely. At some stage, the force of air resistance or drag, will equal the weight of the falling object. At this point the forces on the object will balance, the object will stop accelerating and it will continue to fall at a constant speed, known as its terminal velocity. As an example, the terminal velocity of free-fall parachutists is about 120 mph (193 kph).

The third law of motion

The third law of motion states that **every action has an equal and opposite reaction**.

Imagine a 1 kilogram mass placed on a table. Because of the acceleration due to gravity, the 1 kilogram mass is exerting a downward force of 9.8 newtons on the table. The table is solid and rigid, and is not moved by the force of the mass pushing down on it. Instead it provides a reaction or contact force, exactly equal and opposite to the force applied by the 1 kilogram mass, and this reaction force supports the mass in a stationary position on the table surface. It is conventional, as in the diagram below, to represent the size and direction of the forces concerned by arrows of appropriate length and direction. The forces in this instance constitute a balanced pair, and the 1 kilo mass remains stationary.

This is a difficult concept. Some accounts describe the table in the first example as 'pushing back' on the 1 kilo mass, and many people find it hard to accept that the table actively 'pushes' the mass with exactly enough force to keep it in position. An easier concept, in my opinion, is the idea that the force provided by the 1 kilo mass produces an equal and opposite reaction force on contact which *supports* the mass in position. If there were no reaction force, the 1 kilogram mass would 'sink' into the table surface!

Balanced forces can also affect moving objects, and this too, seems difficult to understand. Surely, common-sense would tell us that if forces on an object were balanced, then it would not move? Newtonian physics suggests however, that if balanced forces are acting on a moving object, then the object will continue to move at a constant speed. For example, any object (such as a stone) dropping in 'free fall' towards the Earth will eventually be 'acted on' by a balanced pair of equal and opposite forces – the pull of gravity will be balanced by the force of friction supplied by the air resistance or drag on the object. The result will be constant motion towards the Earth, at a terminal velocity which reflects the mass and shape of the object concerned (see Fig. 4.21).

A 'personal' experiment may help here. Stand facing a wall at a distance of about 50 cm, and place your hands flat against the wall at about shoulder height. Gently bend your elbows so that you lean against the wall slightly, and then push against the wall to recover your original position. You should have performed a 'standing-up' press-up against the wall. The wall has provided an equal and opposite reaction force to your push which has caused you to return to your starting position. Repeat the process, but this time push much harder against the wall. In this case the equal and opposite reaction force provided by the wall enables you to 'push' yourself vigorously away from the wall – it is you, of course, who supply the energy of the push. In similar fashion, a slow 'knees bend' followed by the straightening of your legs allows

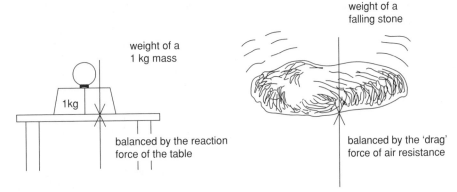

Fig. 4.21 *Equal and opposite reactions: forces in balanced pairs*

weight of a 1 kg mass

weight of a falling stone

balanced by the reaction force of the table

balanced by the 'drag' force of air resistance

you to stand upright (the floor provides the equal and opposite reaction force), whilst a violent knees bend followed by a vigorous push with your legs results in you leaving the ground in a vertical jump – again, the floor provides the reaction force which allows you to do this.

A combination of the first and third laws of motion shows us that when objects are acted on by forces which have an equal and opposite effect – balanced forces – the result will be that stationary objects will remain stationary, and moving objects will continue to move at a constant speed. Hence, the 1 kilo mass remains stationary on the table, and the stone continues to fall at terminal velocity.

Conversely, if the forces acting on an object are not balanced, i.e. if one force is larger than another, acceleration of the object will occur. This may take the form of a stationary object beginning to move, a moving object beginning to speed up or slow down (and stop), or a moving object changing direction. It is important to keep in mind the distinction between objects moving at a constant speed (which may have balanced forces acting on them on Earth, or no forces acting on them in deep space), and objects which are accelerating, which will have unbalanced forces acting on them. As examples of the effect of unbalanced forces:

- if a force (an upward pull) of more than 9.8 newtons is applied to the 1 kilogram mass, the mass will be lifted from the table;
- when a free-fall parachutist pulls the ripcord and the parachute opens, the force of friction is increased because of the air resistance of the large area of the canopy, and the parachutist is slowed down (decelerated) from terminal velocity (after a time the forces will once again balance and the parachutist will descend at a (slower) constant speed with the canopy open);
- a snooker ball, moving across a table, makes contact 'at an angle' with a stationary ball. The stationary ball a) applies a reaction force to the moving ball which is deflected from its original path, and b) receives a 'push' from the moving ball and itself starts to move (see Fig. 4.22).

The effects of forces: change of shape

When forces act on materials, a number of effects may be noticed, depending on the properties of the materials concerned (see also Key Idea 3.1: The Physical Properties of Materials):

Fig. 4.22 An example
of the effect of
unbalanced forces

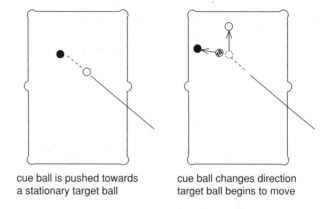

cue ball is pushed towards
a stationary target ball

cue ball changes direction
target ball begins to move

If the material will sustain plastic deformation, the movement of the material caused by the application of a force may result in a change of shape. Imagine a piece of playdough being squeezed between finger and thumb. The opposite 'pushes' from the finger and thumb are large enough to move particles of the material relative to each other, and the playdough is flattened.

If the material is elastic (see Key Idea 3.1: Elasticity, and Key Idea 4.1: Strain Energy), the forces acting on the material will cause the molecular bonds in the material to 'stretch', as in a rubber band, or to 'compress', as in the coil spring of a car's suspension system. When the material concerned is under such tension or compression, the forces of attraction between the molecules tend to restore the molecules to their original positions. This tendency in the material causes the application of a force both within the material, and also to any objects attached to the material. So a pile of papers is 'pulled together' by the force applied by a rubber band stretched around them, and the compression and resultant recoil of a car spring results in a smoother ride for the motorist.

Note: the elasticity of a material is not in itself a force; it is a property of the material. But the molecules in an elastic material under tension or compression, i.e. which have been moved out of place by the application of a tensile or compressive force, will themselves apply an opposing force as they tend to resume their original positions in the material.

FURTHER CONCEPTS TO SUPPORT KEY STAGE 2

Pressure

Pressure is defined as **force applied per unit area**, measured in newtons per square metre (N/m²), a unit also known as a Pascal (Pa). Pressure is therefore a measure of the concentration of a force, and the concentration (or dissipation) of a force has a number of practical applications (and implications).

If for any reason, a material is to be pierced, the concentration of an applied force through a very small area will have the greatest effect. This is exemplified by needles piercing fabrics, and nails and screws piercing wood and masonry. If the pushing force on a needle were to be 9.8 newtons (imagine the weight of a 1 kilogram bag of sugar), and assuming that the area of the point of a needle was one thousandth of a square centimetre (0.001 cm²), the pressure produced at the needle point would be:

$\dfrac{9.8}{0.001}$ = 9,800 N – equivalent to the weight of a 100 kilo (15.7 stone) person!

This effect can also be seen (usually in the form of damage to the floor) when the pressure of a person's weight is applied through the small contact areas of stiletto-heeled shoes. Similarly, if water is flowing through a hosepipe, the pressure of the water leaving the pipe can be raised by reducing the diameter of the pipe (by placing a finger or thumb over the end of the pipe, or by squeezing it). This will have the effect of reducing the area over which the force of the water is acting, and water will leave the pipe at an increased pressure (the same effect will result from placing a finger under a tap). This effect is immediately obvious when using a hosepipe with a 'variable' nozzle, and can be seen when firefighters use a narrow hose nozzle in order to increase the pressure (and therefore the range) of the water used by their appliances.

Conversely, pressure can be lowered by 'spreading' the applied force over a larger area, and this effect can be seen in a number of applications. The spreading of weight over a large area of a suspect surface will minimize the likelihood of the surface giving way – so rescuers approach a hole in an ice-covered pond by crawling rather than standing on the ice, and by spreading their weight on planks of wood or ladders. The effect of this action is to reduce the overall pressure by causing their weight to act over a larger area of the surface. Snow shoes produce a similar effect for people walking in deep snow, by increasing the surface area of the wearers' boot soles and therefore spreading their weight over a larger area of snow.

Forces in action   Key Idea 4.1 (The Primary Sources of Energy), suggested that four forces – the strong and weak nuclear forces, electromagnetic, and gravitational forces – are responsible for all the energy transfers in the universe. The effects of some of these forces have already been described elsewhere, including:

- the force of gravity (see above, and Key Idea 4.1: Potential and Kinetic Energy);
- the forces of magnetic attraction and repulsion (see Key Idea 3.1: Magnetic Properties);
- the forces of tension and compression in elastic materials (see above, Change of Shape, Key Idea 3.1: Elasticity, and Key Idea 4.1: Strain Energy).

Two further forces are now described, and these are the forces of friction, and upthrust.

Friction

Friction is the force which opposes the motion of objects. When the molecules on the surface of an object come into contact with those of another surface, or with the molecules of a fluid (a liquid or a gas), forces of attraction between the molecules – the frictional forces – tend to 'stick' the surfaces of objects together, or to slow down the movement of a solid material through a fluid. When objects are slowed down by frictional forces in a fluid, the effect is known as drag – air resistance, for example, is a form of drag.

When friction is overcome, and movement results, two other effects can be noticed. Firstly, the force applied in order to overcome the force of friction causes the conversion of energy as heat – moving surfaces heat up when they are rubbed together. Secondly, moving surfaces which are in contact tend to suffer from wear.

The force of friction, like the force of gravity, is always present on Earth. In everyday terms, it is practically impossible to produce a completely friction-free system, although in industry and commerce, much time, money and effort is spent in the attempt to minimize the effects of frictional forces between materials. The effects of the force of friction can be both advantageous and disadvantageous.

Some advantages of friction:

- frictional forces allow us to move. The soles of our shoes 'grip' the ground, and the tread of car tyres grip the road – if surfaces in contact simply slid apart, no movement would be possible;
- the braking systems in vehicles rely on the friction between brake pads and discs (or brake shoes and drums) to slow the vehicles down;
- the tuning pegs of violins, and fastenings such as nails and screws rely on friction to remain in place;
- friction allows us to warm our hands by rubbing them together on cold days;
- air resistance slows down the descent to Earth of parachutists, and of space capsules (space capsules which return to Earth from beyond the atmosphere are slowed down to such an extent by the friction of the atmospheric air molecules that their surfaces glow red hot).

Some disadvantages of friction:

- friction slows down vehicles and machinery. The effect of friction is counteracted by minimizing the area of surfaces in contact – perhaps the greatest discovery in this area was the wheel, which reduces the ground contact points on a vehicle to a minimum – and by 'streamlining' the design of the vehicle to minimize drag – the frictional effect of air resistance;
- friction heats up, and wears out machinery – these effects of friction are minimized by lubricating moving parts so that a thin film of oil or water is placed between the surfaces. Wear is minimized because the surfaces 'slide' over each other more easily, and the heat generated by friction is conducted away by the lubricant.

Obviously, different surfaces will have different frictional properties. Smooth, rigid, and/or polished surfaces will produce less friction than will rough and pliable surfaces. Surfaces which can 'mould' together are much more likely to 'stick' together. So, steep ice provides less friction, and is therefore harder to climb, than rough rock. Similarly, skates will slide smoothly on ice (too smoothly for beginners!), but will not slide at all easily on a wooden surface or a carpet. Riding a cycle on rough ground is harder work than riding on the road, because there is more friction between the rough ground surface and the 'chunky' tyres than there is between the tyres and the flat road.

The differences in friction between different surfaces can be investigated by finding out what force (using a forcemeter) is necessary to cause a block of wood covered with different fabrics to begin to slide on a 'standard' surface. Before you start, an interesting exercise is to predict what you think the 'rank order' of the fabrics and materials will be, from the 'slippiest', i.e. that needing the smallest force to overcome the force of friction, to the 'grippiest', i.e. that needing the largest force to produce the same effect. The diagram (Fig. 4.23) shows the set-up for the experiment, and the table gives some typical results for the forces needed to make a wood block covered with different materials begin to slide on a horizontal table top.

Type of material covering the block	Force needed to start the block sliding (newtons)
corduroy	1.0
felt	0.90
fine sandpaper	0.85
coarse sandpaper	0.80
satin	0.75
lycra	0.65
polycotton	0.50

Fig. 4.23 *Investigating the force of friction*

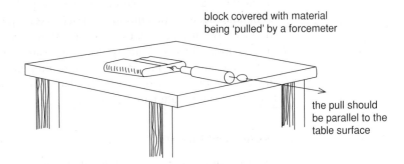

block covered with material being 'pulled' by a forcemeter

the pull should be parallel to the table surface

The values for sandpaper seems at first to be anomalous. Surely sandpaper would provide a good grip, i.e. need a large force to overcome the friction between itself and the table top? Consideration of the nature of the sandpaper surface may give us a clue here. The small sand grains, glued onto the paper, will act like roller bearings and will minimize the contact area between the sandpaper and the table top, so *less* force will be needed to overcome the friction of the sandpaper-covered block than for the felt or corduroy fabric, where the surface of the fabric can 'mould' to the table top with a consequently higher frictional force.

Upthrust

When a liquid is placed in a container, the weight of the liquid, (its mass, which is being pulled downwards by the force of gravity) creates a pressure – a force per unit area – within the liquid. This pressure acts *in all directions* in the liquid, so in addition to the downward pressure on the bottom of the container and the sideways pressure on the sides of the container, there is an upwards pressure 'pushing' towards the surface of the liquid, and the force producing the upward pressure is known as **upthrust**.

It is easy to feel the upthrust produced in a container of liquid. Screw the cap tightly onto an empty plastic bottle and push it into a bowl or tank of water. You can feel the bottle being pushed back up to the surface, and the 'push' is the upthrust force provided by the water. If you hold the bottle stationary under water, the force which you need to apply to the bottle to keep it in position is equivalent to the upthrust force – the forces are balanced and in opposition.

The upthrust force in a liquid acts on the surface of any objects which are placed in the liquid, and one way to look at it is to imagine that the volume of liquid which has been 'pushed out of the way' – displaced – by the object, is 'pushing back' in order to resume its original position in the body of the liquid (an example of the 'action and reaction' forces of Newton's third law).

Displacement

If you place a stone in a measuring cylinder of water, the water level will rise in the cylinder. The rise in level occurs because the stone has displaced (literally, taken the place of) a volume of water equal to its own volume (volume is sometimes seen as the amount of space taken up by an object, and is measured in cm^3). The displacement method is often used to find the volume of irregularly shaped objects – simply note the volume indicated by the water levels in the measuring cylinder before and after immersion – the volume of the immersed object can then be calculated by subtracting the original volume from the volume after immersion.

Floating and sinking

What governs whether an object floats or sinks?

When any object is placed in water (or any other liquid) it will displace a volume of water (or other liquid). The weight of the volume of water displaced by the object is considered to be equal to the upthrust on the object in the water. When the weight of the volume of water displaced is equal to the weight of the object, the forces are balanced and the object will float at the water's surface. If the total weight of the object is more than the weight of the water it displaces, the object will sink.

Some figures may help here. Three common objects were each placed into a measuring jug containing a known volume of water. In each case, the volume of water displaced by the objects was noted. The objects were then carefully lifted from the water, dried off, and their mass was measured on a kitchen scale (note the paradox – the mass in grams was 'weighed' on a spring loaded scale). The table below shows the results.

Object	Volume of water displaced (cm^3)	Mass (g)	Floated/Sank
apple	125	125	floated
orange	235	235	floated
egg	55	60	sank

Using the knowledge that 1 cm³ of water has a mass of 1 g, it can be seen that the apple and the orange both displaced a volume of water the weight of which (equal to the upthrust) was equal to their own weight – hence they floated. Conversely, the egg had a higher mass, i.e. it weighed more, than the mass of water which it displaced, and it sank.

How can we predict whether a solid object will float or sink? To be able to do this we need to know something about the density – the mass per unit volume – of the objects to be tested. If the object is less dense than the liquid into which it is placed, it will float on the surface; if the object is more dense than the liquid, it will sink. In order to find the density of an object (expressed in g/cm³) we need to know both its mass and volume.

Returning to the objects in the table above (the masses of which had already been measured), each was replaced into the measuring jug so that their volumes could be calculated. The egg presented no problem because it sank of course, but the apple and orange were each held just below the water surface using the end of a teaspoon handle, to ensure that the total volume of each was measured. The results are tabulated below.

Object	Mass (g)	Total volume (cm³)	Density (g/cm³)
apple	125	170	0.73
orange	235	290	0.81
egg	60	55	1.09

Since the density of water is 1.0 g/cm³ (1 g of water has a volume of 1 cm³), it is possible to predict, knowing the relative densities of the three objects, that the apple and orange would float, because their densities are lower than that of water, and that the egg will sink in water, because it has a higher density than water. It is interesting to make a similar comparison with the 'properties of materials' table in 3.1. Those materials with densities greater than 1.0 g/cm³ will sink, whilst those with densities lower than 1.0 will float.

And yet we know that ships made of steel and concrete will float. How does this happen? A solid block of steel, with a density of 7.86 g/cm³, would rapidly sink if it were placed in water. It is possible however, to *shape* the steel so that it displaces a volume of water whose mass (and therefore weight) is larger than its own mass (see Fig. 4.24). Under these conditions the steel will float. What has happened is that the shaping of the steel (into a boat hull, for example) effectively increases the volume, and therefore decreases the over-all density of the structure. Obviously, under these circumstances stability is important – if the boat tips too far sideways, or is 'holed' below the water-line, water can enter the hull, and the 'increased volume' effect is lost, with potentially disastrous results.

The same principle is operating when lumps of plasticene (sinkers) are turned into 'boat' shapes (floaters), in a classroom. If the exercise is carried out using a suitable measuring container, the volume (and hence the mass) of the water displaced by the 'successful' plasticene boats will be found to be larger than the volume of the lumps of plasticene from which the boats are made.

Fig. 4.24 *How the shaping of a hull effectively increases a vessel's volume*

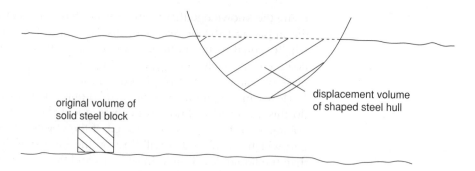

original volume of solid steel block

displacement volume of shaped steel hull

Fig. 4.25 *Forces acting on a mass being weighed in air and water*

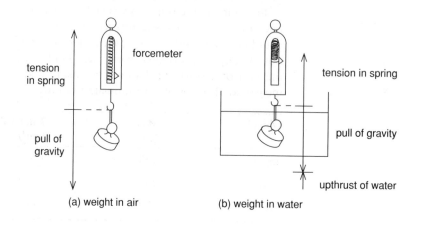

tension in spring

forcemeter

tension in spring

pull of gravity

pull of gravity

upthrust of water

(a) weight in air

(b) weight in water

Objects weighed in air and water

If an object which is a 'sinker' (a 200 g mass, for example) is hung from a forcemeter and weighed in air, and then carefully immersed in water and weighed again, a weight loss will be found to have occurred, and this weight loss is equivalent to the upthrust of the water on the object.

If the weight loss is then converted into an 'apparent loss' in mass (this is easy with forcemeters which are graduated both in newtons and grams), it should be the case that this apparent loss in mass is equal to the mass of water displaced by the sinking object (which can be found using the displacement method in a measuring cylinder).

The forces acting on a mass which was weighed in air and in water are illustrated in Fig. 4.25.

In Fig. 4.25a, the forces of gravity acting on a mass of 200 g, and the tension in the spring of the forcemeter, represent a balanced pair of forces, i.e.:

force of gravity (is balanced by) spring tension (2.0 newtons)

In Fig. 4.25b, where the 200 g mass has been immersed in water, the balance occurs between gravity – the force acting downwards – and a combination of upthrust and spring tension. Since gravity is assumed to remain constant, the upthrust of the water 'pushing' against the 200 gram mass, lessens the effect of gravity on the extension of the spring, hence:

force of gravity (is balanced by) upthrust of water + spring tension (1.75 newtons)

The upthrust, equivalent to the weight loss, has therefore provided a force of 0.25 newtons, a force produced by a mass of 25 grams. The displacement due to the immersion of the 200 g mass was 25 cm³, also equivalent to a mass of 25 grams. The weight loss in water (expressed in grams) is therefore equivalent to the mass of water displaced by the immersed object.

We can use this piece of information to calculate the density of the object concerned. Since density is mass per unit volume, and we know that the 200 g mass (weight = 2.0 N) displaced 25 cm³ of water (registering a weight loss in water of 0.25 N), the density of the material from which the 200 g mass is made is:

$$\frac{200 \text{ g}}{25 \text{ cm}^3} = 8.0 \text{ g/cm}^3$$

The 200 g mass used for the investigation was made of brass, and the value of 8.0 g/cm³ is close to the conventionally accepted value of 8.5 g/cm³ for the density of brass.

The Earth and beyond

Introduction

It is in astronomy, perhaps more so than in any other field, that those who study science are on the boundaries of knowledge and belief. For many centuries, people have looked into the night sky and wondered if there was anything (or anyone) 'out there', and the 'heavens' have been peopled with supernatural deities, the activities of whom have been used to explain the apparently inexplicable. There have been gods of thunder, and of rain, and a god who drew the sun across the sky each day in a fiery chariot.

As our understanding of the Earth's place in the universe has widened, many of the 'supernatural' explanations for natural events have been superseded by more rational accounts of the processes involved. It is not the place of science (and particularly of primary school science) to demolish sincerely held beliefs about the nature of the universe, but it is appropriate to consider alternative theories which may offer more convincing explanations of the processes of the natural world.

A religious account of the 'creation' constitutes one theory, the 'big bang' explanation of the origin of the universe is another. In the final analysis, people may (some might say should) make up their own mind about the nature of things in the light of the evidence presented to support the theory being advocated. Whatever seems to them to be a reasonable (or convenient) explanation will become incorporated into their own personal system of knowledge and belief. It is perhaps worth remembering that it is easy to offend religious sensibilities by offering theoretical explanations as 'facts'.

Without going too deeply into the philosophy of science, it is assumed that all teachers of science would acknowledge the provisional nature of science knowledge, and would endorse the view that what we offer in the way of scientific explanation represents the theory with the current best fit to the observable evidence. The following sections are presented with that thought in mind.

CONCEPTS TO SUPPORT KEY STAGES 1 AND 2

The solar system

The **Earth** is one of nine **planets** which orbit the Sun. The **Sun** is a **star** – a burning ball of gas – which emits light and heat energy as deuterium (heavy hydrogen) atoms fuse to form helium atoms (see Key Idea 4.1: Nuclear fusion). The planets do not emit light of their own, and can be seen because they reflect the light of the Sun from their surfaces.

A useful mnemonic for remembering the names of the planets, from the innermost (nearest to the Sun) outwards, is:

My Very Easy Method Just Shows U Nine Planets,

and a table of data relating to the solar system is included below.

	Distance from Sun (millions of kilometres)	Diameter (kilometres)	Axial rotation	Time for 1 orbit
Sun		1,384,000		
Mercury	57.9	4,840	59 days	88 days
Venus	108.1	12,400	243 days	225 days
EARTH	**149.5**	**12,742**	**23h 56m**	**365.25 days**
Mars	227.8	6,800	24h 37m	687 days
Jupiter	777.8	142,800	9h 50m	11.86 years
Saturn	1,426.1	120,800	10h 14m	29.45 years
Uranus	2,869.1	47,600	10h 49m	84.01 years
Neptune	4,495.6	44,600	15h 40m	165.79 years
Pluto	5,898.9	14,400?	16h	248.43 years

The Sun contains more than 99% of all the matter in the solar system, and it is the mass of the Sun which provides the gravitational force which keeps the planets in their orbits. Each planet describes a more or less elliptical orbit round the Sun, and with the exception of Pluto, these orbits are all roughly in the same plane. As can be seen from the table above, the Earth completes an orbit round the Sun once every 365.25 days. This gives rise to our Earth year of 365 days, with the 0.25 days adding up to the extra day in the 'leap year' once every four years.

In addition to the major planets, the solar system also contains smaller planetary fragments or **asteroids**, some of which are concentrated in a belt between Mars and Jupiter, and **comets,** which are clusters of rock and ice (including ice formed from gases such as methane and carbon dioxide). Comets, in particular, travel in long elliptical orbits which may carry them far beyond the orbit of Pluto before they eventually return towards the Sun again. When comets break up (sometimes due to the melting of the ice which binds the fragments together) pieces of the resulting debris become visible from Earth as **meteors** or **'shooting stars'** as they 'burn up' due to the heat generated by friction with the Earth's atmosphere.

Day and night At the same time as the Earth is travelling on its annual orbit round the Sun, it is also rotating on its own axis. A mental model sometimes used is that of a spinning top, and whilst this may be helpful in imagining axial rotation, it is misleading when considering the relative speed of rotation. Similarly, the globe which can be seen rotating on the screen before the start of BBC TV programmes is also travelling far too fast – to get a scaled-down idea of the speed at which the Earth is spinning on its axis, imagine the speed at which the hour hand of a 24-hour clock would travel around the clock face – in relative terms, the Earth is turning slowly.

Since the Earth is bathed in the light from the Sun, it is possible to imagine that one hemisphere will be in sunlight whilst the other is in darkness, and that because of the axial rotation, a fixed point on Earth will experience a period

Fig. 4.26 *Simulating day and night*

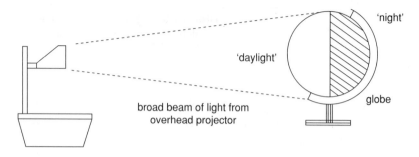

of light (daytime), followed by a period of darkness (night) in any given 24 hours (the period of axial rotation).

This process can easily be simulated by slowly rotating a globe on its axis in a beam of bright light – that from a slide- or overhead projector, for example (see Fig. 4.26). The darker the room, and the brighter the light source, the more pronounced the 'shadow' effect will be on the side of the globe away from the 'Sun'. As a point on the Earth's surface (or a small 'person' attached to the globe) rotates in the 'sunlight', sunrise, the apparent change in height and position of the Sun during the day, sunset and darkness can all be visualized. The Earth rotates on its axis from west to east, so in any simulation the surface of the globe facing the observer should be moving from left to right. This ensures that the Sun 'rises' in the east and 'sets' in the west!

The seasons　We know from our own experience that as the year progresses, the seasons change. The effects of these changes are seen and felt particularly in terms of daylight length and ambient temperatures. What causes this annual and predictable cycle of seasonal change? It occurs because the Earth's axis is tilted (at an angle of 23.5° from the vertical) relative to the direction of the light (and heat) from the Sun. Before considering the effect of this axial tilt, it is interesting to imagine what would be the case if the Earth's axis were not tilted, but was exactly perpendicular to the light from the Sun? In this case, *there would be no seasons*. Day and night would each be exactly 12 hours long, and for any given place on Earth the daily weather patterns would be predictable and identical, although the patterns would vary from place to place – equatorial regions would still be warm and polar regions would still be cold.

Figure 4.27 shows the effect of the axial tilt on the length of daylight experienced on Earth at different times of the year. During northern hemisphere summer, when the northern hemisphere is, as it were, tilted towards the Sun, places in the northern hemisphere experience longer days than nights, i.e. in a 24 hour period, they are 'in the Sun' for longer periods than they are 'in the dark'. In June in the U.K. for example, the summer days are about 18 hours long, whilst at the 'extremity' of the northern hemisphere, places inside the Arctic circle experience 24-hour daylight in the 'land of the midnight Sun'.

Six months later, when the Earth has travelled half way round its orbit, the northern hemisphere is now 'titled away' from the Sun, northern hemisphere winter nights are longer than days, and the Arctic circle is in darkness for 24 hours a day. At this time the southern hemisphere is tilted towards the Sun, and it, in turn, experiences longer days than nights, with the Antarctic becoming the land of the midnight Sun.

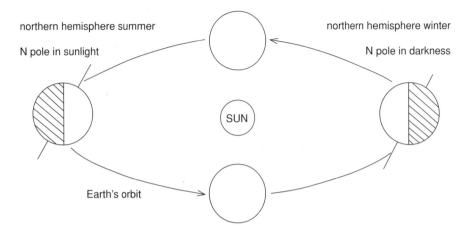

Fig. 4.27 *Summer and winter: the positions of the Earth and Sun*

At the intervening times between summer and winter (in March and September), the position of the Earth on its orbit round the Sun, coupled with the Earth's axial tilt, results in an even distribution of hours of daylight and darkness. This results, on 21st March and September respectively, in the vernal (spring) and autumnal equinoxes, each having 12 hours of daylight and 12 hours of darkness.

The Earth and the Moon

Just as the planets of the solar system are satellites of the Sun, some of the planets have orbiting satellites of their own. Jupiter has at least 12 satellites, four of which are visible through ordinary binoculars, whilst Saturn has 10 satellites in addition to its 'rings'.

The orbit and rotation of the Moon

The Moon is the Earth's satellite, and is our closest celestial neighbour. It has a diameter of 3,456 kilometres (2,160 miles), and it orbits the Earth at a distance of about 382,400 kilometres (239,000 miles). A complete orbit takes just less than 28 days (a lunar month), and during the orbit the moon itself rotates once on its axis. The effect of this axial rotation is that it is always the same hemisphere of the Moon which is visible from Earth.

Note: strictly speaking, the Moon does not simply 'go round' the Earth, but both bodies, held in position by gravitational attraction, rotate around a common centre of mass. Since the Earth is about 80 times as massive as the Moon however, the centre of mass of the Earth-Moon system lies inside the Earth, so effectively the Moon is in a simple orbit round the Earth.

The phases of the Moon

As with the Earth, the Moon is also bathed in light from the Sun. During its 28 day orbit round the Earth therefore, the appearance (not the shape!) of the Moon changes as parts of the hemisphere which faces Earth move into and out of the sunlight. These changes in appearance are described as the phases of the Moon, and are summarized below:

Day of lunar orbit	Phase of Moon	Description of appearance
1	new Moon	Moon invisible
8	first quarter	'half Moon', right side visible
15	full Moon	complete disc visible
22	last quarter	'half Moon', left side visible

Fig. 4.28 *Simulating the phases of the Moon*

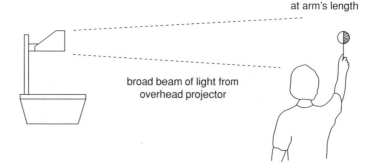

observer holding a 'moon' at arm's length

broad beam of light from overhead projector

The Moon's phases can be readily simulated by holding a suitable ball (the Moon) at arm's length, and then rotating the person (arm, ball, and all) in a bright beam of light (see Fig. 4.28). The person (the viewer as from Earth) then sees the progression of the changing shadows on the 'Moon' (the phases) during a single orbit. If a suitable mark is placed on the ball, the effect of the Moon's single axial rotation can also be seen. In order to keep the same 'side' of the Moon facing the observer, the Moon will need to be turned once on its own axis during its travel round the orbit.

To summarize the relative places and movements of the Earth and Moon in the solar system:

- the Sun, a star, is at the centre of the solar system;
- the Earth is one of nine planets in elliptical orbit round the Sun, with an orbiting period of 365.25 days;
- the Earth is also rotating on its own axis, with an axial rotation every 23 hours, 56 minutes;
- the Earth is orbited by the Moon, with an orbiting period of 27 days, 8 hours;
- the Moon is also rotating on its own axis, with an axial rotation time which is the same as its orbiting period, hence the same hemisphere always faces Earth.

The solar system and beyond

In the whole of science, perhaps one of the most difficult things to visualize and comprehend is the scale of the universe. This final section attempts to take us beyond the solar system, in order to gain some insight into the orders of magnitude involved when considering the component parts of the universe.

Fig. 4.29 *The orbits and axial rotation of the Earth and the Moon*

Fig. 4.29 *The orbits and axial rotation of the Earth and the Moon*

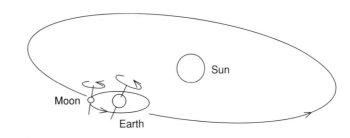

Fig. 4.30 *The relative sizes of the Earth, the Sun and Betelgeuse*

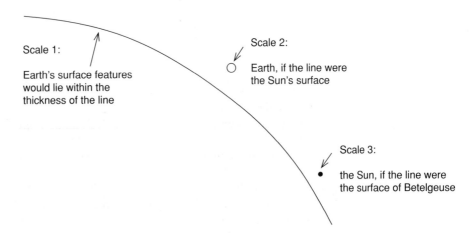

Scale 1:

Earth's surface features would lie within the thickness of the line

Scale 2:

Earth, if the line were the Sun's surface

Scale 3:

the Sun, if the line were the surface of Betelgeuse

In order to do this in any easily understandable way, it is necessary to use a variety of different scales and units. Fig. 4.30 represents a composite diagram for use with a variety of 'celestial scales'. The line is drawn with a radius of 15 cm and a thickness of 0.5 mm.

Scale 1   If the curved line were to represent the curved surface of the earth, then all the physical features of the Earth's surface, from the top of Mount Everest to the bottom of the deepest ocean trench, would fall within the thickness of the drawn line.

Scale 2   If the line were then to represent the curved surface of the Sun, then the arrowed circle (3 mm in diameter) would represent the size of the Earth, drawn to the same scale.

Scale 3   If the line were to represent the surface of the star Betelgeuse (a red giant visible in the 'top left' corner of the constellation of Orion), then the arrowed dot (1 mm in diameter) would represent the Sun drawn to the same scale!

Betelgeuse is so large (with a diameter of 400 million kilometres) that the entire orbit of the Earth round the Sun could be contained within its own diameter.

So much for size, but what about distance? On a universal scale, the solar system is so small and isolated that once we leave its confines our units of linear measurement are of limited value to us. In order to appreciate the distances involved if we were able to make a journey beyond the solar system, we need a different unit of measurement, and one which has been found convenient is the **light-year.** A light-year represents the distance travelled by light in a year, i.e.:

300,000 (the speed of light in kilometres per second) multiplied by $365 \times 24 \times 60 \times 60$ (the number of seconds in a year),

$= 9.46 \times 10^9$ m, or 9.46 billion kilometres.

In terms of the solar system, the light reflected from the Moon takes 1.25 seconds to reach the Earth, and the light from the Sun takes about 8.25 minutes. It is a measure of our isolation in the universe that our nearest stellar neighbour – the closest star – lies at a distance of four light years away!

Galaxies

The Sun is a medium sized star in a collection of stars – a star system known as a **galaxy.** The galaxy which contains the Sun – 'our' galaxy – is of a type known as a spiral nebula, and has an estimated population of 100 billion stars, of which only some 6,000 are visible to the unaided eye, even though some stars are many times larger than the Sun. The size of Betelgeuse has already been described, and the star named Antares in the constellation Scorpio, is large enough to contain the orbit of the planet Mars round the Sun.

The shape of 'our' galaxy has been described as a flattened disc of stars and star clusters. It has been estimated to be 100,000 light years in diameter, and up to 20,000 light years thick at its centre. The Sun is positioned along one of the spiral arms of the galaxy, about 32,000 light years from its centre. When we look at the 'Milky Way' in the night sky, we are looking through the galactic disc 'end on', hence the concentration of light in that area. Even the small magnification provided by binoculars can bring into range countless stars which are invisible to the unaided eye, and the Milky Way seen through a telescope is an awesome sight.

In terms of movement, the entire galaxy is itself rotating in space. It has been calculated that the Sun is moving at about 240 kilometres per second about the galactic centre, and will take about 200 million years to complete one galactic revolution.

Inter-galactic space

But even the size of the galaxy pales into apparent insignificance when we realize that only three of our 'neighbouring' galaxies are visible to the unaided eye (the Large and Small Magellanic clouds and the Andromeda nebula). However, the 200 inch reflecting telescope at the Mount Palomar observatory in California (one of the largest optical telescopes in the world) is capable of photographing *1 billion* galaxies. The most distant objects in the universe which can be located by astronomers are estimated to be of the order of 9 billion light years distant, and the light which we now detect from these objects was emitted by them nearly 4.5 billion years before the Earth came into existence!

One final idea relates to the 'big bang' theory of the origin of the universe. Evidence exists that all objects in the universe are receding from each other at great speed – the universe is expanding. 'Our' galaxy is rapidly moving away from all its neighbours, and from all other galaxies, further into the empty regions of deep space.

To bring us back to Earth again, and to summarize what we know of the relative movements of the Earth and the Moon in relation to the Sun and the galaxy, let us consider how it is that all of us on Earth are moving in four different directions at the same time:

- the Earth is turning on its axis;
- the turning Earth is orbiting the Sun;
- the Sun is moving round the galactic centre as the galaxy rotates in space;
- the galaxy is moving apart from all other galaxies.

A cosmic address In terms of orders of magnitude, it is interesting to consider where an individual person may be placed in the context of the size of the known universe. So what might our cosmic address be, in universal terms?

How about:

Room	year 3 classroom
Building	Lingmill Primary School
Town	Anytown
County	Barsetshire
Region	South-west England
Country	England
Sub-continent	Europe
Continent	Eurasia
Planet	Earth
	The solar system
	'Our' galaxy
	'Our' galaxy cluster
	The currently observable universe?

Physical processes: National Curriculum coverage

Below is listed each of the component parts of the relevant programme of study of science in the National Curriculum (SCAA, 1995). In the bracket below each component the relevant Key Idea is shown, together with the section heading(s) in the book where further specific details may be found.

Pupils should be taught:

1. Electricity
a that many everyday appliances use electricity;
b to construct simple circuits involving batteries, wires, bulbs and buzzers;
   (KEY IDEA 4.1: Electricity in simple circuits)
c that electrical devices will not work if there is a break in the circuit.
   (KEY IDEA 4.1: Electricity in simple circuits)

2. Forces and motion
a to describe the movement of familiar things, e.g. cars getting faster, slowing down, changing direction;
b that both pushes and pulls are examples of forces;
c that forces can make things speed up, slow down or change direction;
d that forces can change the shapes of objects.
   (KEY IDEA 4.2: The effects of forces)

3. Light and sound

Light and dark

a that light comes from a variety of sources, including the Sun;
b that darkness is the absence of light;
(KEY IDEA 4.1: Sources of light, Light and seeing, Light and dark)

Making and detecting sounds

c that there are many kinds of sound and many sources of sound;
d that sounds travel away from sources, getting fainter as they do so;
e that sounds are heard when they enter the ear.
   (KEY IDEA 4.1: Sound)

Pupils should be taught:

Simple circuits

1. Electricity
a that a complete circuit, including a battery or power supply, is needed to make electrical devices work;
   (KEY IDEA 4.1: Electricity in simple circuits)
b how switches can be used to control electrical devices;
   (KEY IDEA 4.1: Switches)

c ways of varying the current in a circuit to make bulbs brighter or dimmer;
(KEY IDEA 4.1: Electricity in simple circuits, Series circuits, Parallel circuits)

d how to represent series circuits by drawings and diagrams, and how to construct series circuits on the basis of drawings and diagrams.
(KEY IDEA 4.1: Circuit diagrams)

2. Forces and motion

Types of force

a that there are forces of attraction and repulsion between magnets, and forces of attraction between magnets and magnetic materials;
(KEY IDEA 3.1: The physical properties of materials: Magnetic properties)

b that objects have weight because of the gravitational attraction between them and the Earth;
(KEY IDEA 4.2: Gravity, The difference between mass and weight)

c about friction, including air resistance, as a force which slows moving objects;
(KEY IDEA 4.2: Forces in action, Friction)

d that when springs and elastic bands are stretched they exert a force on whatever is stretching them;

e that when springs are compressed they exert a force on whatever is compressing them;
(KEY IDEAS 3.1: The physical properties of materials: Elasticity; 4.1: Strain energy; 4.2: The effects of forces: Change of shape)

Balanced and unbalanced forces

f that forces act in particular directions;

g that forces acting on an object can balance, *e.g. in a tug of war, on a floating object*, and that when this happens an object at rest stays still;
(KEY IDEA 4.2: The effects of forces: The laws of motion)

h that unbalanced forces can make things speed up, *e.g. an apple being dropped*, slow down, *e.g. a shoe sliding across the floor*, or change direction, *e.g. a ball being hit by a bat*.
(KEY IDEAS 4.1: Potential and kinetic energy; 4.2: The effects of forces: The laws of motion)

3. Light and sound

Everyday effects of light

a that light travels from a source;

b that light cannot pass through some materials, and that this leads to the formation of shadows;

c that light is reflected from surfaces, *e.g. mirrors, polished metals*;

Seeing

d that we see light sources, *e.g. light bulbs, candles*, because light from them enters our eyes;
(all KEY IDEA 4.1: light, The behaviour of waves, Light waves, Straight

line travel, The reflection and absorption of light, Shadows, Transmission, Refraction)

Vibration and sound

e that sounds are made when objects, *e.g. strings on musical instruments*, vibrate but that vibrations are not always directly visible;
(KEY IDEA 4.1: Sound waves)

f that the pitch and loudness of sounds produced by some vibrating objects, e.g. a drum skin, a plucked string, can be changed;
(KEY IDEA 4.1: Sound waves, Pitch, Loudness)

g that vibrations from sound sources can travel through a variety of materials, *e.g. metals, wood, glass, air*, to the ear.
(KEY IDEA 4.1: The reflection of sound, The absorption of sound, The transmission of sound)

4. The Earth and beyond

The Sun, Earth and Moon

a that the Sun, Earth and Moon are approximately spherical;

Periodic changes

b that the position of the Sun appears to change during the day, and how shadows change as this happens;

c that the Earth spins around its own axis, and how day and night are related to this spin;

d that the Earth orbits the Sun once a year, and that the Moon takes approximately 28 days to orbit the Earth.
(all KEY IDEA 4.3: The solar system; Day and night; The seasons; The Earth and the Moon)

Useful references

SCIENCE SUBJECT KNOWLEDGE

ASIMOV, I. (1992) *Asimov's New Guide to Science*, London, Penguin.
PEACOCK, G. and SMITH, R. (1992) *Teaching and Understanding Science*, London, Hodder and Stoughton.
SHREEVE, T. (1983) *Discovering Ecology*, Harlow, Longman.

THE MANAGEMENT OF PRIMARY SCIENCE

NORTHAMPTONSHIRE INSPECTION AND ADVISORY SERVICE (1994) *Success with Managing Primary Science*, Hatfield, Association for Science Education.
SHERRINGTON, R. (Ed) (1993), *The Primary Teacher's Handbook*, Hemel Hempstead, Simon and Schuster.

SCIENCE ATTAINMENT TARGET 1

GOLDSWORTHY, A. and FEASEY, R. (1994) *Making Sense of Primary Science Investigations*, Hatfield, ASE.

Appendix:
Symbols used in drawing circuit diagrams

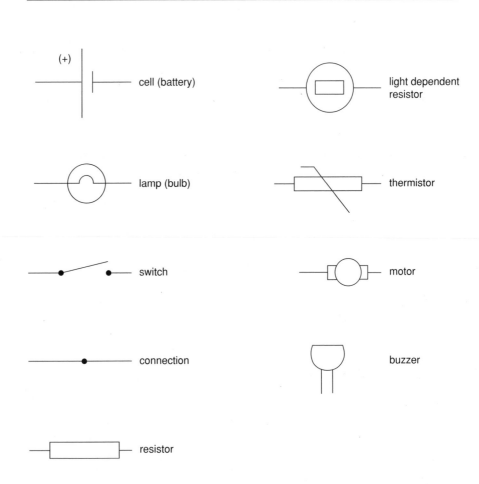

Index

acceleration 158, 161
adaptation 61
aerosols 106–7
air 79
alcohol 44
allotropes 99
amplitude 147
asteroid 177
atom 97–8

bacteria 47
bending 102
blood 15–16
bonding 99
  covalent 100–1
  ionic 100
  metallic 101
bone 20
breathing 18
burning 108

carbon cycle 68–9
carbon dioxide 34
cardo-vascular system 15–19
cartilage 20
ceramics 81
changes of state 95–6
chemical reactions:
  endothermic 108
  exothermic 108
circuit:
  diagrams 133
  parallel 131–2
  series 130–1
circulation 15–17
classification 46
  animals 51–3
  plants 48–9, 51
comet 177
compound 97
compressability 88
condensation 96
conduction of heat 143
conductivity:
  electrical 89–90
  thermal 88–9
convection of heat 143
current 128

Darwin, Charles, observations and
  deductions of 56–8
day and night 177–8
defence systems of the body 39–40
density 84–5

diet 40–1
differences between plants and
  animals 12
digestion 13–15
dispersal 33
displacement 172
distilation 106
drugs 44

ear 24–5
Earth 176
elasticity 86–7
electricity:
  generation 135–6
  in a simple circuit 128
  what is 127–8
electromagnetic spectrum 138
element 97
emulsion 106
endocrine (hormone) system 27–8
energy:
  chemical 125–6
  definitions of 121–2
  law of conservation 122
  transfer 65–6, 70, 126–7
evaporation 96, 105, 115
excretion 11
exercise 38, 43
eye 23–4

fabric 83
feeding 11, 13–15
filtration 106
floating and sinking 172–4
foam 107
food 35
  chains and webs 66–7
  cycle 67
forces 157
  balanced and unbalanced 166–7
frequency 147
friction 169–71
fungi 48

galaxies 182
gamma rays 140
gas 79, 95
  compression 97
gaseous exchange 18–19
germination 32, 34
glass 81
gravity 141, 163–4
growth 12

habitats 61–3
hardness 85
health 34–7
heat 108, 142–4
heating and cooling 103–4, 107–8
hormones 27–8
hydroelectric power stations 136–7
hygiene 42–3

identification of plants and animals
  using keys 53–5
immune response 40
infection prevention 40
infra red radiation 139
isotopes 99

joints 22–3

keys:
  dichotomous 53–5
  lateral 55
kinetic energy 141–2
kinetic theory 95

life style 40, 43–4
ligaments 21
light:
  absorption 148–9
  and dark 146
  reflection 148
  refraction 150–1
  and seeing 145–6
  sources 144–5
  transmission 150
  visible 139
  waves 147–8
liquid 95
living things, characteristics of 9
loudness 156

magnetism 90
mass 108, 158
materials:
  case study 94
  characteristics 91
  choice of 93–4
  composite 91
  manufactured 79–80
  natural 78–9
  properties 83–91
  uses 92–3
matter, states of 95
menstrual cycle 31
metal 80–1

meteor 177
microwaves 139
mixture 97
  separation 104
momentum 161
Moon 178–9
motion, laws of 158–67
movement 12, 21–3
muscles 21–2
musculo-skeletal system 20

natural selection 56–63
nervous system 23, 26–7
Newton, Sir Isaac:
  laws of motion 158
  light refraction 150
Newtons 164
nitrogen cycle 70
nuclear:
  energy 122–3
  fission 124
  fusion 124–5
  power stations 136
nutrients 34
nutrition systems 13–15

Ohm 129
organ systems 9–10
oxygen:
  availability 34, 37
  change 108–9
  cycle 69–70

paper 82–3
periodic table 98–9
photosynthesis 13, 34, 65
pitch 155–6
planets 176
plasma 15
plastic 81–2
platelets 16
pollination 32, 35
potential difference 129
potential energy 141
power 122
precipitation 115
pressure 168

protoctista 47–8
puberty 30–1

radiation, heat 144
radio waves 138
radioactive decay 123
red blood cells 15
reproduction 12
  asexual 28–9
  flowering plants 31–3
  human 29–30
  sexual 29
resistance 129
respiration 11–12, 17, 34
  cellular 19, 109
rest 38, 43
rocks 78
  igneous 110
  metamorphic 112–13
  sedimentary 110–12
rocky shores 62–3
rubber 82
rusting 109

safe site 37–8
scale of Universe 182–3
seasons 178–9
seed and fruit development 32–3
sensitivity 12
shadows 149–50
shape, change in 102–7, 167–8
sieving 105
skeleton 20–1
skin 25
smell 25
soil 78–9, 113–14
solar system 176
  and beyond 180–2
solid 95
solubility 105
sound:
  absorption 154–5
  reflection 154
  speed 153–4
  transmission 155
  waves 152–3
speed 147, 158

squashing 102
static electricity 137–8
stiffness 87–8
strain 86
strain energy 140–1
strength of materials 85–7
stress, material 86–7
stretching 103
sublimation 96
Sun 176
sunlight 34
suspension 105
switches 132–3

taste 25
teeth 41–2
temperature 142–4
tendons 22
thermal power stations 136
tobacco 44–5
toughness 88
transpiration 115
twisting 102

ultraviolet light 140
upthrust 171–2

variation:
  environmental 59–60
  genetic 59
  sources of 58–9
velocity 148, 158, 161
virus 46–7

warmth 34, 37
water 79
  availability 34, 37
  cycle 67–8, 115
wavelength 146–7
waves:
  behaviour 146
  longitudinal 153
  transverse 146–7
white blood cells 15
woodland 61–2
work 121

x-rays 140